SLAVES AND SLAVERY IN MUSLIM AFRICA

VOLUME II
The Servile Estate

SLAVES AND SLAVERY IN MUSLIM AFRICA
Volume I
Islam and the Ideology of Enslavement

By the same author
STUDIES IN WEST AFRICAN ISLAMIC HISTORY
Volume I
The Cultivators of Islam
(edited with an Introduction by John Ralph Willis)

*The Passion of Al-Hajj 'Umar: An Essay
into the Nature of Charisma in Islam*

SLAVES AND SLAVERY IN MUSLIM AFRICA

VOLUME II
The Servile Estate

Edited by
JOHN RALPH WILLIS
Professor in the Department of Near Eastern Studies,
Princeton University

FRANK CASS

First published 1985 in Great Britain by
FRANK CASS AND COMPANY LIMITED
Gainsborough House, 11 Gainsborough Road,
London E11 1RS, England

and in the United States of America by
FRANK CASS AND COMPANY LIMITED
c/o Biblio Distribution Centre
81 Adams Drive, P.O. Box 327, Totowa, N.J. 07511

Copyright © 1985 Frank Cass & Co. Ltd.

British Library Cataloguing in Publication Data

Slaves and slavery in Muslim Africa
   Vol.2: The servile estate
   1. Slavery in Africa—History
   I. Willis, John Ralph
   306'.362'096   HT1326

ISBN 0-7146-3201-5

Library of Congress Cataloging in Publication Data

Slaves and slavery in Muslim Africa

   Bibliography: p.
   Includes indexes.
   1. Contents: v. 1. Islam and the ideology of enslavement — v. 2. The servile estate.
   1. Slavery—Africa. 2. Slavery and Islam—Africa.
I. Willis, John Ralph.
HT1321.S56 1985   306.3'62'096   83-24313
ISBN 0-7146-3142-6 (v. 1)
ISBN 0-7146-3201-5 (v. 2)

All rights reserved. No part of this publication may be reproduced in any form, or by any means, electronic, mechanical, photocopying, recording, or otherwise, without the prior permission of Frank Cass and Co. Ltd. in writing.

Typeset by Essex Photo Set, Rayleigh.
Printed and bound in Great Britain by
A. Wheaton & Co. Ltd, Exeter

CONTENTS

Preface	vii
Acknowledgements	xii
Notes on Contributors	xiii
I. The 'Ulama' of Fas, Mulay Isma'il, and the Issue of the Haratin of Fas *Aziz Abdalla Batran*	1
II. Notes on Slavery in the Songhay Empire *J.O. Hunwick*	16
III. Comparative West African Farm-Slavery Systems *Polly Hill*	33
IV. Ahmad Rasim Pasha and the Suppression of the Fazzan Slave Trade, 1881-1896 *B.G. Martin*	51
V. Slavery and Society in Dar Fur *R.S. O'Fahey*	83
VI. Al-Zubayr Pasha and the Zariba Based Slave Trade in the Bahr al-Ghazal 1855-1879 *Lawrence Mire*	101
VII. The Ethiopian Slave Trade and Its Relation to the Islamic World *Mordechai Abir*	123
VIII. Black Slavery in Egypt During the Nineteenth Century as Reflected in the Mahkama Archives of Cairo *Terence Walz*	137
IX. The Slave Mode of Production Along the East African Coast, 1810-1873 *A.M.H. Sheriff*	161
Glossary	182
Index of Arabic words and terms	184
General Index	187

PREFACE

Slavery in Islamic Africa has been a fascinating subject to which many scholars have referred, but of which no detailed monograph has emerged. If the subject of Islamic slavery in Africa has failed to arouse the interest which has attended the trans-Atlantic slave trade[1] to the New World, it must be said that it compares with the latter in scale and scope, and out-distances the more popular subject in its length of duration.[2] Indeed, so pervasive is the subject of slavery in African societies, that one cannot appreciate fully the social, economic or political dimensions of the African past and present without some reference to it. Moreover, slaves of African origin formed a vital thread in the living lines of economic production in the Near and Middle East[3] and formed the cord of economic activity in Islamic Africa itself. Slaves sustained the salt pits and date palms of desert societies;[4] they worked the spice plantations of the East African littoral – became the porters and placemen in the trans-Saharan trade;[6] and they constituted the entourage – the veritable wealth and currency – of the notables of Islamic societies. Thus in O'Fahey's Dar Fur they stand as "marks of favor" in the gift of the strong, a kind of investment "hedge" against the vagaries of the nomadic orb; or, as Martin underscores for the Ottoman court, slaves become "gestures of friendship and submission" bestowed by worthies within the Ottoman sphere. Yet again, as Hill reminds us, they were by the fact of their uprooting strangers who had been reduced to things that could be owned.

Our visions of slavery in the New World spring from the spectral image of the torn and tormented male figure. That males dominated the dreary head counts of the trans-Atlantic trade suggests something of the nature of slavery in the Americas: the excessive reliance of plantation sugar and tobacco, coffee and cotton upon the sinews of forced labor. Yet the face of servility in societies under Islamic influence must focus in a different light. For the very moment when Africans were kicking out their men at the Atlantic end of the continent, we find the exit of thousands of women[7] and children[8] cross the Sahilian shores of the Sahara – through the commercial channels of the Indian Ocean and Red Sea. In African societies, where status and wealth were measured by the length of the master's line, the production of progeny[9] – the motive force behind the institution of concubinage in Islam – became a reflection of the prestigious self. Women were the vessels of male *hubris* – the reproducers of that malleable material which would be shaped to the master's will. They plumed the entourage of personages of power; formed the circulating medium of foreign exchange. And, as Hunwick shows, women slaves in the market place unveiled and open to public view could conduct affairs in a manner denied the free. Moreover, in the large households to which they were attached, women slaves presided over the cultivation and preparation of food, the fabrication of clothing, the nurture and upbringing of infants. These tasks, added to the duties of the market place, composed the routine chores of the domestic day. Finally, female slaves were the mats of the male pleasure-ground; unlike their counterparts among the freeborn, they could be folded up and transported over long distances against their will.[10] Hence, the master's sexual exploitation was, in Walz's phrase, "a right which brought no blame."

The better part of the essays in these volumes has its ancestry in a conference held at Princeton University during the Summer of 1977 under the title: "Islamic Africa: Slavery and Related Institutions". At that international gathering, four principal themes dominated discussion: the servile estate, its genesis and composition; the master-slave connection and the post-servile condition; patterns and perspectives of slave trading; the legacy of Islamic slavery in Africa to contemporary societies. While the primary focus of attention remained on Africa, questions ranged well beyond the continent, pursuing, as it were, the path of the slaves themselves. In these volumes, we have maintained a similar thematic concentration. While the angle of our attention has been formed by two principal lines of interest (the ideology of enslavement under Islam and the evolution of the servile estate within Africa), we have had to range well beyond the boundaries of the continent and consider these questions within the wider context of universal Islam.

And what is "Islamic" about the institution of slavery as it evolved within the categories under discussion? Several points can be advanced in response to this question. It must be remembered that Muhammad, the Prophet of Islam, was at once a slaveholder and a practitioner of polygamy and concubinage. And since the tenets of Islam are tethered so tightly to the *sunna* (model) of its prophet, it is of no surprise to discover that slavery and polygamy command such a wide presence in the social annals of Islam. Again, concubinage, that

Preface

forceful feature of universal Islam, fed the insatiable demand for females and placed an unmistakable cachet upon the character of slavery in Muslim lands. Secondly, is the known practice of the Muslims to liquidate men in *jihad* and take captive women and children for use in the domestic scheme. Indeed, the sunna of the Prophet summoned the incorporation of slaves into the kinship structure of ancient Arabia, thereby calling into existence a mass of rootless people who had no previous identity. And when incorporation was coupled with conversion to Islam, a way was found to shade the difference between the servile and the free. Finally, the stress on the sensual in the paradaisical passages or the Qur'an could hardly serve to remedy the Eastern malady (pederasty) or discourage the importation of youthful slaves for sexual purposes.

The study of slavery in Islamic societies is still in its infancy, and these essays are only the embryo of a growth that promises to be rapid in the coming years. In the first volume we have been able to isolate the germ of the institution in the morbific influence of certain ancient beliefs. The ideology of enslavement in Islam came to rest upon the premise that the servile estate was somehow preordained – that some persons were predestined to servility as surely as other were foreordained with the gift of prophesy. Yet Muslims themselves were able to view the condition of slavery as an aberration – as a non-convergence of the rays of infidelity to the single focus of Islam. Again, while such a view did not prove fatal to the essential belief in the liberty of the individual, it served as a brake on the forward movement towards abolition. Indeed, that conversion to Islam offered no infallible specific is seen by the frequent enslavement of Muslims of color despite their religious beliefs. Nor did incorporation into the lineage network always serve to mend the aberration and release the brake on the acceleration towards freedom. The voices of abolition come through faintly in these essays, but it is possible that we have not given them their due.

Nor have we been able to portray with sufficient clarity the various orders of the servile estate. The eunuch order holds a particular fascination given the power and peculiarity of this especially "Eastern" degree. Nor again have we probed very deeply the forbidden degrees of the *ghulam* order wherein young boys were shackled to the perverse tastes which the Prophet of Islam so roundly condemned. If we are to understand the unique aspects of the institution of slavery under Islam, we must come to understand the workings and interconnectedness of these orders, as we must somehow penetrate the intimacy and inner secrecy of the *harim*. Finally, there is little in these essays that enlightens our knowledge of the marketplace and allows a comparison of the different slave emporia of Islam. All this and more is the promise of future research, and it is hoped that these volumes point the path in the right direction.

J.R.W.

NOTES

1. Controversy continues to convulse discussion of the question of quantitative estimates for the Trans-Atlantic slave trade (c.1450–c.1900). Curtin's assertion that the total estimate is unlikely to exceed 10,500,000 brought forth a vigorous challenge from J.E. Inikori who condemned *The Atlantic Slave Trade: A Census* (Madison, 1969) for "an inbuilt tendency to under-estimate the number of slaves imported". See J.E. Inikori, "Measuring the Atlantic Slave Trade: An Assessment of Curtin and Anstey", *The Journal of African History*, XVII, 2, 1976, pp.197-225; and "Discussion: Measuring the Atlantic Slave Trade", by Philip D. Curtin, Roger Anstey, and J.E. Inikori, *The Journal of African History*, XVII, 4, 1976, pp.595-627.
2. Professor Ralph A. Austen (University of Chicago) offers a working figure of 17,000,000 for the Islamic slave trade out of Africa (Trans-Saharan, Red Sea and Indian Ocean). The period covered is from c. 650–1905. (The figures are based on a personal communication to this writer.)
3. For an introductory statement on slavery in the Near and Middle East, see the stimulating essay by Bernard Lewis, *Race and Color in Islam*, N.Y., 1971, which draws usefully upon the work of G. Rotter, *Die Stellung des Negers in der islamisch-arabishen Gesellschaft bis zum XVI Jahrhundert* (Bonn, 1967).
4. The role of slave labor in salt production remains a subject for scholarly attention, but see J. Clauzel, *L'Exploitation des Salines de Taoudenni* (Alger, 1960). Saharan palmgroves were cultivated by the Haratin (sing. = Hartani), a sedentary population of apparent slave origin (see article, "Hartani", *The Encyclopaedia of Islam,* (new edition), by G.S. Colin, p.230-231.
5. There is no satisfactory monograph on this subject, but see F. Cooper, *Plantation Slavery on the East Coast of Africa,* (New Haven, 1977).
6. See *wakil, infra,* p.3.
7. The principal distinction enunciated here is between the Trans-Atlantic trade, which attracted males (predominantly), and the trade to Islamic lands, which attracted females and children (predominantly). Within this distinction, it must be noted that females and children were in demand both in Islamic lands within Africa and beyond. On the preference for females and children, cf. the following: P.D. Curtin, *The Atlantic Slave Trade, A Census,* 1969, pp.19, 28, 41, 46 (high ratio of young males to young females). See the same author's *Economic Change in Precolonial Africa: Senegambia in the era of the Slave Trade,* 1975, pp.175 *et seq.*, where the "retention" of females in Africa is advanced over the notion of "preference" for males in the New World; Suzanne Miers and Igor Kopytoff (eds.), *Slavery in Africa: Historical and Anthropological Perspectives,* 1977, pp.53, 62, 72, 108, 162. See also, E.A. Ayandele, "Observations on some Social and Economic Aspects of Slavery in Pre-Colonial Northern Nigeria", *Nigerian Journal of Economic and Social Studies* (Ibadan), IX, 1967, pp.329-38; p.332, following F. Horneman (The Hakluyt Society: *Mission to the Niger,* vol. IV, *The Bornu Mission,*

1822-1825, edited by E.W. Bovill, Cambridge, 1966): "The statistics that have survived show clearly that most of the slaves exported [from Northern Nigeria] were women of from ten to twenty years – a class of people not required for farm labour. Next to them were children of less than eighteen. Youths of eighteen to thirty years were hardly ever sold".

8. While it has been stressed by many authors that a principal attraction of adolescent slaves was the ease with which they could be incorporated into the family structure, reference should be made to the point raised by Bosworth and Hardy (to quote the former) that, "in considering the personal relationship between master and slave, the sexual aspect should certainly not be neglected; the ethical climate of Persia in this period (c.540/1145) condoned homosexual liaisons..., and the master of youthful slaves was well placed for indulging unnatural and sadistic tastes" (C.E. Bosworth, "Ghulam", New *E.I.*, section II, Persia, and P. Hardy, "Ghulam", New *E.I.*, section III, India, pp.1082 *et seq.*). From the last days of the Roman Empire, when eunuchs were "fabricated" for the sensual gratification of Roman dames (and to the eternal delight of Chinese ladies of court) the eunuch order seems to have served a sexual purpose. Castration preserved the boyish and beardless "innocence" of these fondlings (perhaps "pets" would be more appropriate) and enhanced their appeal to both female and male companions. Cf. Alhaji Sir Abubakar Tafawa Balewa, *Shaihu Umar*, Longmans, 1967 (for a Nigerian example of the appeal of the *ghulam*); Taisuke Mitamura, *Chinese Eunuchs*, Vermont, 1970, p.37; and, "Eunuch", *The Encyclopaedia of Religion and Ethics*, vol. III p.580. C. Snouck Hurgronje, *Mekka in the Latter Part of the Nineteenth Century* ("... the very widely spread paederasty... a conspicuous result of that West Arabian Babel-culture which is abhorred of the Central Arabians"), 1931, p.11. Al-Jahiz (Abu 'Uthman 'Amr b. Bahr al-Fuqaymi al-Basri, c.776–869) wrote a bristling satire on sodomy in his *Kitab al-Tarbi' wa'l-tadwir* (ed. Ch.Pellat, Damascus, 1955).

9. These slaves are termed *"tilad"*: "slaves or pasturing beasts that breed at one's own abode, or home, and become old, or long possessed...." (E.W. Lane, *An Arabic-English Lexicon*, Book I, Part I, p.312). See Mahmoud Kati ben El-Hadj El-Motaouakkel Kati [*sic*, Ibn al-Mukhtar], *Tarikh el-Fettach ou Chronique du Chercheur pour servir à l'histoire des villes, des armées et des principaux personnages du Tekrour*, French translation and Arabic text, O. Houdas and M. Delafosse (reprint edition, Paris, 1964, Arabic text, p.56, translation, p.107).

10. The pull of family obligations militated against the prolonged separation of a free woman from her people (it should be noted, her main source of protection). On the other hand, the extended absence of a husband from his wife (be it for religious or business reasons) was a situation to be tolerated – even to the point of allowing him to take on another woman in a temporary "marriage" of pleasure (*mut'a*). M. Gaudefroy-Demombynes, *Muslim Institutions* (London, 1950), p.133.

ACKNOWLEDGEMENTS

Parts of the Preface and of the Introduction to Volume I have appeared previously in my "Islamic Africa: Reflections on the Servile Estate", *Studia Islamica*, fasc. LII, 1980, pp.183-197. The editor wishes to thank the *collegerunt* of this journal for permission to incorporate certain materials, and to extend his thanks to the Ford Foundation for its support of the Princeton conference (Islamic Africa: Slavery and Related Institutions, 12th-15th June, 1977) which made these volumes possible.

NOTES ON CONTRIBUTORS TO VOLS I AND II

John Ralph Willis (professor of history and Near Eastern studies, Princeton University) is an authority on the evolution of Islamic culture in Africa.
Paulo Fernando de Moraes Farias (lecturer, Centre of West African Studies, University of Birmingham) has made numerous contributions on the diffusion of Islam and the attitude of Muslim geographers and historians towards the peoples of Africa.
Akbar Muhammad (professor, State University of New York, Binghampton) has been concerned with the scholarly tradition in the Western Sudan and the image of the African in early Arabic literature.
Ephraim Isaac has investigated early Coptic manuscripts and their importance for the history of Ethiopian civilization in the pre-Muslim period.
William John Sersen has conducted research on Muslim attitudes towards the environment (especially as seen in proverbs and other popular literature), and has specialized in early Islamic sources for the history of science.
Mervyn Hiskett (professor of Hausa Studies, Bayero University, Kano, Nigeria and formerly lecturer on Hausa literature, SOAS, University of London) has written extensively on the early development of Islam in Northern Nigeria.
Bernard Barbour is exploring the origins of slavery in the Western Sudan from the perspective of external and internal Arabic sources.
Michelle Jacobs has studied the social status of women in early Islam with special reference to the institution of marriage.
Constance Hilliard has pursued the role of the Torodbe in the dissemination of Islam in the Western Sudan.
Nehemia Levtzion (professor, Hebrew University, Jerusalem, and Director, Harry S. Truman Research Institute for the Advancement of Peace) has focused on economic and religious factors in the spread of Islam in ancient Ghana and Mali, and is concerned with the phenomenon of conversion to Islam from the earliest times.
Daniel Pipes (lecturer on history, Harvard University) has published

studies on slave soldiers in Middle Eastern states and the role of Islam in the development of political power in the modern Middle East.

Aziz Abdalla Batran (professor, Howard University, Washington, D.C.), has investigated the importance of Sufism and religious brotherhoods in West African Islam and the evolution of a tradition of scholarship within Muslim communities of the Western Sudan.

J.O. Hunwick (professor, Northwestern University) has been the editor of the Centre of Arabic Documentation, University of Ibadan, *Research Bulletin*, and directs the *Fontes Historiae Africanae* of the International Academic Union.

Polly Hill (Cambridge University) has written widely on the contribution of farmers in Ghana and Northern Nigeria to the formation of economic and social institutions in those regions.

B.G. Martin (professor and director, Middle East Studies Program, Indiana University, Bloomington) has contributed numerous articles on the relations of African Muslims with the wider Muslim world, and the importance of religious brotherhoods in the diffusion of Islam in Africa.

R.S. O'Fahey (professor, Bergin University) has studied early Funj (Eastern Sudanic) institutions in the development of Islamic states in the Sudan of the pre-colonial period.

Lawrence Mire has been interested in the impact of the West in the modernization of Egypt and the Sudan, and has conducted research on pre-modern political and social structures of Eastern Africa.

Mordechai Abir (professor, Hebrew University) has published extensively on the Islamic factor in the development of the Ethiopian state.

Terence Walz has used the Mahkama Archives of Cairo for several studies of demographic patterns in the spread of slavery throughout the Muslim world.

A.M.H. Sheriff (lecturer, Dar es-Salaam University) has analyzed the mode of production as a phenomenon in the economic history of Eastern African peoples.

I

The 'Ulama' of Fas, M. Isma'il and the Issue of the Haratin of Fas

Aziz Abdalla Batran

When M. Isma'il ibn al-Sharif ascended the throne in 1672, the 'Alawite regime which his half-brother, M. al-Rashid (reg. 1668-1672) had founded (mainly with tribal support) was barely six years old. With determination and political astuteness, the young monarch (M. Isma'il was then twenty-six) directed his energies towards the consolidation of his power, the expansion of the state, the suppression of internal dissent and the repulsing of the European and Ottoman threat. To achieve these aims, he recognized the need for a strong stable army that was intensely loyal to him and dedicated to the preservation of the regime. Tribal support and loyalties, had essentially proven to be unreliable. In a letter addressed to Sidi Muhammad ibn 'Abdal-Qadir al-Fasi (d. 1704/5), the great sage and scholar of Fas (Fez), M. Isma'il spelt out the reasons that motivated him to establish a professional army. He wrote:

> the Khilafa must have an instrument to prop it up. This is a (standing) army ... that protects the Muslim Community, guards its ports, keeps security on its roads and repulses whomever covets it. And when Allah charged us with this responsibility (the Khilafa) we re-examined the composition of the state armies, which are the main-stay of the Khilafa's authority. We do not know of a civilization that depended on factional loyalties, nor did we find a single tribe in the Maghrib that was devoted and strong enough to provide the main prop of the regime.[1]

Indeed no viable state can afford to depend exclusively on tribal alliances for its authority and defense. Tribal support could be withdrawn at any time and at any sign of discord with the central government. Moreover tribal soldiers were not always readily available, for they "were primary producers, bound for their subsistence to animals and land. Consequently, their ability to fight was constrained by seasonal cycles of agriculture and pastoral transhumance."[2] M. Isma'il recognized this fact. In his letter to Sidi

Muhammad ibn 'Abdal-Qadir al-Fasi, he explained that soldiers other than those whom he intended to "own", "would not forget their homes, their flocks and farms. They would, at any sign of laxity in discipline or whenever the chance presented itself, desert the army and rejoin their tribes having already squandered public funds which they received in salaries."[3]

M. Isma'il, therefore, decided to free himself from the shackles of tribal whims and not to rely solely on unpredictable tribal loyalties and support. For instance, he accused the people of Fas of slackening off in furnishing him with soldiers at times of need. "Whenever we requested 2000 or 3000 soldiers," he alleged, "the people of Fas complain that they were unable to raise that number. We therefore neglected them and sought conscripts from other towns, villages and tribes. But these too were of no use and were good for nothing." M. Isma'il henceforward, says Akansus, "gave up total reliance on tribal support and dropped his policy of setting one tribe against the other."[4]

The creation of an army large and powerful enough to sustain the 'Alawite regime was indispensable. M. Isma'il elected to choose for this purpose the 'Abid (slaves) and the Haratin of Morocco, two "social and cultural categories which had no reference to any (Moroccan) corporate group . . . landless, vulnerable and despised, and therefore had neither sentimental nor material commitments to groups with interests independent of the Makhzan (central government)."[5] Unlike free men, slaves and Haratin exhibited admirable qualities that fascinated the Sultan and encouraged him to establish the 'Abid al-Bukhari army or the slave army. "The slaves," M. Isma'il proclaimed, "possess the bravery, the resoluteness, the aptitude and the endurance that are lacking in free men." Once they were bought and conscripted, M. Isma'il continued to say, they would dedicate their lives and energies to serving in the army.[6] He thus decided to buy, he claimed, all the legally owned slaves in Morocco.

The Faqih Muhammad 'Alilish (d. 1711) is said to have been the one who drew the attention of M. Isma'il to the existence of a register that contained the names of all the Sa'dian soldiers (daftar bi-asma' al-'abid alladhina kanu fi 'askar al-Dhahabi al-Sa'di).[7] The Sultan subsequently charged him with the responsibility for their "collection". 'Alilish became the chief recruitment officer, assisted by court officials, governors of towns and tribal chiefs.

When the recruitment began is not known for certain. However by the opening months of 1677 the collection was at its height.[8]

The 'Ulama' of Fas, M. Isma'il and the Haratin of Fas

According to 'Alilish, registers (*dawawin*) of slaves from every town, village and tribal homeland were prepared after thorough and painstaking investigations. The registers were then presented to the Qadis and 'Ulama' of Fas for further scrutiny and approval.*

Only those registers which they approved were submitted to the Sultan. Instructions were immediately issued authorizing the purchase of all those in the registers, at a fixed price of 10 mithqals per head irrespective of sex or age. Unowned slaves were recruited free of charge.[9]

The success of the recruitment drive was immeasurable. Within a short time every black man, free or slave, in and around Marrakush and the northern face of the Atlases, was collected.[10] The collection was thus indiscriminate, covering free-born Muslims, and according to the 'Ulama' and the Talaba of Fas, illegal. Sidi Muhammad ibn 'Abdal-Qadir al-Fasi articulated, in a tactful way, the disapproval of the 'Ulama' in a letter that he addressed to M. Isma'il. "The basic condition of man," he wrote, "is freedom. If the slave-status of a person cannot be justifiably established, then we can say no more than that such a person is the master of his soul. Therefore no one has any authority over him and he cannot be traded. This opinion is based on the Kitab, the Sunna and the Ijma'."[11]

Refuting these allegations, M. Isma'il, it is claimed, sought and received the approval for his action from the 'Ulama' of the Orient. On the other hand he attested that he never ordered the collection of slaves and Haratin unless the registers were approved by the 'Ulama' themselves and concrete evidence of original slave-status of those in the registers was presented. He claimed that "the status of every person is probed and thoroughly investigated until we are certain of his or her slave-status and that he or she was legally owned. Concrete proof, confessions, public opinion, testimony by persons of repute are the determinants of a person's original status."[12]

In an angry move, M. Isma'il humiliated the Qadi of Fas, Burdula (d. May 7, 1721) whom he dismissed and reinstated several times; and he accused the 'Ulama' and Talaba of Fas of being lax in their studies. However, in a more sober note, he asked, "if the 'Ulama' allege that it is not permitted to buy these slaves for the public good, then (they) must tell us, who in the entire Maghrib, in its towns and villages, will undertake this religious duty?"[13]

---

*The 'Ulama' of Fas, especially those of the Qarawiyin Mosque, had always been highly respected by the Moroccan sovereigns, who sought their support and counsel in secular and religious matters. A powerful and popular intelligentsia, they were the recognized leaders and representatives of the 'Ulama' of the entire nation.

Be that as it may, the fact still remains that free born black Muslims were recruited, often by force. The 'Ulama' of Fas led by the aged Qadi Burdula agitated ceaselessly against what they referred to as "the enslavement of free born Muslims", much to the consternation of the Sultan.

Things, however, came to a head between M. Isma'il and the 'Ulama' of Fas on July 18, 1698, when the Sultan ordered the "collection" of the Haratin of Fas. The term Haratin, according to al-Nasiri, is used in the Maghrib to designate "a manumitted man, or a free man of secondary rank."[14] However, the etymology of the term is still a subject of debate.[15]

Although the origin of the Haratin is shrouded in mystery, it is generally believed that they were indigenous to the north Saharan oases, hybrids between an ancient black population and Berbers, and most of them had dark skin and negroid features.[16] The Haratin did not constitute a tribe, rather they were groups of families scattered amongst North African and Saharan Arab and Berber tribes. Though the Haratin were free men, they were generally considered to be of inferior social status, between slaves and free men (hur thani). Most of the Haratin were farmworkers and not landowners, receiving a fifth (*Khammas*) of the harvest from Arab and Berber landlords, for their work. In general, the Haratin were a class of people "who were in many ways like slaves: i.e. non-tribal, economically vulnerable, socially debased and pheno-typically distinct."[17] Their negroid features, their lowly social status, their economic dependency and hence vulnerability, their non-tribal composition and their propensity to discipline and loyal service to their patrons, interested M. Isma'il in them.

By the second half of the seventeenth century large groups of Haratin could be found in almost all the major towns of Morocco. Droughts, famines and political disturbances, such as those that took place following the death of M. Ahmad al-Mansur al-Dhahabi in 1603, sent droves of Haratin cultivators from the Saharan oases to the urban centres of Central and Northern Morocco. Explaining this phenomenon to M. Isma'il, 'Alilish is claimed to have said: "you are aware, may Allah make you victorious, that not long ago a series of famines and political disturbances had struck the Maghrib, forcing people to wander from one place to another. The first to suffer and hence to start the exodus (to the towns) were the brown-skin Haratin (*ahmar al-jilda*)."[18]

It is not surprising that Fas, which 'Alilish described as a prosperous metropolis, a leading industrial and commercial centre, absorbed a huge number of Haratin emigrants. By 1690 the emigrant Haratin were completely urbanized, sharing in the economic activity of the town, while some of them, no doubt, worked in the farms of Fasi landowners. Some of the Haratin became eminent citizens, married into free Fasi families and made a final break with the past.[19] Why the 'Ulama' and citizens of Fas vehemently opposed M. Isma'il's orders, is obvious. The conscription of Haratin would not only deprive them of farm labour, but also of artisans, acquaintances, friends and kith and kin.

On the morning of July 18, 1698, the Governor of Fas, Qa'id Abdalla al-Rusi, met the 'Ulama', the Shurafa and Haratin dignitaries in the Qarawinyin Mosque. He conveyed the Sultan's orders to them: the Haratin of Fas were to be collected, military registers of the Haratin to be prepared and the 'Ulama', the Qadi and court officials should sign the registers. The Sharifian orders were discussed at length. The assemblage resolved to send a petition to the Sultan, humbly requesting him to rescind his decision. It was also suggested that a respected sage be sent to Meknes to intercede with the Sultan. According to Ibn al-Hajj, the Sultan acquiesced.[20] This was communicated to the people of Fas on July 22, 1698. It was a time of tumultuous rejoicing. The 'Ulama' and the Haratin who had gone into hiding reappeared. But that was only temporary. Four months later, on November 19, 1698, Governor 'Abdalla al-Rusi received firm orders from M. Isma'il to collect the Haratin and to chastize the 'Ulama' and the dignitaries of Fas. According to Ibn al-Hajj, M. Isma'il changed his mind after reviewing the whole question of the recruitment of the Haratin with his chief recruitment officer, 'Alilish and his courtiers. The Sultan came to realize that to spare any group of Haratin would create dissent amongst those already recruited.

In a letter which he addressed to Sidi Muhammad ibn 'Abdal-Qadir al-Fasi, M. Isma'il insisted that the Haratin of Fas were originally slaves.

> No matter how long the Haratin, especially the brown-skin Haratin (ahmar al-jilda), have been urbanized, many of them are, nonetheless, slaves. They have indeed severed all ties with their patrons and forgotten their (slave) origin. Some of them do not even know that they are originally slaves. Others are aware of this fact, but they will not acknowledge it, either because they do not wish to debase themselves after having become urbanized and have made a final break with their patrons and with those who know their origin, or because they hide behind baseless evidence in the Holy Law that proves they are free born. We must, for this reason, investigate the background of the Haratin of Fas, so that every one of them will know his origin and his long forgotten patron.[21]

In another letter M. Isma'il argued that "many Haratin have attached themselves to persons other than their masters. They overpowered their (new patrons) and arrogated to themselves equal rights . . . in this they were either motivated by worldly desires or they were aspiring to marry free women. In fact they (freely) married unto the families of their masters. Therefore, it is our duty to unearth their background."[22]

The Governor of Fas, 'Abdalla al-Rusi, took it upon himself to intercede personally with the Sultan in Meknes. His intercession, however, failed. Upon his return on November 27, 1698, he summoned the 'Ulama', the Fuqaha' and the dignitaries of the town to a meeting in Zawyat Sidi 'Abdal-Qadir al-Fasi and read to them the new orders.

Eight days later (Dec. 5, 1698) Governor 'Abdalla al-Rusi received a Sharifian letter. The orders that it contained were specific: all the Haratin of Fas should be registered; the register should be in three copies, each gilded; one of the copies to be sent to the Sultan, the second to be kept in a safe place in the library of the Qarawiyin Mosque; the Qadi, the Fuqaha' and court Witnesses must individually sign all the registers.[23]

The Governor proceeded to collect the Haratin, thus creating great confusion and fear in Fas. Many Haratin fled the town and likewise did some of the 'Ulama' and court Witnesses who refused to sign the registers. The Governor prepared three registers, specifying the names, families and living quarters of about seven hundred Haratin. He is also claimed to have forced some of the 'Ulama' and dignitaries of Fas to sign the registers. He then led the Haratin to Meknes.

It seems that Qa'id Abdalla al-Rusi, who showed much sympathy to the cause of the people of Fas, did not, as it were, collect the cream of the crop. His seven hundred recruits were found unfit for military service and were promptly sent back to Fas.[24] The Governor was then transferred to Meknes. M. Isma'il appointed in his place Hamdun al-Rusi who was in turn replaced by Abu 'Ali al-Rusi in 1703/4.

The "collection" of the Haratin of Fas was laid to rest until c. 1708. The reason for this, says Ibn al-Hajj, was that M. Isma'il directed his energies towards more urgent and serious problems such as the rebellion of his son Sidi Muhammad al-'Alim (May 1702-1704).

On Sunday, May 28, 1708, 'Alilish and the ex-Governor of Fas, 'Abdalla al-Rusi, arrived in the town to collect the Haratin. The unwelcome recruiters were met with great hostility. The 'Ulama' refused to cooperate and even the Governor, Bu 'Ali al-Rusi, was reticent. The mission was a total failure.[25] Governor Bu 'Ali was consequently dismissed and Hamdun al-Rusi, who had held that position between 1701/2 and 1703/4 was reappointed in his place. At the same time M. Isma'il invited the 'Ulama' of Fas to an audience with him in Meknes. Eight of the leading 'Ulama', led by Sidi al-Hajj Abdal-Salam ibn Jasus, arrived at the Sultan's court.* A lengthy debate ensued between the 'Ulama' of Fas on the one hand and Faqih 'Alilish on the other in the presence of the Sultan who listened to the opposed views of the two parties. It is claimed that before the debate ended, the Sultan rose and prepared to leave, upon which Jasus held him by the hem of his robes and said, "be seated and listen to what your Grandfather (the Prophet), peace and blessings of Allah be upon him, said." According to Ibn al-Hajj, the Sultan pulled his robes around him and left the audience in a rage.

The views of the 'Ulama' of Fas can be discerned from the two *fatwas* of Sidi al-'Arbi Burdula and 'Adbal-Salam Jasus.[26] The main contention of the 'Ulama' was that the Haratin were free born Muslims and that their forced recruitment was nothing less than the enslavement of free Muslims (*istirqaq*). The Law, they maintained, was specific on this: Free born Muslims could not be enslaved. Burdula announced, "the primary condition of man is freedom. Opinions do not differ on this . . . this basic condition of man cannot be reversed unless concrete evidence to the contrary is produced. This evidence must establish beyond a shadow of a doubt an original slave status. The evidence should be in accord with the Shari'a, free of bias, coercion and the like."[27] Jasus, on the other hand, agreed that it was indeed necessary for a Muslim state to establish strong and sizeable armies. But he reminded M. Isma'il that "This does not mean the enslavement of free men, for joining the army is of one's own free will."[28] The forced recruitment of the Haratin, he claimed, was " . . . an unashamed enslavement of free men and reducing them to servitude with no legal justification." "The Haratin of Fas," he attested, "are free like all other free born Muslims. Their free status is well known and is unquestionable. Therefore, any admission by them that they are slaves of named or unnamed persons, or any testimony given by others accusing them of being slaves, irrespective

---

*These were Sidi Muhammad al-Masnawi, Sidi Muhammad ibn al-Shadhili al-Dala'i, Sidi Muhammad ibn Zakri, Sidi Muhammad al-Mashshat, Sidi Al-'Afya al-Zawwaq, Sidi Muhammad ibn Yada ibn al-Hajj, Sidi al-Hassan ibn Rihal and 'Abdal-Salam Jasus.

of why such testimony was presented, is indeed the result of pressure and coercion. This is witnessed and seen and there is no lack of evidence to support it."[29]

The 'Ulama' of Fas charged that the Haratin were forced to admit to slave-status, while they ('Ulama') were forced to sign the registers. Jasus states in his fatwa that the recruiter "publicly announced to the multitude, the learned and the unlearned that he would make an example of them if they do not comply with this enslavement. He warned them saying that he would inflict on them unbearable penalties such as death, the disgrace of their families and intolerable fines." Forced admissions and forced testimonies are basically wrong and contrary to Muslim law. Jasus asked, "how can one rely on these admissions and accept these confessions? Moreover, how could a person be enslaved or manumitted on the weight of these admissions and testimonies? The legal texts of the A'imma are replete with the opinions that any admission and any confession given under pressure or coercion is null and void and cannot be relied on."[30] According to Jasus admission by the Haratin "to slavery, even if it were of their own volition and not forced on them is invalid. According to the Holy Law, they cannot be subjected to slavery nor bound by their admission. Their freedom is a right that Allah bestowed on them. Therefore, they have no right to choose to enslave themselves."[31] There was no doubt in Jasus' mind as to the free social status of the Haratin of Fas: "We grew up together in the same town. We know them well. We know their free status and nothing pertaining to their condition is hidden from us. But now we have been coerced to retract our firm beliefs and what we are certain of."[32] In conclusion Jasus asked M. Isma'il,

> is it not appropriate for a man of integrity to see to it that these basic principles (of the Holy Law) are observed? In whose name, may we ask, are these authentic legal texts compromised and twisted? How could these abominable distortions and falsifications (of the Holy Law) and all that they engender, which are essentially improper, unsound and do not conform to any legal principle, be perpetrated . . . ? This ignominious (crime) has engendered evil deeds and hideous sins.

Al-Hajj 'Abdal-Salam Jasus was immediately seized, after the audience, and imprisoned in Meknes for three months (June 4-September 8, 1708). A number of the 'Ulama' of Fas, fearing for their lives, fled the town. Sidi Muhammad al-Mashshat for instance fled to Wazzan, returning only after the murder of Jasus. Jasus was released on September 8, 1708 on the condition that he paid a large fine and promised not to agitate against the "collection" of the Fasi

Haratin. However, he was neither able to pay the fine nor prepared to be quiet. Bu 'Ali al-Rusi, who was reinstated to the Governorship of Fas, reimprisoned the Shaikh, tortured him, and confiscated all his and his family's property, even his books.[33]

On July 4, 1709, M. Isma'il ordered that Jasus be killed. The following morning the Faqih of Fas was strangled to death. It is however claimed that before his death he left a note under his pillow. It reads.[34]

> Praise be to Allah. I, the undersigned, attest, may Allah, his Angels and all his creation be my witness that I have refused to agree to the enslavement of those whom they (Isma'il and his Agents) enslaved only because I found neither justification nor any guiding principles in the Shari'a that authorizes this action. And if I acceded to it, voluntarily or under duress, I would have betrayed Allah His Messenger and the Shar'. I am afraid that Hell would then be my eternal abode. I have studied the histories of the earlier A'imma (*imams*) who were coerced to agree to issues that had no legal base in the Shar'. Invariably they neither compromised the Shar' nor did they alter it, even when their lives and possessions were in jeopardy. Let it be known to whomever hoped that I might compromise the Shar' and to whomever fabricated or lied about what I said or did that we will eventually meet before Allah.

There was nothing to constrain M. Isma'il. The "collection" of the Haratin of Fas, it seems, continued unabated. Whether the lips of the 'Ulama' remained sealed as a result of the murder of Jasus is not known. The sources however claim that M. Isma'il went to great lengths in patronising the 'Ulama' of Fas. For instance, he is said to have personally attended the celebrations that were organized in Fas in honour of Sidi Muhammad al-Mashshat upon the latter's completion of the Mukhtasar of Khalil.

APPENDIX I

Fatwa of Abu Muhammad Sidi al-Hajj 'Abdal-Salam ibn Ahmad called Hamdun ibn 'Ali Ibn Ahmad Jasus d. July 4, 1709

... We have been repeatedly informed that his (M. Isma'il's) profound concern with regard (p.198) to the collection of the Haratin and his confirmed interest in this is motivated by nothing more than his sound judgment and firm intention to build extensive armies which are the instrument by which the Faith is upheld and Muslim Lands and the Muslim Community are protected. For it is he (M. Isma'il) who lit the luminous light of the Faith. It must however be said that by this endeavor, he did not crave for a mundane desire, though there are those who thought otherwise. Having misconstrued his intentions, they proceeded to collect the Haratin in a manner that was not only unjust but also contrary to the fundamental precepts of the Holy Law and even to his intentions, may Allah preserve his lofty rank. What else can be said since he (M. Isma'il) has repeatedly announced that he ordered the collection of the Haratin in fulfillment of a religious duty? There is no man of integrity, of learning and piety who denies the fact that his (M. Isma'il's) intentions to increase the size of the armies do not mean the enslavement of free men, for joining the army is of one's own free will. Having thus ascertained all this and that the issue is no longer obscure even to the confused, this calamity that has befallen us at the present time, that is the unashamed enslavement of free men and reducing them to servitude with no legal justification, should be immediately stopped. The manner in which it (enslavement) is carried out, the pretexts given and all the mortal sins and the prohibited acts that are committed in its pursuit should be made public. Its place within the Holy Law should be determined and clearly stated. Such an issue can neither be ignored nor tolerated. And why should it not be so? It is an issue that (p.199) engenders distortion and suppression of the law. And if we agree that the issue is as we said, then may I be permitted to disclose it to Mawlana whose commands are promptly executed and may his firm authority prevail over the evil-doers and the unruly. It is a well known fact those who are today marked out for collection (enslavement) in the town of Fas are free like all other free Muslims. Their free status is well known and is unquestionable. Therefore, any admission by them that they are slaves to named or unnamed persons, or any testimony given by others accusing them of being slaves, irrespective of the manner in which such testimony is presented, is indeed the result of pressure and coercion. This is witnessed and seen and there is no lack of evidence to support it. This is the truth, since the person who is charged with this responsibility (the collection of the Haratin) has publicly announced to the multitude, the learned and the unlearned that he would make an example of them if they do not comply with this enslavement (istirqaq). He warned them saying that he would inflict on them unbearable penalties such as death, the disgrace of their families and intolerable fines. And if we agree on these facts, then how can one rely on these admissions and accept these confessions? Moreover, how could a person be enslaved or manumitted on the weight of these admissions and testimonies? The legal texts of the A'imma are replete with the opinions that (p.200) any admission and any confession given under pressure or coercion is null and void and can not be relied on. Ibn Yunis surmised that Malik had said, "a person under coercion is not bound by forced divorce, forced marriage, forced manumission and the like." According to Ibn 'Arafah the divorce of a person under coercion and all his deeds are invalid. Ibn al-Hajjib stated that forced divorce is inadmissible and likewise are forced marriages and forced manumissions. It has been explicitly stated that if confession, before an interrogator, is suspected of having been given out of fear, it is void and inoperative. In al-Kafi of Ibn 'Abdal-Bar, "the confession of a minor is conceivable without qualification or evidence, only if the interrogator is not known for his ruthlessness and oppression." Those who are today enslaved are free and their free status is well known. Their admission to slavery, even if it were of their own volition and not forced on them, is invalid. According to the Holy Law they cannot be subjected to slavery nor bound by their admission. Their freedom is a right that Allah bestowed on them. Therefore, they have no right to choose to be slaves. Sahnun surmised, "we unanimously agreed on the case of a woman whose descent and free status were well known and whose parents were free, that her confession to being a slave is null and void." Muhammad Ibn Abdal-Hakam said, "if a person is known to be of free origin and he admits that he is a slave, his admission is invalid. A free man has no right to reduce himself to slavery." With regard to this issue, it is more appropriate to take into consideration a person's known and evident status, (p.201) rather than his confession. Moreover, is it not appropriate for a man of integrity to see to it that these basic principles are observed? In whose name, may we ask, are these authentic legal texts compromised and twisted? How could these abominable distortions and falsifications (of the Holy Law) and all that they engender, which are essentially improper, unsound and do not conform to any Legal principle, be perpetrated, when this is known to whomever has the minimum knowledge of the Law and can see that they are used as pretexts to justify the enslavement of free men and trading in them like chattel? And we ask, in the light of the legal texts cited above, are these not alterations and distortions of the Holy Law? This ignominious (crime) has engendered evil deeds and hideous sins. Of these, we enumerate the following. (1) False testimony and its presentation under coercion. The Prophet, peace and blessings of Allah be upon him, explained that false testimony equals polytheism. Abu Da'ud related [the following] (the text which we quote below is his), as did Al-Tirmidhi and Ibn Majah from Fatik, may Allah be pleased with him, the Messenger of Allah, peace and blessings of Allah be upon him, one day led the Dawn Prayer. And upon its conclusion he stood up erect and said three times: "False testimony is equal to polytheism!" Imam (p.202) Ahmad related from Abu Huraira, may Allah be pleased with him, who said, "I heard the Messenger of Allah, peace and blessings of Allah be upon him say: whomever gives a false testimony against a Muslim, will occupy his (deserved) seat in Hell." (2) Of these are forced admission of slave status and forced bondage. He who enslaves a free man is one of the three whose prayers Allah does not accept. Abu Da'ud and Ibn Majah related from 'Abdal-Rahman Ibn Ziyad who transmitted from 'Amran who transmitted from 'Abdallah Ibn 'Umar, may Allah be pleased with both of them, who said, "the Messenger of Allah, peace and blessings of Allah be upon him, said: there are three (men) whose prayers Allah does not accept. A man who leads a people who detest him, a man who observes the prayers *dabari*, that is to say, after the prescribed time has elapsed and a man who enslaves a freed man." He is also one of the three about whom Allah had said that He would be their adversary in the Day of Judgement. Al-Bukhari, Ibn Majah and others transmitted from Abu-Huraira, may Allah be pleased with him, said that the Messenger of Allah, peace and blessings of Allah be upon him, said, "there are three (men) whose adversary I will be at the Day of Judgement, and I will then litigate against whomever is my adversary. There is a man who supported me and then betrayed me; a man who sold a free man and used up the sale price, and a man who hired another, and upon completion of the job did not pay him his dues: (3) Included in these is also the passing of judgments and the giving of Fatwa under coercion. Justice is thus lost to falsehood and error. Allah's commands are neglected, the Sunna of the Messenger of Allah (p.203), peace and blessings of Allah be upon him, is contravened and what Allah has prohibited is made legal. Allah's warnings against this abound. Al-Shaikh Abu-Talib al-Makki surmised in *Al-Qut*, "it was transmitted from Ibn 'Abbas who transmitted from the Prophet (peace and blessing of Allah be upon him), who said: Allah the Glorified and Exalted has three angels. One angel is above the Sacred House of Allah, the second is over the Mosque of the Messenger of Allah, peace and blessings of Allah be upon him and the third is over Jerusalem. They speak out daily. The one over the Sacred House of Allah says: whomever does not observe Allah's prescribed duties will not be under His protection. The angel over the Mosque of the Messenger of Allah (peace and blessings of Allah be upon him), says: whomever contravenes the Sunna of the Messenger of Allah (peace and blessings be upon him), the Messenger of Allah (peace and blessings of Allah be upon him) will not intercede on his behalf. The angel over Jerusalem says: whomever legalizes a prohibition will not find redemption and remorse and tears are of no avail to him." (4) Included in these is also the abolition of the right to manumission and to the freeing of men who were slaves. Free men who were never enslaved and whose forefathers had never been slaves are at the present drawn into slavery. The manumission of such persons has no (legal) basis. The issue opens the door for indiscriminate enslavement so much so that it is impossible to predict who will be affected from amongst this community. Those of noble descent and even the reciters of the Qur'an and the learned men and others may not be spared. (5) Included in these is what is realized today as a result of this affliction (the collection of the Haratin), that is the closure of the door of manumission through which the faithful draw nearer to Allah. At the present time (p.204) there is no certainty that a manumitted person would continue in his new status and join the free Muslim folk. The Lawgiver's sincere love of manumission, His encouragement of it and His promises of abundant rewards for those who manumit their slaves are well known. Let us ponder on what this innovation which has afflicted no other country than this Maghribi country, and no other generation than the present generation, has caused. It is pertinent upon a man of integrity to put a decisive end to it and close the door in its face. We humbly invoke Allah, praise be to Him, to guide Amir Al-Mu'minin to realize its harmfulness and to save us from it. The high and the low are weary of it, for it is an affliction on both the Faith and the World. Because of it, there are those amongst the faithful who wish that they are not amongst the living. In conclusion, it is tantamount to total rejection of the Holy Law; nay, it is tantamount to the casting of the Holy Law behind one's back and the association of an evil innovation with the Shari'a that would become an accepted tradition, so much so that the Holy Law will forever remain an object of ridicule. Allah forbid, for such a thing will not happen in the presence of Amir al-Mu'minin. Besides, the 'Ulama' and 'Ilm, the custodians of the Faith, are forever vigilant. One may ask the question, why have you waited all this time to bring these views to light when similar issues (the collection of the Haratin) did in fact take place in the past? You have never before expressed such opinions nor have you argued for the arresting of such activities? Nay, you have indeed expounded the views which command the collection of the Haratin. The answer to this is, these who were enslaved (p.205) in the past inhabited areas that were far removed from us. We do not know their families, their forefathers, nay, even their names, and much less their free or slave status. As to our views concerning the obligatory nature of enslavement we wished to draw the attention of the collectors to the conditions under which enslavement is permitted, having already seen the signatures of the judges of those far removed areas (in the slave registers). The responsibility for the strict observance of these conditions rests with the judges, the men of note and repute of these areas. As for those who are today marked out for enslavement and who are our immediate concern, we grew up together in the same town (Fas). We know them well. We know their free status and nothing pertaining to their condition is hidden from us. But now we have been coerced to retract our firm beliefs and what we are certain of. On the whole the evils that are associated with this issue are indeed innumerable. May Allah preserve us from error and may He guide our every step. We have said all this because giving of advice is a religious duty. We invoke the Lord, praise be to Him, to forgive us for what still remains in our conscience and for what we have neglected to mention all that is connected with the issue. And I greet his Highness; with blessed and genial greetings.

APPENDIX II

Fatwa of Abu-'Abdallah Sidi Muhammad al-'Arabi
Ibn Ahmad Burdulah Qadi of Fas
(December 15, 1632-May 7, 1721)

(p.189) Our master the Iman, the supported, the gallant, protector of the Faith and the Faithful, humiliator of the aggressor, repressor of the erring and the wrongdoer, leveler of the path for all worshippers, the Khalifah who is loyally followed, the victorious, the praiseworthy, the honoured, the noble, Abu-al-Nasr Mawlana Isma'il, may Allah elevate him and may his days last forever. Peace; Allah's compassion and blessings be with Mawlana. Furthermore, we have received the letter from Mawlana, may Allah protect and support him, and may his armies multiply and grow in size. We studied the letter to the end and understood its contents. We say that although (in general) we agree with its contents we humbly beg to differ. As far as the Khilafah is concerned, evidence for it is in the Book, the Sunna and the consensus opinion of those amongst the community whose opinion carries weight. Why should it not be so, since with it law is preserved, the Faith is spread far and wide, Islam is elevated, roads are kept safe, justice is maintained and dissent is overpowered. Heaven and earth have not existed except by justice and for it; and the Muhammadan Community has not maintained its integrity without the observance of the Law. But what law would prevail amongst the mob or in times of chaos? Be that as it may, Allah has given the responsibility for protecting the Faith and the lands of Islam to you, His Khalifah, the gallant, the victorious . . .

(p.190) Concerning the issue of ownership of slaves (we say) it is based on the sale (of slaves) to the buyer. Opinions do not differ on this. Allah, the Almighty said: Whereas Allah hath permitted trade and forbidden usury (Q. II: 275). The one who is sold is the one who is owned. Whomever is bought from an owner could legally be resold. But if he is bought from a person other than the owner, his sale should be revoked and the slave should be returned to the owner.

Above all, the primary condition of man is freedom. Opinions do not differ on this. According to some learned men, the 'Ulama' are unanimously agreed on this basic condition of man which cannot be reversed unless concrete evidence to the contrary is produced. This evidence must establish beyond a shadow of a doubt that a person is originally a slave. This evidence should be in accord with the Shari'a, free of bias, coercion and the like. If ownership is affirmed, then it becomes the rule of Law . . .

NOTES

1. Al-Fasi, p. 48. The Sharifi 'Alawi dynasty whose descendent, King al-Hassan II, today rules Morocco, claim descent from Prophet Muhammad. They settled in the region of Tafilalt in either the 13th or 14th century. The Sharifs took advantage of the political disturbances that broke out in Morocco at the beginning of the 17th century to establish a dynasty that still holds power in the country.
2. Meyers, p.113.
3. al-Fasi, p.49.
4. Akansus, p.114; al-Aqqad, p.69.
5. Meyers, pp.57 and 114. The conscripted 'Abid and Haratin were at first stationed in two training camps, Mashra' al-Ramal (between Meknes and Sale) and Wujih 'Arus (near Meknes). The soldiers together with the Sultan took an oath of loyalty on Sahih al-Burkhari (a collection of authentic traditions of the Prophet), hence the name 'Abid al-Bukhari.
6. al-Fasi, p.49.
7. al-Zayani, p.15; Akansus, p.94; al-Nasin, p.56.
8. al-Zayani, p.14; Akansus, p.94. Meyers, pp.84-85 suggests that the recruitment must have started sometime between 1674 and 1676.
9. al-Fasi, p.55; Akansus, p.95. Moroccan sources claim that the 'Abid al-Bukhari was 150,000 strong.
10. al-Zayani, p.15; Akansus, p.94.
11. al-Fasi, p.29. See also pp.42, 49-54.
12. al-Fasi, p.54.
13. al-Fasi, p.50.
14. al-Nasiri, p.58.
15. For the etymology of the term Haratin see Colin, G.S., *Encyclopaedia of Islam*, vol. III, n. ed., p.230-31; *Le Sahara*, Ch. 2 and 8.
16. See Gellner and Micaud L. (eds.), pp.53-54 and 95-96; Meyers, pp.63-64; Colin, p.230.
17. Meyers, pp.63-64.
18. al-Fasi, p.56. This argument lends support to the suggestion (see Meyers, pp.92-95) that M. Isma'il must have recruited Abid al-Bukhari from the black slaves who had once worked in the sugar industry in Southern Morocco and had

dispersed throughout the country following its collapse in the first half of the 17th century.
19. al-Fasi, pp.56 and 61.
20. Ibn al-Hajj, vol. 6, pp.389-390.
21. al-Fasi, p.56.
22. al-Fasi, p.61.
23. Ibn al-Hajj, vol. 6, pp.393-394.
24. Ibn al-Hajj, vol. 6, p.395.
25. Ibn al-Hajj, vol. 4, pp.184-187.
26. Ibn al-Hajj, vol. 4, pp.189-205; see also Appendix I and II. For the biographies of Burdula and Jasus, see al-Kattani, vol. 2, pp.14-15 and vol. 3, pp.138-139; al-Nasiri, p.94-95.
27. Ibn al-Hajj, vol. 4, p.190.
28. Ibn al-Hajj, vol. 4, p.198.
29. Ibn al-Hajj, vol. 4, p.199.
30. Ibn al-Hajj, vol. 4, p.200.
31. Ibn al-Hajj, vol. 4, p.205.
32. Ibn al-Hajj, vol. 4, p.201.
33. Ibn al-Hajj, vol. 4, pp.210-211; al-Kattani, vol. 2, p.15, al-Nasiri, p.94.
34. Ibn al-Hajj, vol. 4, p.212; al-Nasiri, p.95.

BIBLIOGRAPHY

Al-'Aqqad, Salah, *al-Maghrib al-'Arabi*, Cairo, 1966.
Akansus, Abi 'Abdalla Muhammad b. Ahmad, *al-Jaysh al-'Aramram al-Khumasi*, al-Khizana al'Amma, Rabat, No.26.
Colin, G.S., "Haratin," in *Encyclopaedia of Islam*, vol. III, n. ed., pp.230-231.
Delafosse, M., "Les débuts des troupes noires du Maroc, " in *Hésperis*, III, 1928, pp.1-12.
Gellner, E. and Micaud, C., *Arabs and Berbers*, London, 1972, Chs. by David M. Harr and Ross E. Dunn.
al-Fasi, Muhammad, in *Hésperis Tamuda*, special issue, Rabat, 1962; *Majalat Tatuan*, special issue, 1962, pp.27-28.
Ibn al-Hajj, *al-Dur al Muntakhab al-Mustahsan*, al-Khizana al-'Amma, Rabat, No. 1875.
Le Sahara: Rapports et contacts humains, Aix-en-Provence, 1967.
Meyers, A.R., "The 'Abid'l'Buhari: Soldiers and Statecraft in Morocco, 1672-1790," Ph.D. Thesis, Cornell, 1974.
al-Nasiri, Ahmad b. Khalid, *al-Istiqsa Li-Akhbar Duwal al-Maghrib al-Aqsa*, vol. 7, Casablanca, 1966.
Salim, Mahmud Abdal-'Aziz, *Al-Maghrib al-Islami*, 2 vols., Cairo, n. d.
Yahya, Jalal, *al-Maghrib al-Kabir*, 4 vols. Cairo, 1966.

II

Notes on Slavery in the Songhay Empire

J.O. Hunwick

This paper is an attempt to assemble and, so far as is possible, to analyse the information available on the institution of slavery in a single African state. Although there was a Songhay state from as early as the eighth century in all probability, virtually nothing is known of its history and institutions until the time when it expanded from its nucleus in Songhay proper[1] to become an imperial power in the second half of the fifteenth century, asserting its complete domination over the Middle Niger "from Kanta to Sibiridugu"[2] and raiding and exacting tribute from a much wider belt of the Sahel from the R. Senegal to the Air massif and northern Hausaland.[3] Slavery, of course, existed in the area long before the fifteenth century and continued to exist long after the destruction of the Songhay empire by the forces of the Sa'dian sultan al-Mansur. But the particular interest in restricting this inquiry to the epoch of imperial Songhay (roughly the period 1450-1600) lies in the light such an inquiry may throw on the social and economic institutions of a single cohesive and highly organised African state and of the ways in which Islam may have affected traditions of slavery and servitude in such a state. The period is treated as a unity despite the change of dynasty from the Sunnis to the Askias in 1493. The change appears to have had no influence on slavery as an institution, except in so far as the enslavement of Muslims under the Askias was much less common.

The sources upon which this study is based are regrettably very limited. There are the two well-known chronicles, the *Ta'rikh al-Sudan* written in Timbuktu in c.1655 by 'Abd al-Rahman al-Sa'di[4] and the *Ta'rikh al-Fatash*, a work written by several hands and compiled in its original form c.1655 by Ibn al-Mukhtar, a descendant of the *qadi* of Tindirma Mahmud Ka'ti.[5] In addition there are two works of a juridical nature: the "Replies" of the North African scholar al-Maghili to the questions of Askia al-hajj Muhammad I, written probably in Gao, c.1498,[5a] and the replies entitled *Mi'raj al-su'ud* or *al-Kashf wa'l-bayan li-asnaf majlub al-sudan* written by the Timbuktu jurist Ahmad Baba in 1608 in reply to questions sent to him from the Saharan oasis of Tuwat.[6] The final source is the seventh part of Leo Africanus's *Della Discrittione dell'Africa* first published in 1550 and containing information on the Middle Niger gathered by the author in the course of two journeys in the area in the early years of the sixteenth century.[7]

These works are of unequal value for the present study. Those written by al-Maghili and Ahmad Baba were conceived from the viewpoint of Mulim jurists endeavouring to explain and uphold the law of Islam (*al-shari'a*) by defining what categories of person might be enslaved or be retained in slavery. Though often general and theoretical, both contain some information of interest to the social historian. The two local chronicles, though written two generations after the overthrow of the Songhay empire, both draw on earlier written sources or accounts handed down orally from the sixteenth century. The *Ta'rikh al-Fattash* presents special problems which have been ably exposed by Nehemiah Levtzion.[8] While in the present state of knowledge about the textual history of this work his conclusions cannot be said to be definitive, it is clear that the material found in Manuscript C (the only "complete" one) which does not appear in Manuscript A/B represents an insertion posterior to the composition of A/B and it must be suspected (though it cannot at present be proved) that the social situations depicted in such passages belong to a period later than that to which they allegedly refer.[9] This includes nearly all the material on the so-called "servile tribes" which Askia Muhammad I was supposed to have "inherited" from Sunni 'Ali who "inherited" them from the ruler of Mali. Not surprisingly under the circumstances there is no mention of these twenty-four "servile tribes" in any of the written or oral accounts concerning the Mali empire. Such an argument *ex silentio* does not, of course, *prove* that such servile groups did not exist in the Middle Niger area in the 15th-16th centuries, but in view of the legitimate doubt surrounding their existence during the period of the Songhay empire, no mention will be made of their role, except for the Sorko and Arbi who appear also in Manuscript A/B.[10] Leo Africanus's material has the advantage of being based on its author's eye-witness, for though doubt may be cast on his claims to have visited Mali, Jenne, the Hausa states and Bornu, it seems most likely that he visited at least Timbuktu, Kabara and Gao. Its disadvantage is that Leo only recorded his impressions (at least in book form) some fifteen years later, writing in very poor Italian (which was polished by his publisher Ramusio) rather than his native Arabic.[11] Though his account of the area contains some manifest inaccuracies on points of detail his few remarks on slavery are consistent with what is known from other sources.

The Middle Niger to as far downstream as Gao had come under the domination of Mali in the late thirteenth century and remained within its political orbit for approximately a century and a half. When Mali's power began to decline in the late fourteenth century its grip on its eastern provinces began to loosen. By 1433 they had lost Timbuktu to the Touareg and it was no doubt at the same period that the Songhay re-established their control over Gao. By the middle of the century the Sunnis were already flexing their muscles to supplant the Malians in the west; Sunni Sulayman Dama is said to have raided as far afield as Mema to the west of the Middle Niger flood plain. But it was only under Sunni 'Ali (1464-1492) that the Songhay began to embark on a wide-ranging movement of expansion along the river Niger and into its hinterland on both the right (*gurma*) and left (*hausa*) banks, establishing an empire that stretched from beyond Jenne to the borders of Kebbi and included much of the mountainous region between Hombori and Bandiagara and the desert regions from Walata to Azawad. Askia al-hajj Muhammad I, who seized power from 'Ali's son and successor Abu Bakr within a matter of months, consolidated these gains and extended the sphere of his authority, however precariously, westwards into the northern provinces of Mali and eastwards to the northern Hausa states and Air. He came to terms with the Tuareg and forged a marriage alliance with their chief in the Timbuktu region and it was under him that the salt pans of Taghaza came under Songhay control. To the south relations remained hostile. There were several raids on the Mossi and Gurmantche and unsuccessful forays were made into Borgu.

The motives and mechanics of these wide-ranging conquests and raids need not concern us here. What does concern us is the fact that these military activities resulted in the seizure of many captives who were brought back to the central lands of the empire and especially to the royal city of Gao. Thus, after the much-vaunted jihad which Askia Muhammad I waged against the Mossi in 1498, so many captives were brought back to Gao that a special quarter had to be built for them.[12] In a raid on Dialan in Mali in 1501-2 many captives were taken, including a woman called Maryam Dabo who became the mother of Askia Isma'il.[13] Similarly a raid on Borgu in 1505-6 produced large numbers of captives, among whom was the future mother of Askia Musa.[14] A raid into "Gurma" (inner buckle of the Niger) during the reign of Askia Isma'il (1539-1549) produced so many slaves that their price on the Gao market fell to a paltry 300 cowries.[15] Many raids probably had no other motive than obtaining slaves. One of Askia Dawud's sons boasted that even his younger brother could go out with a raiding party (*sariyya*) and come back with 10,000 slaves and, although this is doubtless a much exaggerated claim, it does seem to indicate that forays of this kind were fairly commonplace.[16] Leo Africanus also indicated that many slaves had been obtained in the course of expeditions against the Hausa States – information he could well have obtained at Gao rather than from any alleged visit to the states in question.[17]

Sunni 'Ali is reported to have amassed slaves and wealth from many different quarters.[18] He did not respect the prohibition on enslaving his fellow-Muslims; indeed, many of the territories he conquered were inhabited largely by Muslims. Askia Muhammad, who sought to legitimise his seizure of power by posing as the champion of Islam who had abolished the "pagan" rule of Sunni 'Ali,[19] naturally had to take a firmer line on such questions and the scholars of Timbuktu who gave his rule a strong moral prop, were there to see that the norms of the *shari'a* were upheld. Islamic law, as Ahmad Baba pointed out,[20] rules that the sole reason permitting the enslavement of a man is his being an "unbeliever" who is not a protected person (dhimmi) belonging to a group that has not made a pact of peace with the Muslims. He should have been captured in a jihad after having refused the summons to Islam. The born Muslim, or one converted before such a jihad takes place, is *ipso facto* a free man. A non-Muslim converted to Islam only after capture, however, remains a slave until formally liberated through one of the many channels that Islamic law provides.

The problem which Askia Muhammad had to face after his accession was what to do with the large number of men and women who had been enslaved by Sunni 'Ali or his officials and who claimed that they were Muslims at the time of their capture. On the advice of al-Maghili, to whom he put this problem,[21] he set at liberty all those who claimed that they were free-born Muslims. A similar view of the problem is attributed to the *qadi* of Timbuktu Mahmud b. 'Umar (held office 1498-1548) who ruled that all those slaves who claimed to be free-born Muslims should be set free and the burden of proof in the matter should rest upon their owners.[22] The Askia also asked al-Maghili about the position of children born of the concubines of Sunni 'Ali and his officials when these concubines had been obtained from the booty of campaigns. He ruled that the children should be considered free, though their mothers could be sold.[23] The argument seems to have been (though not stated clearly in such terms) that the fathers were, at least in origin, Muslims and hence free, even if they had apostatised through their acts, and in Islamic law the child follows the status of its father. Similar problems seem to have been current in the Air region at the same period, to judge from the questions which Muhammad al-Lamtuni addressed to al-Suyuti in 1493.[24]

The problem evidently did not end there. There were many who claimed to be Muslims, but whose practice of the faith was so tainted with non-Islamic customs and beliefs that, according to al-Maghili, they could legitimately be re-enslaved; the particular group referred to in the "Replies" appear, from his description of their "cult of the fox" to have been Dogon.[25] Even if the Askias upheld the Islamic position with regard to enslavement (and not all of them may have been as rigorous as Muhammad I), their officials may not always have followed their example. In the reign of Askia Isma'il, Farina 'Ali Kushiya made himself notorious for enslaving freeborn Muslims. Fate had its revenge, however. Having fled following an abortive attempt on the Askia's life, he ended up as the slave of a desert Arab.[26] In periods of weakness or inadvertence the Muslims of the Middle Niger area were liable to be attacked and carried off into slavery by powerful non-Muslim neighbours. The celebrated Mossi attack on Walata in 1480 originally led to the capture of many families, though these were subsequently released. When Songhay authority collapsed following the Sa'dian invasion of 1591, raiding Fulbe, Bambara and Dyawambe (Zaghrani) in the west, carried off many Muslims – especially women – into slavery. Revenge was taken on the Dyawambe by the Moroccan *qa'id* Mami who raided them and carried off many women and children who were sold in Timbuktu for prices of 200–400 cowries.[27]

The cumulative evidence of the two chronicles shows that very large numbers of slaves were amassed in the area of the Middle Niger in the sixteenth century. What, one may ask, was the economic motive for the acquisition of all these slaves and what roles did they play in the economic and social life of the Songhay empire? Firstly, though our sources are strikingly uninformative on the subject, it is evident that some of these slaves were sold to North African traders. Some must also have been sold to the Arabo-Berber tribes of the southern Sahara whose economy has traditionally been heavily dependent on slave labour for tending crops in oases and on lake and river banks, for pasturing flocks, drawing water and serving in numerous capacities in the desert encampments. Slaves provided the labour force at the salt pans of Taghaza and later Taoudeni.[28] They smelted copper at Takedda in Ibn Battuta's day (1353)[29] and, no doubt, until production ceased. Leo Africanus reports that the merchants of Agades used slaves to form armed escorts for their caravans to Hausaland and Borno.[30]

If the chronicles are virtually silent on the trans-Saharan slave trade, it is only fair to point out that they say little about trade of any sort except by implication,[31] though we know from the little they do say that Timbuktu was a very prosperous city of commerce. It may be suggested that an activity such as selling off slaves for transportation to North Africa was such a commonplace activity, so much part of the fabric of normal life as to require no comment. The one time when our attention is drawn to an Arab slave-dealer is when he becomes involved in trying to negotiate the purchase of a lot of five hundred slaves which had come into the hands of Askia Dawud from the inheritance of one of his officials.[32] But the point of the passage is not to inform us about the slave trade, but rather to show the generosity of the Askia who disdained the merchant's price of 5,000 *mithqals* and chose to parcel them out as gifts.

A better piece of evidence for a flourishing trans-Saharan trade in slaves comes in the reply which Ahmad Baba sent to the men of Tuwat on this matter. The Tuwatis were concerned about which slaves they could deal in with good conscience on the clear understanding that they would not be Muslims. Ahmad Baba advised that any slave who claimed his origin was from Bornu, Kano, Katsina or Songhay should not be taken as a slave since these were lands of Islam. He also pointed out (quoting Ibn Khaldun) that the people of Mali were long-standing Muslims and he declared the Fulbe to be Muslims, except for some living beyond Jenne. At the end of his *Mi'raj* is a list of the non-Muslim groups of West Africa known to him who could be retained in slavery in good conscience. This list is appended as an after-thought, it seems, and may be a later addition. Nevertheless, apart from one or two names it represents the ethnic groups against whom the Askians did in fact make raids: Mossi, Gurma, Busa, Borgu, Kotokoli, Dagomba, Yoruba (?), Bobo, Tombo (hill Dogon), Kambe (or Kambebe, Dogon of the plain). The importance of Tuwat in the trans-Saharan slave trade was earlier emphasised by Antoine Malfante writing from there in 1447 and he remarked on the cheapness of slaves there "which the blacks take in their internecine wars".[33]

The slaves who were retained within the lands of the Middle Niger were put to various uses. Many, perhaps most, of the nubile females were taken as concubines by the Askias, high officials of state, army commanders and merchants. In periods of glut even the common man could no doubt afford to purchase. Sunni 'Ali is reputed to have built up an enormous harem, not bothering whether the women he selected for it were free-born Muslims or slaves.[34] According to Leo Africanus,[35] Askia Muhammad also possessed "an enormous number of wives, concubines, slaves and eunuchs". These, in defiance of Islamic law, were taken over *en bloc* by his rebellious son Musa when he seized power.[36] Except for Muhammad I himself, all the other Askias were sons of concubines. The large number of sons produced through concubinage meant that on the death of an Askia the contenders for the throne were very numerous and hence the new Askia generally had to spend the early days of his reign eliminating the most dangerous of the pretenders. Once such a purge had been carried through the remaining brothers of any rank were appointed to state offices. Thus, to a large extent the Songhay state became a family oligarchy.

There is some evidence of other occupations engaged in by female slaves. Leo Africanus mentions that food sales in the Timbuktu market were in the hands of slave women who could appear there unveiled and conduct business openly whereas free women had to be veiled and were, no doubt, kept mainly within their houses[37]. This practice has been retained down to the present century. Miner, writing about conditions at Timbuktu in 1940 remarks: "The women, who are the principal sellers in the market, are all slaves or serfs. Alfa and Arab women not only do not sell in the market, they may not even buy there. Their slaves or husbands do the shopping."[38] Slave women were also engaged as singers at court, a practice common in many Muslim kingdoms. Askia Muhammad Bunkan (1531-1537) introduced many innovations at his court including some new musical instruments and singers both male and female (*qayn/qayna*, the words indicating in themselves a slave origin).[39] After a raid on northern Mali in 1550 Askia Dawud had to establish a special quarter in Gao for the numerous Fulbe of the Maabe caste who were singers and weavers by profession.[40] When the Balama al-Sadiq fled after being defeated by Askia Ishaq II in 1588 he took with him three concubines who had accompanied his campaign together with fourteen other women belonging to a blacksmith group who were evidently musicians (*al-haddadiyyat al-zamirat* – singers or, possibly, flutists).[41] The fact that they were clearly under his complete control and obliged to accompany him indicates that they were of slave or servile status. This, then, would appear to be evidence of the unfree status of smiths among the Songhay from as early as the sixteenth century, a status which that society has recognised until modern times.[42]

Reference has already been made to the eunuchs who lived in the

Askia's palace at Gao and whose principal job was, according to Leo Africanus, to guard over the harem. By the time of Askia Dawud (1548-1583) they were very numerous at court. The *Ta'rikh al-Fattash* reports that this Askia was flanked by 700 eunuchs at his Friday audience, an astonishing figure if true.[43] Like the Black eunuchs in the service of the Ottoman sultan, the favoured eunuchs at the Songhay court had intimate access to the ruler. Askia Muhammad Bani's closest personal servant who woke him from sleep was a eunuch; so was the master of the royal wardrobe.[44] One wonders if they ever acquired the same influence at court as those of the Ottoman sultans did in the 17th and 18th centuries.[45] The Askia's army also contained a sizeable eunuch corps which seems to have constituted an important part of the royal cavalry. Figures of 2,000 and 4,000 are mentioned in the two chronicles as the number of eunuchs who took the field against the revolted Balama al-Sadiq.[46] They were under the command of the *Hugu-korei-koi*, "Chief of the Palace Interior", a title which could also be read as *Hu-kokorei-koi*, "Chief of the Palace Eunuchs". In another place this official is described as the confidant (*bitana*)[47] of the Askia which is another indication that he may have been a eunuch. Another eunuch foiled a plot to install a son of Askia Isma'il as ruler after the death of Muhammad Bahi. When he was sent to summon Ishaq son of Askia Dawud he disclosed the plot to him, allowing Ishaq to rally his forces and take power himself.[48] The same eunuch, Tabakali who was given the post of Barei-koi (probably meaning "Commander of Cavalry"), played a heroic role in the battle of Tondibi against the Moroccan troops in 1591.[49] There is one recorded case (and there may have been more, of course) of a eunuch holding an important administrative post. In 1588 the post of Kabara-farma, "Customs Collector of Kabara", was held by the "tyrannical, over-bearing and high-handed" eunuch 'Alu.[50] It was his quarrel with the Balama al-Sadiq that sparked off a major revolt against the Askia.

There is no indication where these eunuchs were obtained from or whether they were already operated upon at the time of their capture or purchase or after. According to al-Maghili, Sunni 'Ali used to castrate men, though the way in which this is mentioned makes it seem as if this form of mutilation was used as a form of punishment rather than as a means of producing eunuchs for service.[51] Leo Africanus claims that Askia Muhammad I had some of the sons of the ruler of Gobir castrated for service in his palace when he conquered that territory, but this report must be regarded with some caution, since there is no mention in any of our sources of a Songhay attack on Gobir.[52] One possible source may have been from the very numerous slaves who were obtained from the Mossi and Gurma lands. Certainly, if the operation were carried out after capture a large reservoir of young men would be required since the mortality rate is generally very high.[53] A recent writer reports that the Mossi themselves had the reputation of being skilled gelders, but he gives no source for this information.[54]

As will already be clear, the Askias were major "consumers" of slave labour. We have already noted the employment of eunuchs as cavalrymen and it may be wondered what proportion of Songhay armies as a whole was made up of slaves. This involves a small digression into military organisation. Under Sunni 'Ali armies appear to have been levied for specific campaigns. Each ruler who came to power would no doubt have had his own loyal group of warriors who would serve as commanders; many apparently had to fight their way to power,[55] as did Askia Muhammad I and some of his successors. According to al-Sa'di, everyone had been liable to be called on to fight in Sunni 'Ali's time, whereas Askia Muhammad I "made a distinction between the ordinary citizen (*al-ra'iyya*) and the military (*al-jund*)".[56] This suggests that the Askias had a standing professional army at Gao. The fact that Askia Muhammad Bunkan could be said to have increased the size of the army by 1,700 men again suggests a regular body of troops.[57] Regional commanders had their own troops, of which the only one capable of confronting the "Songhay force" (*jund Songhay*, apparently the Askia's troops) was that of the Kurmina-fari.[58] Though the use of the terminology does not seem always consistent, there appears to be a distinction between the use of the words *jund* and *jaysh*, the first meaning a body of troops controlled directly by either the Askia or one of the regional commanders, and the second meaning the army composed of several of these "regiments" assembled for a major campaign.[59] It would not be surprising if elements in these "regiments", and specifically a bodyguard element were slaves; such a practice was common in North Africa and Egypt. Askia Dawud, in fact claimed that the men of his jund were his slaves and he began the practice of inheriting the entire possessions of a deceased *jundi*. Prior to his time the Askias had only "inherited" the horse, the spear and the shield of a deceased jundi, though they had apparently all felt free to take daughters of their jundis as concubines.[60] This latter practice alone would appear to indicate that members of the jund were of slave status, though the fact that it was only Dawud who started formally to consider them slaves may indicate that they were not war captives (i.e. slaves in the technical Islamic sense), but members of some traditionally "servile" group, perhaps of the Sorko

Slavery in the Songhay Empire

or Arbi whom Askia Muhammad claimed as his personal possessions (*mamluk*) and forbade anyone else to marry into.[61]

The Askias, at least from Dawud onwards, also made extensive use of slaves as agricultural labourers. Dawud possessed (whether by inheritance from his predecessor or otherwise is not known) large tracts of rich agricultural land along the banks of the river Niger from Dendi in the south-east to the Lake Debo area in the north-west. These royal estates were set aside for the production of rice, of which over 4,000 *sunnu* (about 800 tons) were sent back to Gao each year. Production was undertaken by slaves working under "slave captains" (*fanfa*), each of whom might be in charge of between twenty and a hundred slaves.[62] At a large estate called Abda in Dendi there were two hundred slaves working under four fanfas, at the head of whom was a chief fanfa responsible for the whole estate.[63] These plantations and their labour force were the property of the Askia (though whether personally or officially is not clear) and he could give away parts of them, as, for example, Dawud did on one occasion to Alfa Ka'ti.[64] The full extent of this practice is not clear, though other high officials may have also owned farms worked by slaves. When an apparently minor official of Askia Dawud died (himself, perhaps, a slave) he left behind five hundred slaves and the equivalent of about 300 tons of grain which, with the rest of his property, the Askia took for himself, eventually giving away most of the slaves as an act of piety and setting free a group representing three generations of a single family.[65] The very person sent by Dawud to take charge of the estate of the deceased official was called by the Askia "one of my slaves and a member of my jund" and this is only one of several examples that could be given of slaves being sent off on missions of trust to distant parts.

Mention has already been made of the two groups whom the Askia considered to be his mamluks – the Sorko and the Arbi. The Sorko are fishermen and boatmen who move up and down the river Niger seasonally between Kebbi and Lake Debo and are probably a pre-Songhay autochthonous group. It is probably they who are referred to as providing boats for the Askia[66] and they are no doubt those mamluks of the Askia who were said to have a thousand boats ready to ferry the inhabitants of Gao across to the *gurma* bank at the time of the Moroccan invasion.[67] The Arbi are less easily identifiable. The name Arbi simply means "black man" which may indicate that they are descendents of some autochthonous stock also, but associated with the soil rather than the water.[68] These two groups are specifically referred to in the document of privilege (*hurma*) which Askia Muhammad I granted to the descendents of Mori Hawgaro. They were allowed to marry anyone throughout the Songhay realm with the exception of the women of Sorko and Arbi. If, however, they transgressed this rule and married one, the offspring would be free. The woman would only be "free" during the period of the marriage and when that terminated by the husband's death or by divorce, the woman returned to the Askia's ownership.[69] Clearly the Askia was very anxious to retain both of these groups in perpetual bondage, making an exception only if the children were fathered by holy men (something one suspects had already happened by the time the document was drawn up). Possession of these groups of descendents of the aboriginal owners of the land and the water may be seen as a legitimation on the traditional level of the Askia's right to rule the Songhay territory.

There may, perhaps, be a reference to these groups in one of the questions which Askia Muhammad I put to al-Maghili which refers to those who "have among them slaves who are neither sold nor given away. These people say they are slaves of the sultanate to be inherited by whoever inherits it from the deceased, such as the son of the sister for example".[70] At first sight this does not appear to refer to the Songhay state. The question is framed in such a way that it sounds as if a third party is being referred to; secondly the practice of succession passing through a sister's son sounds Tuareg rather than Songhay. However, the question itself, in the form in which it has come down to us, no doubt owes its phraseology to al-Maghili himself and in this fatwa-type literature issues are usually dealt with by discreetly avoiding the mention of specific names. Secondly, according to some sources, Askia Muhammad I was actually the son of Sunni 'Ali's sister.[71] However, whether or not the reference is to Songhay practice, the reply which al-Maghili gave would have served to sanction a custom such as the maintenance of the perpetual servitude of the Sorko and Arbi. He ruled that such slaves are to be considered "like an endowment (*hubs*) from the days of the forefathers who set them aside (as a *waqf*) for those to whom they belong in accordance with their customs".[72]

We know very little about how slaves changed hands or to what extent slaves were liberated during this period. Some light may be thrown on this if we come across more fatwa material dating from the sixteenth century. Many decisions must have been given on matters relating to slavery by the jurists of Timbuktu, Jenne, Goa and other centres. The view of Qadi Mahmud b. 'Umar on granting freedom to all those who claimed it unless their masters could prove the opposite has already been referred to. The jurist Makhluf al-Balbali, a contemporary of Mahmud also held the same view.[73] The replies given by al-'Aqib al-Insamni (or Anusamani) of Takedda to both Askia Muhammad I and Qadi Mahmud may well have contained rulings on such issues, but neither work has yet been recovered.[74]

What we do know is that slaves very often formed gifts or parts of gifts given out by the Songhay rulers and, in at least one recorded case, by a Songhay official.[75] Sunni 'Ali made gifts of slave girls to some of the scholars of Timbuktu after a successful raid on some Fulbe.[76] Askia Muhammad I gave ten slaves and one hundred cows to the great-grandsons of Mori Hawgaro and promised them such a gift annually.[77] Askia Dawud made many such gifts which are dwelt on at length in the *Ta'rikh al-Fattash*. His many expeditions must have produced a great surplus of slaves. These slaves needed feeding, as did the armies that campaigned and seized them. Hence, perhaps, the intense agricultural activity which is evident in his reign and which, in itself, absorbed some of the slave labour.[78] With large numbers of slaves passing through his hands, Dawud could afford to show his liberality and give some away. A few examples will suffice. When Buba Maryam, the ruler of Masina, who had been held at Gao on charges of treachery was released and opted to remain in the Askia's service at Gao, he was given many slaves plus ten horses.[79] On two occasions Dawud gave Alfa Ka'ti gifts of slaves, once tied to a piece of land and on the other occasion as a reward for good advice.[80] When the Sa'dian sultan al-Mansur sent an embassy to Gao with princely gifts, Dawud returned the compliment, including eighty eunuchs and other slaves among his gifts.[81] When Dawud established gardens for the poor at Timbuktu he sent thirty slaves to work them. Askia Ishaq II also made a gift of ten slaves to Alfa Ka'ti[83] and, as part of the deal he tried to effect with the Sultan al-Mansur through his commander the Pasha Judar, he offered a thousand slaves.[84]

References to manumission are equally sparse, though it was probably a common occurrence as it was in most Muslim lands. When the scholars of Timbuktu were given Fulbe slave girls by Sunni 'Ali some of them (including an ancestor of al-Sa'di) married them rather than taking them as concubines.[85] To do so would have meant liberating them first. Askia Muhammad I evidently set free a large number of slaves who came into his possession after overthrowing the Sunni dynasty since many of them claimed to be freeborn Muslims. There is also the case, referred to above, of the slaves of three generations of a single family whom Askia Dawud freed, and on this occasion a deed of manumission was drawn up which some of Dawud's sons witnessed.[86] On another occasion some slaves given by the same Askia to a group of *sharifs* were freed by them and given permission to settle where they pleased.[87] The fact that their freedom to settle where they wished is deemed worthy of mention is perhaps an indication that generally freed slaves continued to be tied to their masters in some way even after being formally freed. It was, in fact, common practice in the central Muslim world for freed slaves to remain clients (*mawali*) of the family of their former master for up to three generations and if such a freedman died without legal heirs the family of the master inherited from him. It also commonly happened that such a freedman's descendants later claimed to belong to the lineage of their former master. In the Songhay case quoted above the freed slaves of the sharifs did later claim sharifian status.[88]

The material presented above, based solely on contemporary or near contemporary sources is very sketchy, due to the nature of the sources themselves. Hence it seemed that the paper deserved no more ambitious a title than 'Notes'. Material relating to later periods has been rigorously excluded (except for an occasional comparison), since the social and economic changes brought about in the region by the Moroccan conquest were certainly very profound. In a period of turmoil with only a weak central authority the social order must have been considerably modified. The Askias of the north were mere puppets, having a relation to the Pashas similar to that of the 'Abbasid caliphs of Cairo to the Mamluks in the period 1250-1517. The Askias of the south were never able to restore any of the glory of their ancestors and their state in Dendi seems to have been of little consequence. Lacking a powerful defender, the peoples of the Middle Niger were themselves raided and enslaved. On the other hand the large numbers of slaves owned by the Askias were no doubt able to assert their freedom when the central authority of the Askias broke down and their armies were scattered to the four winds. The history of slavery and, indeed, the wider social history of the period of the pashalik merits a separate study.

For the fifteenth and sixteenth centuries the best hope for additional source materials is likely to come from juridical literature, despite its generally theoretical bias. At least one collection of fatwas given by the scholars of the Western Sudan has been put together and a copy is known to exist in Timbuktu.[89] A thorough examination of this and other similar material, if such can be found, would doubtless enrich our understanding of matters relating to the ownership, inheritance and manumission of slaves, though they are unlikely to help us with the important historical questions concerning the Songhay empire's economic dependence on slave labour and the slave trade. Short of the appearance of some hitherto unknown sixteenth century chronicle (perhaps the phantom *Durar al-hisan?*)[90] the above materials and any other hints and allusions that can be gleaned from the *ta'rikhs* will have to suffice. Even in their present state it is hoped that these notes will serve as raw material for those interested in undertaking comparative studies.

NOTES

1. That is, along the banks of the Niger downstream of Gao within the present-day Republic of Mali, and within modern Niger along the banks of the Niger down to the border with Nigeria including wide areas of hinterland of the left bank between the Niger and the two dallols, Bosso and Maouri.
2. These are the limits frequently cited in the Timbuktu chronicles. "Kanta" is the state of Kebbi, whose ruler was also known by that title. Sibiridugu was the most easterly province of Mali along the Niger extending downstream to roughly the area of modern Segu.
3. See below, n. 52.
4. Text and translation published by O. Houdas, *Tarikh Es-Soudan*, Paris, 1898-1900. References in this paper are to the Arabic text.
5. Text and translation published by O. Houdas and M. Delafosse, *Tarikh El-Fettach ou Chronique du Chercheur* ... par Mahmoud Kâti ben El-Hadj El-Motaouakkel Kati et l'un de ses petits-fils, Paris, 1913-1914. References are to the Arabic text.
5a. Text and translation in J. O. Hunwick, 'Al-Maghili's Replies to the Questions of Askia al-Hajj Muhammad ...' unpublished Ph.D. thesis, University of London, 1974.
6. Manuscript in the Bibliothèque Générale et Archives, Rabat, D1724, ff. 1v-7r (also paginated pp. 1-12, to which references in this paper refer). Ms. 82/293 of the University of Ibadan Library was also consulted.
7. Published in Giovanni-Battista Ramusio, *Delle navigationi e viaggi*, Venezia, 1550. The translation of A. Epaulard, *Description de l'Afrique*, 2 vols., Paris, 1956, is the reference in footnotes to this paper.
8. "A seventeenth-century chronicle by *Ibn al-Mukhtar*: a critical study of *Ta'rikh al-Fattash*", *Bull. S.O.A.S.*, 34 (1971), pp.571-93.
9. This text has had a very chequered history, even more so than the picture presented by Levtzion's analysis, I believe. A new critical text is called for, but this cannot be prepared until all the mss. used by Houdas and Delafosse have been located and all the fragments brought together.
10. See below, p. 24.
11. See Epaulard's introduction to his translation, p. vi.
12. *Ta'rikh al-Sudan* (hereafter T/S), p.74.
13. *ibid.*
14. T/S, p.96.
15. T/S, p.94.
16. *Ta'rikh al-Fattash* (hereafter T/F), p.105.
17. *Description*, ii, pp. 473, 476-8.
18. J. O. Hunwick, "Al-Maghili's Replies ..." (hereafter "Replies"), p.216. This and all other references are to the Arabic text.
19. Al-Maghili was asked to pronounce on whether or not Sunni 'Ali was an unbeliever. His affirmative reply not only justified Askia Muhammad's *coup*

d'état but legitimised the seizure of all the property of Sunni 'Ali and his supporters.
20. *Mi'raj*, p.2.
21. "Replies", pp. 211-12.
22. *Mi'raj*, p.5.
23. "Replies", 210-11.
24. J. O. Hunwick, "Notes on a late fifteenth-century document concerning 'Al-Takrur'," in C. Allen and R. W. Johnson, *African Perspectives*, Cambridge, 1970; see Section 5 (p.13) and Section 23 (p.17).
25. "Replies", pp. 216-17, 221-22.
26. T/S, p.97.
27. T/S, pp. 143, 157-8.
28. Ibn Battuta, *Tuhfat al-nuzzar*, edited and translated by C. Defrémery and B. Sanguinetti, *Voyages d'Ibn Battuta*, 4 vols., Paris, 1854; see iv, p.378 for Taghaza in 1352. For Taudeni in the nineteenth century see René Caillié, *Travels through Central Africa to Timbuctoo*, London, 1830 (reprinted Frank Cass, London, 1968), ii, p.117.
29. *Voyages*, iv, p.441
30. *Description*, ii, p.473.
31. E.g. by mentioning prices of goods when excessively high or low or by mentioning (T/S, p. 21) that when Timbuktu eclipsed Walata the pious and wealthy came there from all quarters (a long list of towns and countries is given).
32. T/F, p.104.
33. "Letter written from Touat and addressed to Giovanni Marione at Genoa, 1447" in A. J. Crone (ed.), *The Voyages of Cadamosto and other documents on Western Africa in the second half of the 15th century*, London (Hakluyt Soc., series II, vol. 80), pp. 88-89.
34. "Replies", p. 201.
35. *Description*, ii, p.471.
36. T/F, p.43.
37. *Description*, ii, p.467.
38. Horace Miner, *The Primitive City of Timbuctoo*, New York (Anchor Books), 1965, p.69.
39. T/S, p.87. The word *qayn* in Arabic also means "blacksmith" and it may be that members of a certain smithing group were specialised also as singers (praise-singers, griots?). Perhaps these are the same group as the *haddadiyyat zamirat* mentioned below.
40. T/S, p.102.
10. T/F, p.137.
42. Miner, *Primitive City*, p.55.
43. T/F, p.114.
44. T/F, pp. 132, 144.
45. The *Kislar Agha* (chief Black eunuch) "could alone approach the Sultan at all times of the day and night . . . and was the most feared and consequently the most bribed, official in the whole of the Ottoman Empire". N. M. Penzer, *The Harem*, London, 1936, p.129.
46. T/F, p.138, T/S, p.124.
47. T/F, p.132.
48. T/F, p.133.
49. T/F, p.148.
50. T/F, p.126.
51. "Replies", p. 202.
52. *Description*, ii, p.473. However, by the sixteenth century it appears that eunuchs were common in the more important Hausa states, especially Kano, and they were

apparently brought in from Nupe. See the "Kano Chronicle" in H. R. Palmer, *Sudanese Memoirs*, Lagos, 1928 (reprinted Frank Cass, London, 1967), iii, pp. 112, 114. A recent critique of Leo Africanus' material on Songhay intervention in the Hausa states has been published by H. J. Fisher. See his "Leo Africanus and the Songhay conquest of Hausaland", *Int. J. Afr. Hist. Stud.*, 11 (1978), pp. 86-112.

53. H. J. Tremearne in his *The Ban of the Bori* (London, 1914 (reprinted Frank Cass, 1968), p. 62) claims that only 2-3% of men castrated in Zinder, Bornu and Baghirmi survived the operation, but this seems improbably low. Burckhardt (*Travels in Nubia*, 2nd edn., London, 1822, p.295) was told in Asyut that the *fatality* rate among young boys operated on at the nearby Christian monastery was only around 2%. Clearly, everything depended on the "surgery" and the post-operative care.
54. J. Skolle, *The Road to Timbuctoo*, London, 1956, p.62.
55. "Replies", p.198.
56. T/S, p.72.
57. T/F, p.84.
58. T/F, p.93.
59. D. Sourdel in the article *Djund* in the *Encyclopaedia of Islam* (2nd edition, Leiden) remarks: "Under the various dynasties connected with the Maghrib, the term djund kept a restricted sense which is often difficult to define, rarely applying to the whole army. Similarly, with the Mamluks the word djund is sometimes applied to a category of soldiers in the sultan's service, but distinct from the personal guard".
60. T/F, p.116.
61. T/F, pp.73-4.
62. T/F, p.94.
63. T/F, p.94-5.
64. T/F, p.109.
65. T/F, pp.102-3.
66. See J.O Hunwick, "A little-known diplomatic episode in the history of Kebbi (c.1594)", *J. Hist. Soc. Nigeria*, 5, iv (June 1971), p.580.
67. T/F, pp.151.
68. See Jean Rouch, *Les Songhay*, Paris, 1954, p.3.
69. T/F, pp.73-4.
70. "Replies", pp.248-9.
71. See J. Rouch, *Contribution à l'histoire des Songhay*, Dakar, 1953 (Mémoires de l'IFAN, 29), p.188; M. Abadie, *La Colonie du Niger*, Paris, 1927, p.115. T/F, p.48, more generally claims a common ancestry for Sunni 'Ali and Askia Muhammad.
72. "Replies", p.255.
73. *Mi'raj*, p.5.
74. See Ahmad Baba al-Tinbukti, *Nayl al-ibtihaj*, Cairo, 1353 A.H., pp.217-18.
75. T/F, p.130.
76. T/S, p.67.
77. T/F, p.71-2.
78. I cannot agree with Michal Tymowski, in his otherwise most interesting article, that the Askias tried to boost agricultural production because of the diminishing revenue from the gold trade in the sixteenth century. The chief objection to this argument is that food production never bore any relation to foreign trade. It was not food stuffs (apart from dates and other minor luxury comestibles) that were exchanged for gold, but salt and horses in the main. See 'Les domaines des princes du Songhay', *Annales: Economies, Sociétés, Civilizations*, 6 (nov-déc. 1970), pp.1637-1658, esp. p.1645.
79. T/S, p.117.

80. T/F, pp.109, 113.
81. T/S, p.120.
82. T/F, p.115.
83. T/F, p.151.
84. T/F, p.151.
85. T/S, p.67.
86. T/F, p.104.
87. T/F, p.107.
88. ibid.
89. See W.A. Brown "A Monument of legal scholarship: the *Nawazil al-Takrur* of al-Mustafa b. Ahmad al-Ghalawi", *Research Bull.* (Centre of Arabic Doc.), 3, ii (July 1967), pp.137-8.
90. Of Baba Guru b. al-hajj Muhammad al-Amin Ganu whose work is cited several times in the T/F.

III

Comparative West African Farm-Slavery Systems (south of the Sahel) with special reference to Muslim Kano Emirate (N. Nigeria)

Polly Hill

Synopsis

The vulgar search for a single model of West African farm-slavery is a vain one, for although most slavery systems have several common features, including the slaves' rights to live *en famille* with their wives and children and to pursue remunerative non-farming occupations, there are a number of salient variables which must not be ignored in any approach towards a typology, one of them being the distinction between Muslim and non-Muslim systems. Account should necessarily be taken of such variables as the assimilation of slave-descendants (where this occurs), prohibitions (if any) on the sale of slave-descendants, the existence of slave-villages, slaves' rights (including the right of ransom) and the class or political position of the slave owners.

In this presentation the farm-slavery system which existed in Kano Emirate in Northern Nigeria when the British conquerors arrived there in 1903 is regarded as the principal Muslim model with which other systems, both Muslim and non-Muslim, are contrasted and compared.

The definition of slavery

In his article on Slavery in the *International Encyclopaedia of the Social Sciences* (1968) M.I. Finley, the distinguished expert on classical slavery, stated that the Roman definition of slavery, as an institution "whereby someone is subject to the *dominium* of another contrary to nature" may be accepted as "universally applicable", though "without the controversial phrase 'contrary to nature' ", and provided the word *dominium* (which may be translated as "power") is understood to imply the idea of property. He went on to claim that distinctions had to be drawn according to: the type of owner; the existence or non-existence of certain "rights" (such as the claim to eventual manumission or statutory freedom); and the social structure within which slavery functioned. Although, at least in principle, the slave could be distinguished from other servile persons, such as serfs or peons, by the "total of his powerlessness", which sufficiently justified the term "chattel slave", it was Finley's opinion that in any sociological analysis "equal stress must be given to the slave's deracination".

I think it is usually argued that provided systems of pawning and "debt-slavery" are excluded,[1] the definition of slavery in West Africa (south of the Sahel)[2] presents little difficulty: that, indeed, the property aspect of slavery, as it existed in classical antiquity, in Chinese[3] peasant society, in India and elsewhere, was entirely applicable to West African slave-owning societies, where slaves could be bought and sold as though they were plough oxen, and where they were normally strangers who by the fact of their uprooting had been reduced from persons to things which could be owned. It is true that most writers of West African slavery systems have emphasised the relatively humane treatment accorded to slaves[4] by their owners as well as the extent of slaves' rights, but this in itself had presented no definitional difficulties for, as Finley[5] has argued, "one may speak of a spectrum of statuses between the two extremes of absolute rightlessness and of absolute freedom to exercise his rights at all times", while taking for granted that the two extremes have never existed, although the position of the slave in the American South came very near to the former. However, it is one of the themes of this paper that in many, though certainly not in all, West African societies the definition of slavery presents much difficulty, owing both to the gradualness of the process by which slaves evolved into free men and to the existence of the so-called "slave villages" where the "slaves" worked largely on their own account and were subject to no day to day constraint.

Slavery in Kano Emirate

In this presentation the Hausa farm-slavery system which existed in Kano Emirate in Northern Nigeria when the British conquerors arrived there in 1903 is regarded as the principal model with which other systems, both Muslim and non-Muslim, are contrasted and compared. It was a system such that there was no difficulty whatsoever in distinguishing a slave from a free person; it was a system such that the Hausa word *bawa*[6] has to be translated "slave" in the international understanding of that term; it was a system which involved the legal notion of "absolute enfranchisement" when a slave was manumitted or ransomed – there having been no status intermediate between slavery and freedom.

Before I proceed to outline the main features of this Kano farm-slavery system,[7] it is necessary to emphasise that it is correctly denoted a Muslim system – Muslim in terms of the understanding of Maliki Law – despite the fact that there was very little resort to alkali's courts. While we do not know how many alkali's courts there were in Kano Emirate in 1900 (a date which I hereinafter employ to mean "immediately pre-colonial"), the number was undoubtedly extremely small in relation to the rural population of the Emirate, which must have run into several millions,[8] as well as to its vast extent. The great majority of rural dwellers, especially in the very densely populated Kano Close Settled Zone[9] around Kano city, lived dispersedly on the farmland, most of them beyond walking distance of any town where a court was situated,[10] and for this and numerous other reasons we can be sure that, by and large, Kano rural communities "interpreted" Muslim Law for themselves, without the aid of professional legal experts. Since this interpretative task was undertaken conscientiously, as it still is today, for rural populations were (and are) thoroughly conformist in outlook – they were indeed most desirous of demonstrating that they were as much "good Muslims" as were city dwellers – so it is that we are entitled to speak of "Muslim slavery sytems". Indeed it is arguable that rural societies which were inherently Muslim in outlook were more apt to follow the spirit of the law, than those which felt that Muslim courts had been imposed on them. (It is pertinent to note that when present day Muslim populations in rural Hausaland do not conform to the letter of the law on such matters as division of property on inheritance or usury this is not so much because so few cases are actually referred to court (which remain few in number in relation to the size of the population) as that conformity would be inherently impracticable or even impossible.[11] From the point of view of a fieldworker in rural Muslim communities I have found that city dwellers, university students, historians, sociologists and political scientists (among other groups) tend to have little idea of the importance of the economic modifications to Muslim Law which would be required were it to be directly applicable to rural economies. It is, therefore, always necessary to take account of the degree of attitudinal conformity which exists in rural societies, which should not be dubbed "Muslim" without further qualification; and to remember that Muslim slavery systems will necessarily vary greatly in different social contexts).

The dearth of Muslim courts in relation to the vast size of the rural population was, as I have argued, partly a function of dispersed residence. But this is to be insufficiently explanatory. In Kano Emirate, as in many other regions of Northern Nigeria, it was not merely that most people lived in homesteads surrounded by farmland, where nucleated settlements were lacking, but that in socio-political terms they were often not subordinate to authorities resident in towns, or central places, other than Kano city itself – which, for many people, was too far away to be visited more than occasionally, if at all. It is probable that most Village Heads[12] in areas of dispersed settlement were quite unimportant people; their understanding of Muslim Law was greatly inferior to that of the more learned of the numerous religious scholars (malams) who were as apt to reside in the deep countryside as elsewhere. It was because of the long-established tradition of religious learning in the countryside[13] and because Hausa long-distance trade and craftwork were rurally based, that rural communities in districts of dispersed settlement were not isolated or dependent on urban institutions, but rather constituted the general matrix of Hausa civilisation.

The great majority of farm-slaves in rural Kano, as elsewhere in the central Hausa Emirates, were owned by private farmers, who were not correctly denoted as "aristocrats" or "members of the ruling class", as F.D. Lugard, the first High Commissioner of Northern Nigeria, wrongly supposed, though they might have been caravan traders or notable religious scholars. The brief outline of the Kano slavery system which follows thus relates to a situation which involved richer private farmers in acquiring slaves for the primary purpose of increasing their production of basic crops, notably grains, which were both used for household consumption and sold – for, contrary to general belief, there was a flourishing medium-distance trade in grain, the more densely populated districts in the Kano Close Settled Zone being "grain importers". The conventional argument[14] that it was because "labour was scarcer than land" that farmers resorted to the use of captive rather than free labour is entirely false – at least in application to rural Hausaland where the ratio of slaves to freemen may even have been highest in the most densely populated and wealthiest localities, where many free men cultivated insufficient land.[15] The fact of the matter is that farm-slavery systems were far more profitable, as will be seen, than any system that might have involved free labourers – and this quite apart from the fact that the concept of "wage-labour" existed nowhere in the West African savannah in the nineteenth century. As Finley has stated,[16] "the institution of wage-labour is a sophisticated latecomer", which involves two difficult conceptual steps, viz. " the abstraction of a man's labour from both his person and the product of his work" and the establishment of a method of measuring "labour time".

What follows is a summary of certain salient features of Kano farm-slavery.

1. Newly-acquired slaves were strangers and in principle (and often in fact) non-Muslims. However such slaves might have been captured originally (whether in war, by means of deliberate slave-raiding, etc.), they had been converted into *deracinés* marketable chattels before being acquired by the Kano slave-owners, who had had no hand in their capture.

2. It is likely that the numbers of male and female farm-slaves were roughly equal. (One of several justifications for this statement is the likelihood that high proportions of farm-slaves in 1900 were slave-descendants, who had been born locally.)

3. The slave was a chattel because he had a market value, which no one save his owner could realise by selling him; the female slave was doubly a chattel because her children, who were mostly fathered by male slaves, belonged to her owner. (For this reason there is no need to bring in the vexed question of concubinage in justification for the higher prices of female than male slaves.) Whereas in legal principle a slave's property was heritable by his owner on his death, it is doubtful whether most masters laid claim to such property if the slave had children – as most of them had. (In this connection it should be remembered that resort would seldom, if ever, have been made to Muslim courts.)

4. Slaves may have been chattels, but their owners had definite obligations towards them. Among these obligations were the following: When a slave was first acquired, it was the master's duty to provide food, clothing, shelter and other necessities and, as soon as possible, a slave spouse. (It is likely that most slaves lived in their own houses *en famille*.) Then, a master was obliged (though his motives were not wholly disinterested) to provide his slave with a plot of land on which he could work on his own account, and to allow him one or two free days in the week when he could work on his own farm or in

some other remunerative occupation, rather than on his owner's *gandu* farm.

5. As time went by the ordinary slave household became partially self-supporting, at which stage the owner was normally obliged to provide no more than partial maintenance. It was for this reason, in particular, that slave-holding was potentially far more profitable[17] than subsequent farm-labour employment has ever been.

6. Slave-owners were regarded as having a legal right to sell any slave, no distinction having been made between slaves of first and subsequent generations. Although this was so, a slave-owner's freedom to sell any slave living *en famille* was severely limited by local public opinion, which held that children should not be separated from their parents or spouses wrenched apart, unless the owner had become impoverished or the slave were unmanageable, troublesome or criminal.

7. Slaves were regarded as having the legal right of self-ransom – though courts were seldom involved – and they could also be ransomed by third parties. In cases of self-ransom, masters were obliged to allow their slaves time off in which to accumulate sufficient funds by pursuing some remunerative occupation;[18] the general rule was that the ransom should be roughly equal to twice the market value of the slave. (As the stock of slaves was self-reproducing and possibly expanding, it did not necessarily follow that ransoming led to a reduction in the slave population.)

8. A freed slave was free without qualification: in legal language, slaves enjoyed the right of "absolute enfranchisement". There was, in fact, no legal status intermediate between slavery and freedom. On being freed, ex-slaves either migrated or became local farmers on their own account; they were as free as any other resident members of the community to appropriate land for farming, and were sometimes given land by their former owners.

9. It is important to note that the Hausa institution of clientage, which is known as *bara*, was not linked with farm-slavery and that a Kano farm-slave would never have become a *bara* (or servant) of his former owner. In Kano Emirate rural clientage is, and was, notable for its rarity, except so far as the diminutive ruling class is concerned.[19]

As I have emphasised, this summary relates to the great majority of farm-slaves who were owned by non-office-holding, i.e. private, farmers. As for the minority of slaves who worked on estates owned by office-holders, including the Emir of Kano, the Chief Blacksmith of Kano Emirate and the aristocratic title-holders known as *hakimai*,[20] their conditions were probably generally similar to those owned by private farmers. However, two important distinctions should be made: first, the slaves owned by the aristocrats more often lived in separate slave-villages; second, those ex-slaves, or slave-descendants, of the title-holders who had owned official farms,[21] sometimes remained indefinitely on the slave-estate.[22]

Farm-slavery was never formally abolished in Northern Nigeria. Partly owing to the control,[23] which was more moral than actual, exerted by the British administration, but also because of the changed attitudes of the times, the institution petered out by about 1930 – i.e. about a generation after the colonial conquest. As I have argued elsewhere,[24] the transitional period in Kano Emirate was uneventful, and the institution has now vanished without trace. Individual status in rural communities is mainly linked with age, wealth (or economic success) and religious learning and takes no account of descent; virtually all younger people are, in any case, entirely uninterested in whether they themselves, or others in the community, are of slave-origin. Since my statements on this subject are often greeted with hostile scepticism, I conclude this section of my paper with a written statement made by my Hausa assistant[25] in Batagarawa, in Katsina Emirate, in 1969, where the conditions of the slaves had been very similar to those in Kano Emirate.

> You do not hear people saying that "so and so" is of slave descent. Slave descent has no weight at all. Since not all people know who is supposed to be of slave descent, people move and work together in this community with no fear of embarrassment. Even when people talk of slave descent, I am sure they do it in a secret manner. I have never heard of anyone saying to another – "you are of slave descent". Even people whose parents owned slaves and the slave descendants are in Batagarawa, it is hard to get any impression that this is so. These slave descendants are not even servants to their masters' descendants. In fact, there might even be marriages between the two lines . . .

I would add that this disinterestedness does not reflect any prohibition on mentioning the slave origin of others, such as exists to this day in matrilineal Ashanti where slave status was, in principle, never extinguished: on the contrary, no one is interested because status is in no way involved. It was for this reason that in Dorayi, in Kano Emirate, my third-party elderly informants had no more difficulty in helping me to compile genealogies for houses of slave than of free descent – as would not have been the case in Ashanti.

Farm-slavery in Zaria Emirate

This account of the institution of farm-slavery and of the transition from slavery to freedom will astonish those familiar with M.G. Smith's much-quoted findings (on what he always denotes as having been Hausa slavery in northern Zaria) for three main reasons. First, because he insisted that it was "usual for descendants of slaves to seek relations of clientage with the owners of their parents"[26]; second, because he insisted that it was "difficult to appreciate the extent to which servitude continued in Zaria"[27] fifty years after the arrival of the British; and third, because of his emphasis on the fact that second-generation slaves (*dimajo*, pl. *dimajai*) could not be sold.

It is clear from Smith's own account that northern Zaria in 1900 had been a peculiar, peripheral place within the general context of rural Hausaland, both because Hausa and settled Fulani were found living in close proximity almost everywhere and because many of the "local chiefs" who belonged to long-established Fulani lines enjoyed far more political independence, in relation to the Emir, than their counterparts in Kano Emirate for example. It seems justifiable to conclude that the special farm-slavery system that flourished there related to slaves owned by members of a Fulani ruling class[28] (not to Hausa private farmers) and that it was owing to the special political conditions that prevailed there that slaves' descendants paid a rent, known as *galla*, to the former slave-owners. That this is a Fulani, not a Hausa, system is shown by the fact that the main terminology is Fulani: thus, the word *rumada* (pl. *rinji*), which refers to "hereditary settlements of slaves with some free men, but mostly the former, built by nobles and others enjoying similar means"[29] derives from the Fulani word *rumde* (which is sometimes defined as "a wet season slave-farming village"); then, *galla* derives from the Fulani *ngalla* (one meaning of which is "revenue accruing from land"); and *dimajo*, also, is a Fulani word. Nowadays no special Hausa terms for slave-village or rent are ever retrospectively employed in Kano Emirate in relation to systems of farm-slavery involving private farmers and there is no special term, *implying a distinct status*, for slaves of second and subsequent generations: whether his theory is correct or not, it is interesting that R.C. Abraham in his Hausa dictionary should explain that the usual Hausa term *bacucane*, which means a person born in slavery of slave-parents, implies (merely) that such a person knows the secrets of the slave-owner's family and is inclined to "blab" about them.[32]

The main clue to the whole puzzle of the distinction between Fulani and Hausa systems seems to hinge on the meaning of the word *dimajo*, which would often seem to relate to a person who was neither slave nor free.[33] M.G. Smith states[34] that whereas slaves proper were usually employed in direct labour for their owner the *dimajai* were often put on allotted land to farm separately for their own subsistence, being obliged to make payments to their owner. So long as the *dimajai* and their descendants continued to live on the slave estate and to pay rent to the slave descendants, they were a category of "unfree person" – though they were not slaves.

What then becomes of the Muslim doctrine regarding the right of the slave to achieve, by ransom or otherwise, a state of "absolute enfranchisement"? Why did the *dimajai* not demand their freedom? I can only presume that the answer must be sought in terms of the attitudes to (or neglect of) the commands of Muslim Law by the local Fulani ruling class – this being reflected in the peculiar conditions of land tenure in northern Zaria.[35] The system of farm-slavery described by M.G. Smith for northern Zaria, which has always been denoted "Hausa" in all subsequent literature, is, therefore, neither Hausa nor inherently Muslim, unlike that which prevailed in Kano Emirate which, I would contend, is likely to be reasonably typical of Hausa systems in the central Emirates of Hausaland, including Katsina.

Slave-villages

I return now to my contention that in many West African societies, though not in rural societies in the central Hausa Emirates, the definition of slavery presents much difficulty. If the master cannot sell the servile person is he, then, a chattel? Surely the residents of the Zaria "slave-villages" in 1950, whose sole disability lay in their obligation to pay rent to the slave-owners' descendants, were no longer slaves? One of the few scholars to face questions of this kind is W. Derman who, in a book on a former serf village in the Republic of Guinea, argued that the servile farm workers owned by the Fulani of Fouta-Djallon in pre-colonial times did not "fit easily into the categories of either serf or slave."[36] Derman follows the traveller G. Mollien[37] in rejecting the word "slave"; however, although he prefers "serf", he found the literature on the distinction between slave and serf, and particularly the books by J.S. Trimingham,[38] most contradictory and would not wish any analogy to be made with European serfdom. But I do not think that the main justification for the choice of "serf" resides, as he suggests, in the servile persons's self-sufficiency, for the following citation might have happened to have related to Kano slavery, were it not for the reference to the serf-villages (*runde*):

> Although the status of the serfs of the Fouta contained strong elements of what has been considered slavery, there was also a significant way in which they were not slaves; they were economically self-sufficient. They lived in their own villages, they cultivated their own fields and women's gardens (although they did not own the land), owned property and had their own kin groups. On the basis of their economic self-sufficiency we have referred to them as "serfs".[39]

I suggest that the serfs were not slaves for the following three reasons: first, because they were in general not saleable; second, because they were not necessarily strangers;[40] and third, because they lived in "slave-villages" and did not labour directly for their masters. (It is pertinent to add that in pre-colonial times the Fulani masters seldom freed their serfs.)

The slave-owners

I shall return to these questions later in this paper. Meanwhile I want to emphasise that to understand slavery systems it is as necessary to identify the slave-owners as to study the conditions of the slaves. One reason why the literature on West African farm slavery has tended to be so misleading, until quite recently, is that it has been implicitly believed that most of the slaves, particularly in the centralised states of the northern savannah, including the Hausa Emirates, were owned by central officials and urbanised members of the upper classes.[41] Although in Hausaland most farm-slaves were owned by private farmers,[42] F.D. Lugard was so confused on this matter that he thought that a class of free "peasants" only came into existence when the aristocratic slave-owners withdrew to their urban bases as the supplies of slaves began to dry up – in other words he thought that the "peasants" were virtually all ex-slaves.[43] Such general beliefs die hard and it was only recently that I was accused of being "in favour of castration" at a seminar concerned with the conditions of Hausa farm-slaves. Whatever the number of eunuchs who frequented the palaces, the number of farm-slaves owned by private farmers was many hundred times greater, and it was in the interests of all concerned that these slaves should have reproduced themselves as rapidly as possible: indeed, for all we know, birth rates among populations of settled slaves, who were apt to be polygynous, may have been no lower than for free populations, which always included a large element of poor men (see fn 15, p.46). In societies, like the Hausa, where there were no land-owning lineages into which the slaves might have been absorbed (thus becoming unsaleable), an expansion of the stock of slaves (or of the herds of cattle) represented an increase in the value of the agrarian capital owned by the local community. It is indeed surprising that the old myth that slave populations never reproduced themselves should recently have been so strongly revived.[44]

J.L. Boutillier's chapter (in G. Meillassoux's collection of twenty-seven studies on pre-colonial African slavery)[45] is much concerned with the identity of the slave-owners: it is entitled "The Three Slaves of Bouna"[46] and distinguishes the slaves owned by (a) members of the royal clan who did little farming themselves; (b) the Koulango, who were ordinary rural cultivators and pastoralists; and (c) Muslim strangers, known as Dioula or Mande, who were mainly traders and artisans and who owned agricultural slaves, although they themselves lived mainly in towns. In each of these three cases second-generation slaves had ceased (as I would argue) to be slaves proper for the reason that they could not be sold. But the slaves owned by the Muslim strangers did not, thereafter, enjoy progressive assimilation, as did those owned by the other groups, but settled permanently in special "slave-villages"[47] (*djose*), some distance away from their masters' town. The slaves owned by the Koulango were those who were most rapidly assimilated; they lived in their masters' houses and worked alongside them on the fields. As for the slaves owned by members of the royal clan, by the third generation they had a status similar to ordinary commoners, and worked for the most part on their own farms; although they were obliged to undertake certain compulsory labour (*corvée*) there were others who, as Boutillier puts it, were "encore plus corvéable". As with the *dimajai* owned by the Fulani in Zaria, changing status with the generations was indicated by the use of distinct words: the first generation slaves (*zaga*) owned by members of the royal clan evolved into *uroso* and *beni bio* in the second and third generations respectively.

Lineage-organised societies

In West African lineage-organised societies, the conventional assumption (strengthened by the findings of Miers and Kopytoff) has been that the assimilation of farm-slaves was normal, if not universal, in such societies, and that second generation "slaves" could usually not be sold[48] – and had thus ceased to be chattels proper. I make three further assumptions about such societies: first, that farm-slaves were necessarily strangers (in origin) who lacked land rights;[49] second, that the right of ransom normally did not exist or related only to first generation slaves; and third that, for reasons of land tenure, "slave villages", such that the slaves in any village were owned by a number of masters, did not exist.[50]

The question of ransoming has, indeed, not received the attention it deserves. Was the right of self-ransom a special feature of Muslim slavery proper? Or did it commonly occur in non-Muslim, non-unilineal societies, as it did, for example in Benin, where villages, not lineages, were the land-holding units?[51] In lineage-organised societies would "slave-owners" ever have agreed to ransom "slaves" who were no longer slaves proper as they had been partially or wholly assimilated? I doubt if we can answer any of these questions conclusively on the basis of present knowledge.[52]

Non-lineage societies

Although we cannot attempt to make such neat generalisations about farm-slavery in non-lineage societies – which are, incidentally, much more common in West Africa than is sometimes supposed[53] – I offer the following speculations. First, that the only type of assimilation into kin groups that was analogous to that which occured in lineage-organised societies involved the marriage of slave women to free men whose children were always of special status or free from birth.[54] Second, that farm-slaves proper were usually strangers (or the descendants of strangers); insofar as the servile people were indigenes, they usually lived in separate slave-villages,[55] where they worked mainly on their own account, while paying some kind of tribute to their owners, and were thus not slaves proper,[56] though sometimes they might have belonged to different ethnic groups from their masters who constituted some kind of ruling class.[57] As for the right of self-ransom, I suggest that whether or not this was a common feature of farm-slavery systems in non-lineage, non-Muslim societies, it was a right which was actually much more frequently exerted in Muslim than in non-Muslim societies.

Conclusions

As I have paid particular attention in this paper to the system of Muslim farm-slavery which existed in Kano Emirate, it is appropriate to conclude with a few final observations on that system. First, the system did not constitute a pre-capitalist mode of production in the ordinary understanding of that term, so that any surprise that it did not give way to a clientage system is misplaced. I have provided many justifications for this assertion but would here add that as the farm-slaves and the slave-owner's sons worked alongside each other on their owner's/father's fields, under an organisational system which, so far as the sons are concerned, is still known as *gandu*,[58] there was no inherent economic distinction to be drawn between one farmer whose labour force consisted of six slaves and two sons and another who had eight slaves and no sons. The economic conditions of married sons and slaves were remarkably similar, even to the extent that a son who wished to leave *gandu* might have been obliged to migrate – an act similar to a slave's abscondment. Second, if it is necessary to speak in terms of modes of production, the Kano farm-slavery system is appropriately regarded as having been capitalistic, the slaves having been a species of self-propagating agrarian capital – for those who were ransomed could be replaced; the fact that men derived prestige from slave-ownership had nothing to do with the rationale of slave-holding (cattle-holding was likewise prestigious), but everything to do with the close relationship between high status and wealth.[59] Third, the slave-owners as a group were not a class apart but richer farmers, some of whom were women, whose family labour forces were too small to achieve the level of crop production to which they aspired; most slave-owners probably possessed no more than, say, one to four slaves. Fourth, as a form of agrarian capital, slaves were (owing to manu-mission, abscondment[60] and dissatisfaction with a new master) even more apt than other forms to be dissipated on death and, for several reasons, including their relatively high value,[61] were indivisible between the inheriting sons to a peculiar degree: accordingly, while rural economic inequality was much more pronounced than it is today, this did not imply economic stratification. Finally, the fact that present day rural communities are wholly untainted by memories of slavery is due not only to there having been but two statuses under Muslim Law (slave and non-slave or black and white with no grey) but also to the remarkable capacity of Hausa communities to absorb strangers of all varieties, including the slaves' descendants.

NOTES

1. Common in some West African societies where slavery also flourished and unknown in others (such as Kano Emirate), these systems involved temporary servitude only, redemption automatically following the repayment of the debt.
2. Hereafter in this paper the words "south of the Sahel" are implied as qualifying

"West Africa". I exclude that zone intermediate between the savannah and the desert since it seems that types of servitude resembling serfdom rather than slavery more often existed there than in West Africa proper, and also because of the relative unimportance of farming as a means of livelihood.

3. See "Chattel Slavery in Chinese Peasant Studies: A Comparative Analysis" by J.L. Watson, *Ethnology*, Oct. 1976.
4. In Muslim law slaves are sometimes bracketed with animals in this regard. Thus, *La Risala* (on Maliki Law) ed. L. Bercher, 1960, p.323: "On devra traiter avec bonté les esclaves et les animaux dont on est propriétaire et ne pas leur imposer un travail audessus de leurs forces."
5. Finley, *op cit* p.308.
6. F. *baiwa*, pl. *bayi*.
7. See "From Slavery to Freedom: the case of Farm-Slavery in Nigerian Hausaland" by Polly Hill, *Comparative Studies in Society and History*, July 1976. Much of the material in this article, which is mainly based on intensive historical fieldwork in Kano Emirate, as well as on literary and archival sources, is not repeated here. The fieldwork was carried out in 1971-2 in a farming locality, which I denote Dorayi, which is very close to Kano city, where the population density nowadays is about 1,500 per square mile, about a quarter of the population being of slave descent in the male line. A revised version of this article appears as a chapter of my *Population, Prosperity and Poverty: Kano Emirate 1900 & 1970*, 1977 (hereafter, *Population*).
8. In *Population* (see fn 7), I argue that because farm-slaves and their dependants were usually omitted from official population counts, the population of Kano Emirate was grossly under-estimated in the first decades of colonial rule.
9. This densely populated farming zone is an irregularly-shaped ellipse, extending some 60 miles from Kano city to the south-east and some 30 to 40 miles in other directions; it is very much larger and more populous than any other comparable region in savannah West Africa. (See Hill, 1977, *Population*).
10. So far as is known, alkali's courts (as well as Friday mosques) were situated only in towns with a minimum population of several thousand, which were generally lacking in many sections of Kano Emirate. (In Dawakin Tofa District, to the west of Kano city, which may have a population of nearly half a million today, there is still only one court.)
11. If the elaborate formulae governing the inheritance of property were to be applied to farmland in densely populated localities, where farm plots are particularly small, it would be necessary for much of the farmland to be sold on death so that the proceeds could be divided accordingly; and this is but one of the many reasons why inheritance cases seldom reach a court. Rural people feel really embarrassed about their inability to conform to the law and generally refuse to discuss such subjects at all openly. See *Rural Hausa: A Village and a Setting* by Polly Hill, 1972.
12. Commonly known as *dagaci* (pl. *dagatai*) – though there were several other common titles – the Village Heads were the sole resident political authority in most localities. See Hill, 1977, *Population*, on the politico-economic consequences of dispersed settlement.
13. Islam was a religion which appropriately flourished in the open countryside where there were many rooms in private houses which served as small mosques, and where Koranic teaching was conducted in the open air.
14. See, for example, *An Economic History of West Africa* by A.G. Hopkins, 1973, p.24 and "States and Subjects in Sub-Saharan African History" by J.D. Fage, Raymond Dart Lecture, 1973, Witwatersrand University Press.
15. My basic reason for this dogmatic assertion is that in inegalitarian rural communities, such as existed in Hausaland when farm-slavery flourished, the expression "labour was scarcer than land" is meaningless, it being of the nature of

the case that the labour of the poorer households was under-utilised, whereas that of the richer households was over-extended. This over-summarised argument is expanded in Hill, 1977, *Population*, where it is also suggested that the most densely populated localities where agriculture, trading and craftwork flourished integratedly were attractive to strangers.

16. *The Ancient Economy* by M.I. Finley, 1973, p.65. See, also, "A Peculiar Institution?" by M.I. Finley, *Times Literary Supplement*, July 2, 1976, for the author's statement that until recent times wage labour was "spasmodic, casual, exceptional, as it still remains in part of the world".
17. Written records being wholly lacking, and memories of figures (and even of dimensions) being naturally unreliable, there will never be any possibility of assessing the actual profitability of slave-holding in particular cases. However, for all kinds of reasons its general profitability is not in doubt: the institution had an economic rationale – see the last paragraph of this paper. See a similar argument for slavery in the classical world in Finley, *ibid*.
18. I will not here discuss the relevant Hausa, and Arabic, terminology relating to ransoming which is in the literature: it is somewhat confusing.
19. See Hill, 1976, *op. cit.*, p.424.
20. Sing. *hakimi*. Most of those *hakimai* who were the predecessors of the present day District Heads, because they had the right of collecting tax on behalf of the Emir in certain territories, were permanently resident in Kano city; and, in Hill, 1977, *Population*, I am concerned with the inappropriateness of following Lugard's terminology by denoting them "fief-holders". Such slave-estates as they owned were not necessarily situated in their territories.
21. They were few in number. There were probably no more than fifty *hakimai* at the outside and few of them owned official farms.
22. They could not sell the land (for which, however, no rent was charged) and exerted usufructural rights only.
23. Starting immediately after their arrival, the British had issued a series of Proclamations on slavery the main purposes of which were to prohibit slave-raiding and transactions in slaves and to abolish the legal status of slavery – which meant that runaway slaves could not be reclaimed through the courts; it was also declared that all those subsequently born of slave parents would be free.
24. See Hill, 1976.
25. Malam, now Alhaji, Sabi'u Nuhu, who was a native of Batagarawa, the town to which Hill, *op.cit.*, 1972 relates.
26. *Government in Zazzau* by M.G. Smith, 1960, p.260. See, also, Smith's article "Slavery and Emancipation in Two Societies", *Social and Economic Studies*, Dec. 1954, in which he compares slavery in Zaria and Jamaica, with special reference to the fact that Hausa slavery was such that " the ethos of the recruiting group" (p.245) resulted in progressive assimilation, although Muslim Law defined the slave as a chattel.
27. Smith, 1960, *op. cit.*, p.258.
28. I am grateful to Dr Murray Last for suggesting that the emphasis should be as much on the fact that the slave-owners were members of a local ruling class as that they were Fulani not Hausa. See Hill, 1976, *op. cit.*, fn 47, for a brief discussion of the appropriateness of regarding the rural population of Hausaland as Hausa-Fulani, rather than Hausa, which it is there claimed is apt to be rather misleading as in many sections of rural Hausaland there are no separate Fulani communities, and local institutions are culturally Hausa.
29. *The Economy of Hausa Communities of Zaria* by M.G. Smith, 1955, pp.102-3.
30. However, the Fulani plural *rinji* is employed, as though it were a singular noun, to the large slave-estates formerly owned by absentee members of the ruling class. (The famous Hausa lexicographer, G.P. Bargery, was (for once) confused by this word.)

31. The Hausa word *aro* relates to the seasonal borrowing of farm-plots. As land tenure specialists have established, *galla* is never charged in Kano Emirate.
32. The word *dimajo* is unknown to many Hausa speakers.
33. Probably the word had different meanings at different times and places. Thus Stenning, in his study of the Wodaabe pastoral Fulani of northern Nigeria, states that *diimaajo* (p. *rimaibe*) were sons of men (*dimo*, pl. *rimbe*) whose mothers had borne children by their masters so that they had become partially enfranchised on their death. (*Savannah Nomads* by D.J. Stenning, 1959, p.60.)
34. *Op. cit.*, 1955, p.104.
35. Which are not thought to be paralleled elsewhere in Hausaland proper. Such a practical matter as population density can hardly be relevant, for densities were higher in the inner ring of the Kano Close Settled Zone, where slavery has vanished without trace, than in northern Zaria.
36. *Serfs, Peasants and Socialists: A former Serf Village in the Republic of Guinea* by W. Derman, 1973, p.27.
37. Derman cites the following from *Travels in the Interior of Africa to the Sources of Senegal and Gambia* by G. Mollien, 1820 (reprinted Frank Cass, London, 1967). The use of *rumbde*, which evidently has the same root as the Zaria *rumada*, will be noted.

> The *rumbdes* which I have several times had occasion to mention, are establishments truly honourable to humanity. Each village, or several inhabitants of village (*sic*), assemble their slaves, and make them build themselves huts close to each other, this place is called a *rumbde* . . . These slaves, who are so but in name, cultivate the plantations of their masters . . .They are never sold when they are born in the country, any departure from this practice would cause the desertion of the whole *rumbde* . . . (Mollien, pp. 299-300).

38. *Islam in West Africa*, 1959 and *A History of Islam in West Africa*, 1962. In the former book Trimingham viewed the system as one in which the lot of slaves was ameliorated with each generation as slavery advanced through the various grades of serfdom and ultimately to clientship (p.134).
39. Derman, *op cit.*, p.29.
40. There were two social categories: indigenes and those "brought in" as children.
41. The possibility that private farmers might have been engaged in "commercial agriculture", producing food crops for sale outside the local community as much as for household consumption, has usually been ignored. Those who doubt these assertions should turn to pp. 24 and 76 of A. G. Hopkins' highly-regarded economic history of West Africa (*op cit.* 1973) where he asserts that farm-slaves were not used to produce an "export surplus" but rather "to provide foodstuffs for leading state officials, for their immediate circle of dependants, and for the army" and that pre-colonial trade in foodstuffs was strictly local.
42. This assertion is based on numerous sources, including field work. A notable literary source is Lugard's *Memorandum* No. 22, in his series of *Political Memoranda*, 1906, which was entitled "The condition of slaves and the native law regarding slavery in Northern Nigeria", having been based on material provided by Residents in reply to circular questions. See fn. 24 of Hill, 1976, *op cit.*
43. Sceptics may appreciate the following quotation from Lugard's *Political Memorandum* on Lands, 1919, which has been reprinted in *Political Memoranda by Lord Lugard*, ed. A. H. M. Kirk-Greene, Frank Cass, 1970.

> Nothing would so effectively tend to emancipate the peasant class from the servile attitude of mind which long generations of slavery had induced in them, or better promote a sense of individual responsibility, than to become proprietors of their own fields; in other words that the slave, or the communal tenants, should be replaced by the individual occupier. (Kirk-Greene, p.346)

It is doubtful whether Lugard ever became aware that annually cultivated,

44. In his encyclopaedia article (*op. cit.*) M. I. Finley referred to the fictitiousness of the oft-cited "law" that a slave population never reproduces itself.
45. *L'esclavage en Afrique précoloniale*, 1975. French anthropologists are fortunate in being able to draw on a wealth of archival material, such as forms the basis of most of the chapters on West Africa in this book, for this is generally unavailable for territories such as Northern Nigerian where slave-holding had never been legally abolished as it had been in French West Africa (at least on paper) in the early years of colonial rule. So profoundly embarrassed were the Colonial Office and the Northern Nigeria administration about their realistic attitude to the impossibility of suppressing slave-holding in the early decades, that a total ban was placed on any mention of the institution – except of course by Lugard himself, who vanished from the scene for six years as early as 1906. In his detailed instructions to political officers included in his *Political Memoranda*, see fn. 43 above, Lugard made no mention of the unspoken ban, so that, see fn. 8 above, we do not even know whether slave populations were enumerated.
46. "Les trois esclaves de Bouna." Bouna is in the north-eastern Ivory Coast.
47. Considering that the "slave-owners" were Muslims, Boutillier is surprised by the fact that the "slaves" could not be ransomed. But I think this accords with expectations given that the Dioula were strangers in a non-Muslim society and taking account of the nature of these "slave estates".
48. It has to be admitted, however, that some ambiguity attaches to this notion of a "second generation slave"; probably the concept of generation had to do with ownership by the particular master rather than with original capture or arrival in a particular locality. (Parenthetically, it is worth noting that "unsaleability", which is invariably considered desirable owing to the security it offered, was not necessarily advantageous to particular slaves, for in rural Hausaland, for example, a slave might have demanded that his impoverished master sell him to another.)
49. See *Kinship and the Social Order* by M. Fortes, 1969, p.263, on Ashanti and Tallensi slavery. When stating that anyone who was enslaved in Ashanti was "by definition kinless", Fortes is presumably disagreeing with R. S. Rattray who, in *Ashanti Law and Constitution*, 1949, pp. 33 *et seq*, insisted that there had been indigenous slaves, as well as slaves of stranger origin – respectively known as *akoa pa* and *odonko*. Although Rattray stated that the indigene was definitely not a pawn, he thought that, unlike the stranger slave, he might be redeemed. (He stated that both types of slave might have been killed at funeral customs, with the permission of the chief.) (There is surprisingly little on slavery in *Asante in the Nineteenth Century* by Ivor Wilks.)
50. It is to be noted that the Fulani clans of northern Zaria were not land-owning. The expression "lineage-organised societies" ought, therefore, to be qualified in this context by reference to corporate land-ownership.
51. See "Slavery and Emancipation in Benin, 1897-1945" by P. A. Igbafe, *Journal of African History*, 1975, 3, where it is stated (p.410) that the Oba could, if appealed to, "compel owners who refused to accept redemption money to emancipate the slaves affected".
52. Some writers seem to take the right of ransom in lineage-organised societies for granted: thus Fortes, e.g., in *op. cit.*, 1969, p.263, fn.24, mentions, in passing, that in lineage-organised Tallensi society a slave's absentee kin "could of course ransom him if they wished". The information on ransoming in pre-colonial, lineage-organised Yorubaland is too slight for it to be possible to judge whether those ransomed in pre-colonial times were all first generation slaves; slaves were certainly ransomed there in colonial times.
53. Considering that the great majority of the inhabitants of the very populous northern

states of Nigeria belong to non-lineage societies, it may be that taking West Africa as a whole members of lineage-organised societies are in the minority.
54. In many societies the children of such unions had a special status, and there was a word which denoted it; in Kano Emirate there was, of course, no such word, since the children were free without qualification.
55. Another well-documented Muslim slave-village system (in addition to those in N. Zaria, Fouta-Djallon and Bouna which I have already dealt with) was that of Nupe in Northern Nigeria. According to M. Mason (whose account of the Nupe system in "Captive and Client Labour and the Economy of the Bida Emirate: 1857-1901", *Journal of African History*, 1973, 3, differs somewhat from that provided by S. F. Nadel in *A Black Byzantium*, 1942), most residents of these villages were of Nupe origin, and the distinction between ordinary commoners and slaves was "blurred" (p.456) since both paid tribute to those in authority; it should be mentioned that, as with many other slave-village systems, the "slave-owners" were members of an elite.
56. Perhaps the word "client" is more appropriate than Derman's "serf"?
57. It is partly because Marxist anthropologists tend, with some exceptions, to concentrate their attention on slaves owned by members of the ruling class, or other elites, that they are so much concerned to identify a single mode of West African slave-holding – an endeavour which tends to suppress the very variables which it is our duty to expose. (Nor need the alternative taxonomy involve many types, as this paper is designed to show.) Thus, E. Terray in his very long chapter in Meillassoux, *op. cit.*, on slavery in the kingdom of Abron in Gyaman in the Ivory Coast, is concerned only with slaves owned by members of the aristocracy, although, as he says, there were also other important slave-owning groups.
58. For a full discussion of *gandu* both today and in the past see Hill, 1972, *op cit.*, and also *Baba of Karo* by Mary Smith, 1954 (the autobiography of a Hausa woman) which is a very rich and fascinating source on slavery in Zaria Emirate.
59. See Hill, 1972 and Hill, 1977, *Population*. A rich man who was able to retain the services of 8 married sons, who were fully occupied on his *gandu* farm, would have been no less respected than one who owned 8 farm slaves. It is also possible that the Timbuktu writers were employing the term *jund* for cavalry and *jaysh* for the entire force comprised of cavalry and infantry.
60. See Mary Smith, *op. cit.*, 1954, on the fleeing of slaves on their owner's death.
61. A vigorous male or female slave was a far more valuable chattel than any other form of moveable agrarian capital owned by farmers. Prices varied greatly according to sex and "quality" (females being more valuable), but may have been of the order of from 3 to 7 times the value of an adult's annual grain requirements, which was possibly some £1 to £2, though grain prices were subject to much seasonal fluctuation.

IV

Ahmad Rasim Pasha and the suppression of the Fazzan slave trade, 1881-1896

B. G. Martin

I

In a portrait, doubtless painted toward the end of his life, Ahmad Rasim Pasha looks out from behind a full white beard and long moustaches. Portly, and dressed in the long frockcoat of nineteenth century Turkish officialdom, Ahmad Rasim also wears a red fez. A multicolored ribbon crosses his chest, setting off several orders and decorations of large dimensions. Smiling slightly, the Pasha wears an expression of assured benevolence, that of a man satisfied by a long career in the Ottoman civil service. Indeed, Ahmad Rasim had good reason to be proud of his achievements; even now, he is gratefully remembered by some of the older inhabitants of the Libyan capital. Here he served as *Veli* (governor), his last post before his retirement to Istanbul in 1896. He died the following year at the age of 72, and is buried in the Kayalar Cemetery on the European side of the Bosporus, across the harbor from the centre of Istanbul.[1]

Born in the Turkish capital in 1825, Ahmad Rasim had his earliest education in Athens, where he studied Greek, Italian, and French. In 1844, his first government post took him to the Translation Bureau (*Tercüme Odasi*) at the Sublime Porte. He then transferred to the Foreign Ministry, where he was entrusted with the "solution of political problems" at Salonica, Monastir, and the Island of Samos. In 1863, he was appointed Extraordinary *Müteserrif* for Tulja, then for Vidin, in Bulgaria. In 1867, he became *Veli* of Yanina in Albania. In 1872, he was sent with the same rank to Trabzon on the Black Sea. In 1873, he returned to Albania, this time to Üskudar (Scutari), then back to Diyarbekir in Anatolia. After a few years there, he returned to Istanbul, becoming Director of the Sanitary Commission at the Ministry of Public Health and Prefect (*'Amid*) of the capital. In the autumn of 1881, Ahmad Rasim was appointed *Veli* of Tripoli, where he arrived on the fourth of Muherrem 1299, or 27 November 1881.[2]

Soon after his arrival, an official Ottoman annual noted that the new *Veli* had not only made every effort to implement the policies of his master, Sultan 'Abd al-Hamid II, but that

> Since his Lofty Presence [came here], he has restricted the glance of his concern to the betterment of all that he sees less in need of reform, whether fundamental or particular, in all branches of provincial affairs. He has put in order thing after thing, by moves suited to the time and place. He has drawn the attention of his Exalted Government to important measures designed to advance the prosperity of the state and the increase of its wealth. Up to now, he has succeeded in many matters and in many glorious respects, both material and spiritual . . .[3]

These conventional phrases concealed many real achievements. Ahmad Rasim had not only coped successfully with a huge influx of Arab refugees from Tunis into the Ottoman *vilayet*, after the French takeover there in 1881, but had also improved communications there by making strategic extensions to the telegraph network. Within a year after his arrival, Tripoli was newly linked to such important towns as Tarhuna and Misurata, Fassatu and Nalut, and by cable to Istanbul. Ahmad Rasim had likewise improved the provincial postal services, built modern hospitals and schools (including one for girls). He provided Tripoli with its first modern water supply, and tried to revive the cultivation of disused lands in the vicinity of the capital. The *Veli* also despatched one of Tripoli's municipal physicians to the Institut Pasteur in Paris to study the latest cure for quinsy (suppurating tonsillitis), an illness which much afflicted local children.[4]

With his competence in matters of public health, it would not be long before the energetic, humanitarian, and reform-minded *Veli* came to grips with the worst abuse of his time. This was the slave trade from the far side of the Sahara. For years, Tripoli had been known to Turks and North African Arabs as *Suq al-Bashar* – "the slave market".[5] Since 1863, the Ottoman Government had made more than one effort to stop this obnoxious traffic. But until the 15-year tenure of Ahmad Rasim, the Turks had had variable success with this perennial problem.

One of Ahmad Rasim's first measures, and one which he could enforce locally with vigor, was the manumission of all slaves within the town of Tripoli. Before giving an account of the Pasha's other moves against the trade, it seems worthwhile to note some of the landmarks in the history of the Fazzan slave traffic, whose beginnings went far back into the past.

In this paper, it has seemed necessary to treat the slave trade together with the history of the Fazzan, since the two themes are very much intertwined. The economic situation of the Fazzan and its relative richness made it politically attractive as a conquest, or as an area for trade and settlement, particularly in the Islamic period. When the Fazzan trade, especially the slave trade declined, it became of less political importance. Thus the Fazzan became the home region of the Garamantes, with their capital at German or Jarma. Towards the end of the Garamantian era, as the country came into closer contact with Byzantium and accepted Christianity, the slave trade began to grow. In the early seventh century, when the Muslims conquered the Fazzan, it was already known as a source of captives, since the first Arab raiders in the Fazzan wanted tribute from the declining Garamantes in the form of slaves.

Later, under the Banu Khattab bin Izliten, who established themselves at Zuwayla, a slave trade based on trans-Saharan wars and raiding developed to supply slaves to an accelerating Muslim economy which needed them for domestic and industrial purposes. After about three hundred years of profitable dealing from Zuwayla, the Banu Khattab were wiped out by a renegade Ayyubid Mamluk who was drawn to Zuwayla by its reputed wealth. Very soon after, the Empire of Kanem took over the task of slave-dealing, establishing a corridor by the thirteenth century from Lake Chad to the Mediterranean to protect its slave exports, and imports from the north. The fourteenth and fifteenth centuries are obscure in the Fazzan, but after an era of instability and Berber raids a minor dynasty, the Banu Khurman established itself in the Wadi al-Ajal north of Murzuq. It was shortly replaced by the Awlad Muhammad (the founder of which was a migrant from Mauritania), about 1550.

At nearly the same time, strategic considerations, and a lengthy Mediterranean war between Ottoman Turkey and Hapsburg Spain brought the Turks into Tripoli. They were unable to resist expansion southward and made continued efforts to control the Awlad Muhammad, whom they brought into tributary status. At the least sign of Ottoman weakness, the Murzuq dynasty refused the tribute, which led to a cycle of Ottoman incursion and devastation. Throughout its long life, to 1812, the Awlad Muhammad were supported by the slave trade. The Qaramanli dynasty at Tripoli attempted to control the Awlad Muhammad by the same method as the Ottomans, making them pay tribute. After an interval under 'Abd al-Jalil and the Awlad Sulayman Arabs, the Ottoman Turks took over the Fazzan again in 1842. Trade at Murzuq declined again by the end of the 1860s, in favor of Ghat, Ghadamis and other towns. As trade declined, the Fazzan declined farther as the slave trade was slowly throttled under Ahmad Rasim Pasha after 1881. Eventually it came under Italian colonial control in the 1930s, and it is now one of three major regions in an independent Libya.

II

Like the Greek and Roman civilizations of antiquity, and like their Byzantine successor, the medieval Islamic world obtained much of its labor from slaves. These workers by coercion, the "property" of their owners, fell into three categories. They performed agricultural labor in larger or smaller groups, or worked in gold mines or on sugar plantations, or extracted salt from salt pans. These were invariably male slaves. Women and eunuchs were also used, in the *harims* or as house servants, or as musicians or singers or guardians (such as the *kizlar agas* of Ottoman times).[6] Another category, exclusively of male slaves, served as soldiers or mercenaries, usually called *mamluks* if they were whites, or *'abd, raqiq,* or *'abid* if not.

Once the early Islamic state had reached its full spatial dimensions – say by the end of the Umayyad period (750 AD) – a style of Islamic plural society had been established, in which Jews and Christians and Zoroastrians had their accepted places, and likewise their accepted social functions as traders, physicians, or even bureaucrats. As "protected persons" (*dhimmis*), they could no longer be enslaved. This principle was already enshrined in Islamic law. Those who required slave labor, in whatever form, were forced to look beyond the frontiers of the Islamic world for enslavable persons.[7]

Three areas and peoples existed which could supply slaves for export: the Blacks, the Slavs of Eastern Europe and Russia, and the central Asian Turks. The Slavs and Turks had a long history in Islam as eunuchs, servants, or soldiers. Africa remained the last major slaving area. It is accurate to say that Africa provided more slaves, and furnished them over a longer period than any other region – well into the twentieth century. The other two regions had been closed off to Muslim slave purchases or raiding (particularly the eastern Black Sea districts and the Caucasus) when they came under Russian control.[8]

Within Africa, there were many sources of slaves. The East African coast including Somalia and Ethiopia were several such sources. From eastern Tanzania (the Mrima coast), south Kenya, and southern Ethiopia, large numbers of slaves passed into the medieval Islamic world. Many of the boys were forcibly made into eunuchs at intermediate points on the routes towards Muslim territories. Among the survivors of these crude gelding operations, a much smaller fraction reached the places where they were to be used, passing via Socotra Island, or Aden or Zabid in the Yaman en route to the Persian Gulf, or passing through Aswan on their way into Egypt.[9]

In the "far West" of Africa, a great number of routes brought slaves from Takrur or the lands of the Niger bend, across the western Sahara into North Africa. From there sizable contingents passed at times into the hands of the Christian Catalonians and Sicilians.[10]

Between the westernmost parts of North Africa and Egypt to the east, there was also a constant flow of captives over a central route, from the Hausa country and the Lake Chad region into Libya, via the Fazzan and its trading towns: Zuwayla, Sabha, Murzuq, Ghat, and Ghadamis. Since the slave trade and the history of the Fazzan are closely intermingled, and because neither is fully comprehensible without an explanation of the other, it seems essential to give an account of both of these themes simultaneously. In this long series of historical problems, it is useful to go back to classical times, to examine certain facts about the early history of the Fazzan and a people called the Garamantes.[11]

The word "Garamantes" was apparently derived from the name of their best-known town or capital, Garama (now Jarma or Jirma), whose ruins lie along the bed of the Wadi Ajal just north of Murzuq. Often described by classical writers as a poor and nomadic people, the Garamantes were nonetheless traders of repute. They are described by Herodotus, Strabo, Pliny the Elder and Lucian among others. For many centuries, they served as intermediaries between the southern Mediterranean littoral and the Saharan regions, even the countries beyond the Sahara. With their ox, donkey, or horse caravans, or riding in chariots, they traded in animal skins, in salt, copper, gold, and various foodstuffs, including dates. Herodotus says that they also pursued the "fleet-footed Troglodytes," occasionally capturing them for use as slaves.[12]

The Garamantes' best-known export, cited often by contemporary writers, were "carbuncles," likewise called the "Carthaginian" or "Nasamonian" stone. These semi-precious gems, which the Garamantes obtained and sold to the Carthaginians, Romans, or Byzantines, have been identified as red carnelians or garnets. It is more likely that they were of greenish-blue microcline feldspar, a mineral called amazonite, or *fayruz akhdar* ("green turquoise") in Arabic. Following the researches of A. J. Arkell, the Libyan archaeologist Muhammad Sulayman Ayyub traced a source of this mineral to Ighi Zuma in the eastern foothills of the Tibesti. It is still extracted by the Tubu there: polished amazonite is very popular for women's jewelery. It was mined in Pharaonic times, and doubtless considerable quantities of it were exported to Egypt. Amazonite was known to the ancient Egyptian as *temhi* or *temhy* stone; it has been suggested that they knew the Tubu of the Tibesti under the name of Temhu.[13]

What is striking about the carbuncle trade is the frequent comment it drew from classical writers. Yet, virtually nothing is said about any trade in slaves from the Garamante capital of Garama to the Mediterranean coast until c. 500 AD. Of course, slave trading was so commonplace in antiquity as to arouse little comment. Yet it seems certain that the Garamantes were a slave-holding society, perhaps taking some slaves from other local peoples. To these they doubtless added others from south of Garama, such as the "Troglodytes" mentioned by Herodotus.[14]

About 470 AD, matters changed. At that time the Latin poet Florus records (in scatological and racist terms) the importation of Garamantean slaves into Roman Africa (to Hadrumetum, now Sus in Tunisia):

> Faex Garamantarum nostrum processit ad axem
> Et piceo gaudet corpore verna niger . . .[15]

In the same era, another poet Luxorius, notes the importation of Garamantean women into Roman Africa as slaves:

> Ut tibi non placeat Pontica, sed Garamas . . .[16]

By the sixth century AD, the Garamantes had more constant and friendlier contacts with the Byzantines than they had had with the Romans. About 575, the Spanish Abbot John of Biclar noted that the Garamantes had sent envoys to the Emperor Justin at Byzantium asking for peace with "Rome" and indicating their wish to become Christians.[17] Also, writing after 500, Cosmas Indicopleustes recorded that Christian churches existed in the country of the Garamantes.[18] Such details as these hint that by AD 600 the Garamantes were being drawn into closer trade with the Mediterranean world than ever before. At the same time, a small and insignificant slave trade already existed. Ayyub claims that

> archaeological investigations have shown that the number of slaves arriving on the shores of the Mediterranean before the 6th century AD were extremely limited. Slaving was only practised to a restricted extent during the era of the Jarma kingdom: this trade did not expand until a much later period.[19]

In the growth of the Fazzan slave trade, laying the basis for its future expansion (and also the disappearance of the Garamante state) was the acquisition of the camel by Berber nomads. When camels began to be used on a big scale (c. 200 AD?) nomadic groups like the Libyan Lawata, Mazata, and Hawwara Berbers were able to explore the Sahara farther and faster than before. They now obtained the goods in which the Garamantes had dealt more easily and cheaply, nor did they need the people of Garama as intermediaries. The appearance of the camel also doomed the old ox, donkey, and horse caravans: the chariot was likewise made extinct. Soon the Hawwara and their allies took over the oasis of Zuwayla (south and east of Garama, which they called "little Zalla" after another town of theirs further north, which they had been forced to abandon under Byzantine political and military pressure).[20]

According to traditions of the third Muslim raid on Garama (Jarma) by 'Uqba ibn Nafi' (AD 669) related by Ibn 'Abd al-Hakam in his *Futuh Misr*, part of the tribute demanded by the Muslim leader was more than 300 slaves. To what extent 'Uqba's demand represented a sizable expansion of the slave traffic is unclear, but is worth noting that the Arabs wanted slaves, not currency – perhaps reflecting an increased desire for slaves in the Islamic world.[21] Further, the Italian arabist Ettore Rossi, speaking of the Fazzan slave trade, makes the point that "the Fazzan intermittently paid tribute to Arab Muslim governors of Ifriqiya during the Umayyad caliphate and during Aghlabid rule (at Tunis) . . . and paid it from antiquity to recent times in gold and black slaves."[22]

At the start of Islamic times, between 800 and 900 AD, the slave trade through the Fazzan grew enormously. As they entered Libya from the south, from Bilma in the Kawar Oasis, from the "land of the Zaghawa," or from the later Kanem, the victims of the slavers began to move like a human river into the commercial centres of the Fazzan. At this time, these centres were three towns, laid out in a triangle about 400 miles south and east of Tripoli. These three towns were Zuwayla, Sabha and Murzuq. They came into historical prominence roughly in that order.[23]

First, Zuwayla. From c. 850 to 1172, Zuwayla was the capital of the Ibadi Berber dynasty of the Banu Khattab bin Izliten. Writing about 880, the Persian geographer Ya'qubi, writing in Arabic, observed of the people of Zuwayla that they

> exported black slaves, which they get from the Mira, Zaghawa, Marwa (Meroe?) and other black peoples who live in their vicinity. They take them by capture. I have heard that the kings of the Blacks sell them without making war, for very little. Zuwayliya skins come from Zuwayla . . .Fifteen

days' journey beyond Zuwayla (to the south) is a place called Kawar, where there is a Muslim population from elsewhere, most of them Berbers. It is they who bring in the Blacks.[24]

Ya'qubi also notes that the profits of trade at Zuwayla had attracted many non-Fazzanis: Arabs from Kufa and Basra, and men from Khurasan in Persia. In this respect, Zuwayla was no different from other Khariji towns, Tahert in Algeria, Sijilmasa in southern Morocco, which had a lively slave trade. For several centuries after 800 AD, the Ibadis (and other Kharijis) were able to monopolize Saharan trade. From local oral traditions recorded by Ayyub, it seems certain that the Banu Khattab dynasty arose from a group of rich traders, who had made their money sending out large camel caravans. The Banu Khattab also struck "Zuwayli" gold *dinars*, of which Ayyub found a number at Zuwayla. If these were made from West African gold brought to Zuwayla from across the desert, Ayyub does not make this claim. Yet he does suggest that Zuwayla was a large banking, financial, and money exchange centre under the Banu Khattab.[25] Ayyub also observes about the captives in Zuwayla trade, that

> human beings as commercial goods yielded high profits in those days, so that the slave trade was invigorated in remarkable fashion. For the people of Zuwayla, it was only a short way when they set off for the kingdoms of the Blacks south of the desert, where they bought slaves. Largely these were prisoners who fell into the hands of this prince or that during their continuous raiding ... These prisoners were purchased for clothing, weapons, salt, and other goods which these traders brought to them. At certain times these black kings and rulers used the Zuwayla people against their enemies, after which they and the traders divided the unfortunate human spoils.[26]

Making war deliberately to obtain captives was a constant and repetitive theme in the Fazzan trade (see below). To maintain a constant supply of slaves, it is likely that the slavers of this era used a procedure familiar from 19th century Darfur: traders supplied slavers with goods on credit – to be used on a raid. When the slave raid was over and the captives were brought in, they recovered the value of their goods in slaves.[27]

As Zuwayla increased in size and significance, and as the number of slaves there grew, the Banu Khattab rulers used them to dig underground water channels (*fuqqarat*). Like Persian *qanats*, these channels ran from well to well, bringing fresh water from distant sources to the Zuwayla oasis. Although such techniques may have been suggested by migrant Iranian traders, Ayyub states that they were already in use under the Garamantes. Thus the amount of ground under cultivation at Zuwayla was enlarged to support a bigger population: by c. 950, Zuwayla had truly become the "great city of the Fazzan."[28]

Zuwayla's foreign trade connections kept pace with its growth. It seems certain that under the Aghlabids, a steady stream of slaves passed through the town to the Mediterranean coast near Tripoli, and from there to Tunis or to other places in Ifriqiya. Under the Fatimids and Zirids, too, a number of black slaves served in Tunisian armies and in the ruler's personal guard: after c. 980, these developments are well documented. Near the Fatimid capital of Mahdiya in Tunisia was a new town or suburb. Constructed by the first Fatimid caliph al-Mahdi for the "common people," it was also called Zuwayla or Zawila. Why it was given this name, or what its relation was to the original town is unclear. It may well have had a large slave population which had at one time lived, or passed through, Zuwayla of the Fazzan.[29]

In the latter part of the 10th century, after the Fatimids had moved from Tunisia to Egypt, the new dynasty built Cairo, ringed with a city wall. One of the gates was named *Bab Zuwayla*: within the wall was a quarter called *Harat Zuwayla*. According to the historian Ibn Abi Dinar, it was here that the caliph al-Mu'izz li-Din Allah settled contingents from his army, the *Zuwayliyin*. In his chronicle, Ibn Abi Dinar also records (under the year 381/991-992) circumcision gifts for the young Zirid prince Badis ibn Mansur, sent him by his father's "governor in the Fazzan, Ibn Khattab," including a giraffe and other "goods from the Sudan."[30] On the other hand, the Italian historian Enrico Rossi claims that *Bab Zuwayla* marked one end of a commercial artery linking Cairo and Awjila in eastern Libya, to the Fazzan.[31] Many of the details cited by Ibn Abi Dinar and Rossi are confirmed by the Mamluk writer Ibn Duqmaq, and also by that indefatigable Ottoman traveller, Evliya Chelebi.[32]

From the 11th to the start of the 13th century, information about Zuwayla is fragmentary, but there is no hint of any diminution of the slave trade. Writing about 1070, al-Bakri noted that slaves were being despatched from Zuwayla to all parts of Ifriqiya, and that they were exchanged for "short pieces of red cloth."[33] About 1200, the anonymous *Kitab al-Istibsar* mentions that Zuwayla was

> close to Kanem in the Sudan (which became Muslim about 500 H./1106) ... It is an assembly spot for slaves, and a place where they are exchanged, whence they are sent to Ifriqiya and other places.[34]

During the 12th century, a major political change took place in the Fazzan, the overturn of the Banu Khattab dynasty of Zuwayla. This event was followed by the decline of the town, which was superseded by Traghen or Tarajin, about 30 miles away to the west. The Muslim state of Kanem now expanded northward, taking in most of the Fazzan.

The fall of Zuwayla was sudden and unexpected. In 1174, an Ayyubid officer, an Armenian *mamluk* known by the Turkish name Qaraqush ("Vulture"), arrived in Libya from Egypt. A white slave of Saladin's (Salsh al-Din's) brother, Qaraqush was directed from Cairo to reconnoitre (and doubtless to raid) eastern Libya. This venture was undertaken because Nur al-Din, Salah al-Din's master and ruler of Damascus, was having a violent difference of opinion with his famous underling. At one time, Nur al-Din seemed ready to depose him: hence Salah al-Din was looking for some place in the Maghrib to which he could retire if the worst occurred. Then Nur al-Din died conveniently, and the crisis evaporated. By this time, Qaraqush was too far away to recall, for he was already busy surrounding and sacking a series of Libyan cities. Evidently, the legendary wealth of Zuwayla and its lack of walls tempted him. The Tunisian traveller Muhammad al-Tijani, a contemporary, tells of his attack on Zuwayla, his brutal torturing and murder of the last dynast of the Banu Khattab line in order to extract his money and take his possessions. After sacking Zuwayla, Qaraqush found plundering central Libya and eastern Ifriqiya attractive. Eventually he was cornered by one of his rivals. He fought bravely, with one of his sons: when they were taken alive, both were immediately crucified.[35]

Another son of Qaraqush raised a revolt in the Waddan region (north and slightly west of the Fazzan), but was caught and executed by a king of Kanem in 1258. The Kanemi king's motive was obvious, because Kanem's economy had suffered for a long time from the marauding and depredations of Qaraqush and his sons. By obtaining physical control of the northern end of its Mediterranean trade route, the Chadian state could safeguard its vital slave exports. This point is confirmed by the Arab writer Abu'l-Fida' (who composed his *Taqwim* about 1340, but used information which was of a slightly earlier date):

> Fazzan lies east of Waddan. It consists of islands of palm trees with water. It possesses many towns and cultivated tracts, more than Waddan. All of that is now under the control of the King of Kanem.[36]

At Traghen, a Kanemi garrison remained in place for some time, probably between c. 1300 and 1550. It was under the control of a viceroy or sub-king (*mai*). Local oral history at Traghen records the building of a castle by the southern invaders, likewise the grave of a certain Mai 'Ali, said to be of a family called the Banu Nasur. Chapelle suggests that the local dynasty may have been of Tubu origin, perhaps from the region of the Tibesti. Later, possibly by 1400, the control of Kanem gave way to that of Bornu.[37] The French traveller Duveyrier, who visited Traghen in 1860, claimed he knew of old papers in the possession of the Thamir family claiming Bornu as the "place of origin of the inhabitants of that town."[38] The stamp of Kanem and then Bornu on the Fazzan was a lasting one, for streets and quarters in Traghen (and also in Murzuq) still bear Kanembu and Kanuri names. In the local government, the same influence was manifest, a point which will be taken up further below.

By the later 15th century, it may be surmised that Bornu rule had receded somewhat. The Fazzan, like Tripoli itself, apparently became a dependency of the Hafsid state of Tunis, and so fell back into an earlier pattern of political control. Thus in 1463, the Egyptian traveller 'Abd al-Basit bin Halil passed through Tripoli. He observed that the local *qa'id* paid his Hafsid master a yearly tribute of more than a hundred thousand gold *dinars*, weighing a *mithqal* (4.25 grams) each. Rossi, who obtained these details from a manuscript in the Vatican collections, states that the *qa'id* had under his control the regions of Tripoli, Gharyan, Misurata, and the Fazzan.[39] Although this is mere speculation, a part of this tribute money might have come from a direct gold trade through the Fazzan from the south. Equally, a share of it might have come from a head tax on slaves, a common sort of transit toll in this period.

Another significant development took place in the Fazzan about 1500: although the date of the emergence of the Banu Khurman is uncertain, they soon became a political force of consequence. Whether they were Arabs, as claimed by Duveyrier, or Berbers, as stated by Ayyub, is uncertain. Perhaps as Bornu control of the Fazzan ebbed southwards into the deserts they were able to assert themselves, and to rule parts of the province for a short time from Sabha in the Wadi Ajal, not far north of Murzuq. According to both Duveyrier and Nachtigal, they are rememberd as "oppressors and tyrants," who "reduced the Fazzanis to the state of slaves and overwhelmed them with injustice."[40] Both Rossi and Ayyub agree that the name Khurman has something in common with the word "Garamante," Ayyub going so far as to claim that the Banu Khurman were indeed the descendants of the Garamantes, tracing the evolution of their name from Jarma (the Garamantes' capital) to Khurma and then Khurman. In any case, they were soon overthrown and supplanted by another dynasty, that of the Awlad Muhammad of Murzuq, who lasted until 1812.[41]

Traditionally, the founder of the Awlad Muhammad was a *sharif* from Morocco named Muhammad al-Fasi.[42] But more reliable oral traditions gathered by Ayyub at Murzuq suggest that he hailed from the Saqiyat al-Hamra' in Mauritania. These local reports stress the fact that al-Fasi arrived first in the Fazzan as the leader of a pilgrimage caravan from the west, either from Senegal or Mauritania, and that he was requested(?) by the local Fazzani rulers to take over political control there, perhaps because of an intensification of Berber or Tuareg raids on the province.

Muhammad Sulayman Ayyub adds more details to the story of Muhammad al-Fasi's rise. Accepting and retaining the tradition that he came from the west, that he was the leader of a pilgrim caravan and that he was attracted by the commercial possibilities of the Fazzan (including the slave trade, no doubt), Ayyub has elaborated the following interesting hypothesis:

> It seems more reasonable that the pilgrimage route followed the Wadi Barjuj, and the Wadi al-Hufra, where the town of Murzuq (later) arose. The caravans which followed this route did so of necessity, for they stopped to take on water and food, just as they paid passage tolls at the numerous castles standing in the outskirts of Murzuq, in the district called Umm al-Hammam. Many mounds from these castles continue to exist in the region today, like Qal'at al-Manasi, Tamira, and others. These structures are built with walls and many towers, of unbaked brick (*libn*).[43]

Such castles as these had already been noted by Leo Africanus, who commented on "this ample region, with great store of castles ... inhabited by rich people."[44] Leo did not explain the function of these castles, which Ayyub is able to do:

> According to current tradition, these castles were the property of the Amirs of the Banu Khurman. They were constantly at loggerheads with each other ... The acumen of Muhammad al-Fasi led him to use his goods and the armed guards of his caravan to help one of the Khurman *amirs* against another, until he made away with all of them in the district and ruled over it himself. He erected a new castle for himself at Murzuq ... perhaps the ruined one called "Qal'at Awlad Muhammad." Then he extended his rule to Jarma, and united the entire Fazzan under his banner, setting himself up as Sultan of the Fazzan about 1550.[45]

With the establishment of the new Awlad Muhammad dynasty at Murzuq, trade, the pilgrim traffic – and above all the slave trade – revived and expanded as never before. About 1567, Muhammad al-Fasi was succeeded by his son Sultan Nasir.[46] Ayyub claims that the new trade centre of Murzuq (formerly Marzagh) grew to accommodate a burgeoning trade network of which it was now one of the biggest nodes, other adjoining ones being Ghat and Ghadamis – of lesser importance in the late 16th century than later. Hence the political and economic ties of Murzuq were greatly strengthened and extended, drawing in a large share of its trade from beyond the Sahara, from what is now Niger and Chad Republics, likewise northern Nigeria.

Like Zuwayla at an earlier time, political stability and extensive trade fostered Fazzani agriculture. The province now began to export grain: barley, wheat and sorghum (*dhurra*) went north to Tripoli and south to the Hausa states and Bornu. With the growth of trade, Murzuq's markets proliferated, too. Silks, woollens, and cotton textiles from Venice and Genoa could be found there, firearms and swords imported from Spain, glassware, perfumes, and pottery from various Muslim countries. From the Saharan or sub-Saharan regions came animal skins (and occasionally exotic beasts as well), ivory tusks, ostrich feathers, sandalwood, incense, and gold dust.[47]

At this time, Murzuq assumed the outward appearance of a typical Maghribi town, with whitewashed walls and narrow alleys, some of them roofed over against the sun. The town now contained several separate quarters, the biggest of which was called *Hayy al-Ra'is*, the principal commercial section. It extended from the Castle to the south side of the town. Here the wealthy merchants had their shops and houses: the latter were usually of two stories, usually constructed in unbaked brick, with a coating of lime plaster. This old commercial area was by recent report a heap of ruins, mounds of decayed, collapsed, and fallen buildings.

To the east of the Castle, a second quarter (*Hayy al-Nazila*) contained lodging houses, inns, and warehouses, with an open area where caravans could rest overnight. From the east side of the Castle, a broad street traversed the quarters to the East Gate (*Bab Sharqi*), where the slave market was situated. Along this principal artery (called the *dendal* like similar main streets in Kanuri towns) was a third quarter, probably dating from c. 1850, the *Hayy al-Zawiya*, so-called from the Sanusi religious house in the vicinity.

Murzuq Castle, extensively walled in baked brick, surmounts a hill in the northwest corner of the town. Called locally the *Qal'a* or *Qasaba*, it has a number of towers, with slits for the use of archers or musketeers. By local tradition, it was built by the founder of the Awlad Muhammad Dynasty, Muhammad al-Fasi, then enlarged by his son Nasir. It contained the state offices, the *harim* of the Sultan, his residence and that of his sons. It also afforded housing for their retainers. A mosque adjoined the Castle, and there were at least two others in the town, the Hannashi Mosque and the Sanusi Mosque, the latter doubtless being later than the other.[48]

During his visit to Murzuq in 1860, Duveyrier found a Turkish official who told him that in the times of the Awlad Muhammad clan (before 1812), the place had much resembled "the towns of the Blacks."

> The Sultan had a black guard (*ganga*), the language was virtually Kanuri, and all the names given to things and places were in that language – hence the commercial boulevard of the town was called the *dendal*.

Further, an alleged "last descendant" of the Awlad Muhammad informed Duveyrier that under his ancestors

> White merchants could stay for their business only during three months during the winter. When the hot weather began, the Sultan caused a herald to announce that the whites had to depart, under pain of expulsion or a fine, because they were ill and communicated their illnesses to the other inhabitants.[49]

If these late restrictions did not exist in the 16th century, Murzuq in the 1560s had looked forward to a long period of prosperity, based on its far-flung commercial connections. But at Tripoli, an event had already occurred that boded ill for the hopes of the Fazzanis and the Awlad Muhammad for political independence. This was the arrival (in 1551) of the Ottoman Turks in Tripoli. At this time, although they were preoccupied with the Spaniards and the last Hafsids of Tunis, and with reinforcing their strategic position in North Africa, they eventually found the troops to conquer the rest of the Tripolitanian hinterland. In the long run, the Ottoman Turks would find it difficult to let the Fazzan alone, with its gold, its wealthy merchants, its caravans bringing valuable and taxable goods from south of the Sahara, and its slave trade.

The traditional story of Ottoman penetration into the Fazzan is a curious one, related by Ibn Ghalbun. "In 985/1577," he states,

> Khuda bint Sharuma bin Muhammad al-Fasi, the wife of Muntasir bin Nasir ibn Muhammad al-Fasi, sent word to the Turkish troops in Tripoli that they should come to her and take over the country. If they would come, she promised them abundant gifts.[50]

Ibn Galbun goes on to relate that "although Khuda loved her cousin Muntasir, he had another wife at Murzuq." By her, he had "only had a daughter, while by the Murzuq lady, he had had several children." Muntasir spent most of his time at Murzuq, while Khuda lived alone at the Red Castle at Sabha. "That waywardness which enters women's heads got into hers," adds the chronicler, "and that was what she did."[51]

A small party of Turkish soldiers now approached Sabha (about 60

Ahmad Rasim Pasha and the Fazzan Slave Trade 65

miles NE of Murzuq). Unexpectedly, her husband decided to pay Khuda a short visit. But she barred the gates of the Red Castle against him, mobilizing her followers. Although Muntasir besieged the castle for three days, he failed to get in. Shortly after, he "died of grief." Meanwhile, Khuda thought she might deceive the approaching Ottomans by placing men's capes and turbans over some rocks along the skyline of a hill adjoining her castle, to make the enemy think she had reinforcements within call. This trick was of little use. The Turks promptly attacked the Red Castle and took it, seizing the lady and eventually burning her alive, as Ibn Ghalbun reports with great satisfaction.[52]

Seeing that he could make no effective resistance, Muntasir's son Nasir assembled his brothers, his retinue, and his treasures, and set off across the desert for Katsina in northern Hausaland. At Murzuq, the Turks stayed only a short time. They installed the first "Bey of the Fazzan," a man named Mami or Mahmud, with a small garrison. There are some indications that Mami tried to extend Turkish rule southwards towards Bornu, probably along the trade routes, but the evidence is unclear. On their arrival in the Fazzan, the Turks were aided by some of the surviving Banu Khurman from Sabha, doubtless from their old hostility to the Awlad Muhammad. In some way so far uncertain, it is likely that Khuda and her independent ways suited the local political interests of the Banu Khurman.

Shortly after this (c. 1585), the local population rose against the Ottoman soldiers and the "Fazzan Bey," all of whom they massacred. They then sent word to Nasir in Katsina to return home. He did so, and revived the independent rule of the Awlad Muhammad; he continued to govern at Murzuq until his death in 1599. Nasir's flight to Katsina is significant. His chosen place of refuge suggests that he and his family were both well known and well-connected in Hausaland. It may by surmised that Nasir had his trade agents and his commercial allies there – he and his followers could simply wait until the political situation in the Fazzan improved enough for him to go home.[53]

Under Nasir's sons Mansur and Tahir, energetic Ottoman efforts to control the Fazzan and its trade were evident. In 1613-14, Sulayman or Safar Day, the Turkish governer at Tripoli, demanded an annual tribute from the Awlad Muhammad, no doubt requiring supplementary payments to make up for the "missing amounts" from the years of Nasir's independence. Yet Mansur ibn Nasir refused to pay. His refusal triggered a Turkish invasion of the Fazzan, in a cycle of refusal and reprisal which soon became automatic. Mansur was quickly defeated and killed by the Ottomans at Kunayr between Umm al-

'Abid ("the place of slaves") and Ramla, about 50 miles NE of Sabha.

His surviving brother Tahir fled with his wives and whatever he could salvage "for the Sudan." After the Turks had once again sacked Murzuq and departed from the Fazzan, Tahir returned. In 1622-23, he was forced to flee a second time, on this occasion to Bornu. This time, Ibn Ghalbun says, he took "twelve camel loads of gold" with him, presumably the dynastic profits over the preceding decade of trading. However, since he had angered the Mai of Bornu ('Umar al-Maqdisi) by blinding two of his own nephews (who might otherwise have posed a succession problem for him), the Mai captured him, his following, and his gold as they neared Bornu. He tied Tahir and his men into sacks, and drowned them in a river. The gold the Mai kept. Another group of fugitives (including Tahir's brother Juhaym) did not make this error, but went on to Katsina in the usual manner. For this, Ibn Ghalbun offers no explanation.[54]

During the temporary disappearance of the Awlad Muhammad, the Banu Khurman, in the person of Ahmad al-Huwaydi al-Khurmani, took control of the Fazzan again as the open allies of the Turks, acting as their administrators (*'amils*) and helping them to collect the tribute and the *kharaj* tax. But this arrangement was short-lived: in 1639, Muhammad bin Juhaym, a son of Tahir's brother Juhaym (who had died a fugitive in Katsina), returned to Murzuq. He overthrew the Ottoman Bey and assumed control of the province. As before, the Turks retaliated with an attack on the Fazzan and the local dynasty. This time, the fighting was prolonged and destructive.[55]

Appalled by the extent and the seriousness of this conflict, two members of a local "holy family" (the Awlad Hadiri *murabits* of Sabha) intervened to reconcile the opposing sides. Eventually the Turks and the Awlad Muhammad of Murzuq made peace. The stipulations of the armistice reveal many interesting details about the ongoing Fazzani slave trade to Tripoli, c. 1630. As arranged by the two *murabits*, the Awlad Muhammad would pay the Turks each year

> four thousand *mithqals* of gold, two thousand in gold dust [*tibr*], and would render the equivalent of the remaining two thousand in slaves and slave girls. Each male slave would cost 25 *mithqals,* the price of a slave girl would be 30 *mithqals,* and the cost of a eunuch 80. They (Awlad Muhammad) would bear the expenses of the slaves - those who died before they reached Sawkna. Beyond there, the expenses would be borne by the Sultan['s representative at Tripoli], likewise the hire of riding animals for slaves [would be the responsibility] of the Sultan.[56]

Ibn Ghalbun does not mention the provenance of these slaves, nor the eunuchs, nor the gold, but Katsina, Agades, or Bornu seem likely points of origin. It is significant that the two holy men were not only concerned with making peace, but with assuring the smooth functioning of the Fazzani economy on the basis of its traditional "products", slaves and gold. If they were concerned in any way with the moral issues of slavery like their contemporary Ahmad Baba, the chronicler fails to mention it.

It is hard to establish any rigid value for this commerce of 1630, owing to the variable price of the gold *mithqal*. A generally accepted value for this weight is about 1/7 of an ounce (better, 0.15 ounce). If the price of gold is taken as $147.50 to the ounce, then the value of Ibn Ghalbun's four thousand *mithqals* in contemporary money amounts to $88,500 (or $44,250 for the slave component in this tribute). It is obvious that the tribute money paid the Turks must have represented only a tiny fraction of the total trade through the Fazzan. Although it is impossible to quantify the figures of the slave trade in any way, it is likely that the true total represented several times the amount of tribute money, a very large sum even today.

For the remainder of the 17th century, both Ibn Ghalbun and a chronicle of the Fazzan record recurrent pressure by the Pasha or *Veli* at Tripoli on the Murzuq rulers to pay the annual tribute, as established in 1630. When they felt strong enough, the Awlad Muhammad refused to do so (at least three times between 1658 and 1699), exposing themselves to the inevitable punitive expeditions sent out from the capital. Flights of the *Shaykhs* (or *Sultans*) of the Fazzan to Hausaland or Agades occur with great regularity in this period.[57]

About 1690, Qaradaghli Muhammad Pasha al-Imam, the Montenegrin governor of Tripoli, appointed two members of a local family there to head military expeditions against the Fazzan. These two men, Muhammad al-Ghuzayl and 'Ali al-Mukni (or al-Mukkani) were aided by their influential relative, Yusuf Bey al-Mukni. In these years, at the end of the first Ottoman Period in Libya, and later under the independent Qaramanli dynasty, the Mukni family became increasingly prominent in the Fazzan, tending to regard it as their private domain. Some of them became hereditary tribute couriers or "escort beys" (*bey al-nuba*): each year, one of them accompanied a combined slave and tribute caravan from Murzuq to Tripoli.[58]

The forty years' interval from 1680 to 1720 was a period of relative quiet in the Fazzan; it was also an era of commercial revival and the regular passage of caravans. Rossi, quoting some French sources of 1686, 1692, and 1698, remarks that in these years the *Dayi* of Tripoli despatched two caravans a year to the Fazzan. These carried coarse paper, textiles of various grades (made at Venice and on the Island of

Chios) among other merchandise. At Murzuq, it was exchanged for gold dust, *senna* leaves (a kind of cathartic, from the leaves of a *Cassia* shrub), and black slaves coming from Bornu. The identical sort of traffic was noted by another French observer in 1692. Six years later, Venetian cloth worked with gold and silver designs, tobacco, and textiles from Marseille and Leghorn (Livorno) were still being traded for senna, ivory, and slaves.[59]

Rossi also mentions for this period the existence of "fairs" (*fiere*), but perhaps this term should be understood as the normal trading period during the cooler part of the year at Murzuq, from October to February, rather than any special trade festival. At times, this market season must have coincided with the arrival of pilgrim caravans from Mauritania, Morocco, or parts of the trans-Saharan regions and West Africa. Rossi also records the participation of pilgrims from "Guinea, Congo, and Ethiopia" on these commercial occasions, importing goods from those places, "Ethiopian" slaves among them, who were recognizable from "certain marks on their faces, captured and made Muslims."[60]

Towards the end of this time (1711) a new half-Turkish, half-Libyan dynasty emerged at Tripoli, the Qaramanlis. After crushing his many rivals, then annihilating a certain Abu Qila who announced that he was the "Expected Mahdi," Amhad Pasha, the first Qaramanli, moved against the Fazzan. He found the Awlad Muhammad "disrespectful"; once again they had failed to pay the customary tribute. On two campaigns in 1716 and 1718, Ahmad Pasha led an expedition to the Fazzan. He failed to take the walled town of Murzuq, but obtained good service from his deputy Tiryaqi Ibrahim ("Ibrahim the Opium Eater") who ravaged Qatrun south of Murzuq.[61]

Ahmad ibn Nasir, the Sultan of the Fazzan at this time, finally made his peace with the new masters at Tripoli, where he had to go to present his submission. There, in a humiliating ceremony before the assembled Qaramanli *Divan*, the new Pasha sold him to his son Muhammad for two copper coins, then reinstated him as ruler of the Fazzan, on condition that he pay tribute and the *kharaj* tax.[62] For the onlookers, the symbolism of this ceremony would have been easy to comprehend: by this time, many branches of the Awlad Muhammad were africanised, and a report of the late 17th century says that the ruler of that time was a black.[63] Yet, like the later Qaramanlis, it is likely that the dynasty included several lines, some descended from African mothers, some not.[64] Indeed Hornemann (who stayed at Murzuq in 1798 and 1799) found that

> the Harem consists of a Sultana, who by the rules of the empire must be of

the family of the Shareefs of *Wadan* or *Zuila*, and of about forty slaves. These last are often sold and replaced by others, if they do not bear children to the Sultan, or do not otherwise endear themselves to him by superior charms and accomplishments.[65]

In any case these children were *sharifs*, either by both parents, or their fathers alone, and hence the Murzuq dynasty could look down on common Turks like the Qaramanlis. However, the new Tripoline rulers held overwhelming military power. So, to ensure his continuing obedience, Ahmad Pasha appointed a governor, who accompanied Ahmad ibn Nasir home to Murzuq. The governor was instructed to tear down the walls of the town, so effective an obstacle to the invasions of 1716 and 1718. They were only rebuilt about 1750.[66]

During the first four decades of the 18th century, Fazzani commerce continued in an active way, with three caravans a year in January, May, and October. Yet, by the time of 'Ali Pasha Qaramanli in 1756, the French writer Ange de Gardane complained that the countryside was in rebellion, that the Pasha had no money, and that the caravans from

> the Fazzan and Ghadamès, which used to bring blacks, gold, senna and ostrich plumes, and get European goods here (Tripoli) no longer arrive.[67]

Thirty years later, in 1786, the situation still remained much the same. The French Consul at Tripoli, Vallière, reported that

> Today, the Pasha at Tripoli reigns over rebellious subjects, sterile regions, rubbish heaps, ruins. His palace is falling to pieces.... Before these disastrous times, there was a considerable annual export of wheat, barley, and oil.... Luxury goods were of some importance.... France, Italy, the Levant, and Alexandria furnished them, and they were paid for in wool, ostrich feathers, senna, gold dust, slaves, ivory, etc.... Livorno furnished coarse sheeting, some of which was sold in the Fazzan and Bornu. These sheets for blacks were made at Naples from Tripolitanian and Benghazi wool...Livorno was the city with which Tripoli had the most trade; all of it was in the hands of the Jews.[68]

By the turn of the 19th century, matters had improved slightly. The German traveller Hornemann found (1798-99) that Murzuq still had a very extensive trade with "Cairo, Bengasi, Tripoli, Gadames, Twat, and Soudan." Curiously, few Fazzanis or Tripolitanians participated. Trade was "managed" by small "troops of traders" who lived on the routes leading to Murzuq: men from Awjila dealt with the Egyptian trade, traders of Sawkna that from Tripoli, and the Tibbu of Bilma the trade with Bornu. The Hausaland ("Soudan") trade was carried in by Kel Owi Tuareg or persons from Agades. Among the articles traded were

> slaves of both sexes, ostrich feathers, zibette (musk from civet cats?), tiger

skins [sic], and gold, partly in dust, partly in native grains, to be manufactured into rings and other ornaments for the people of interior Africa. From Bornu, copper is imported in great quantity. Cairo sends silks, *melayes* (striped blue and white calicoes [i.e. *milayat*, wrappers, sheeting]), woolen cloths, glass ... beads for bracelets, and an ... assortment of East India goods ... The merchants of Bengasi, who usually join the caravan from Cairo at Augila, import tobacco manufactured for chewing, or snuff, and sundry wares fabricated in Turkey. . . . The caravan from Tripoli deals chiefly in paper, false corals, fire-arms, sabres, knives, and the cloths called *abbes*, and in red worsted caps. Those trading from Gadames bring nearly the same articles.[69]

In keeping with a still depressed but reviving economy, Hornemann noted that the Awlad Muhammad, during their twilight period, still reigned over their domains "with unlimited power," but that the Sultan held them "tributary to the Bashaw of Tripoly: the amount of the tribute was formerly 6000 dollars (Spanish *Douros*, Maria Theresa dollars?), it is now reduced to 4000. . . . An officer of the Bashaw comes annually to Mourzouk to receive this sum, or its value in gold, senna, or slaves."[70] Hornemann also recorded other interesting details during his visit: Kanuri influence was strong as ever, with such Bornu titles as *Galadima* and *Kaygama* for the ruler's first and second "ministers," both free-born men. The court of Murzuq likewise employed white *mamluks* ("Europeans, Greeks, Genoese, or their immediate descendants"), and many black slaves, purchased "whilst yet boys ... and educated for the court according to their dispositions and talents." Financially, the ruler was still well situated, for he gained "further income from duties on foreign trade, paid by the several caravans." Cairo merchants had to pay "six to eight dollars" for a camel load, and the Bornu and Hausa caravans had to hand over two gold *mithqals* for every slave on sale. Further, the "present sultan had made great additions to his treasures by predatory expeditions, which he occasionally directs against the Tibboes of the tribe of Burgu."[71]

Hornemann was evidently the last European visitor to see and observe the trade and state of the Awlad Muhammad at Murzuq before their demise in November-December 1812. The last ruler, Muhammad al-Sharif, refused to pay the tribute. The Mukni family, still powerful at Tripoli, and the last effective Qaramanli Pasha, Yusuf – known for his ferocity, energy, his huge debts, his avarice, his wars with foreign powers – including the United States – now jointly mounted a major military expedition. On his arrival at Murzuq, Muhammad al-Mukni killed, or arranged for the deaths of, Muhammad al-Sharif, his two sons, many of his relatives, and the principal personages of the local court. He then became master of the

Fazzan, something his clan had aimed at for a long period. According to the Tripoli chronicler Ahmad Bey al-Na'ib al-Ansari,

> In that year (1227/1812-13) Shaykh Muhammad Sharif... became careless about sending the *kharaj*, preoccupied with riches and engrossed with the society of buffoons and clowns neglecting his duty. Yusuf Pasha (Qaramanli) became annoyed at that, and despatched troops under Muhammad al-Mukni against him. When he reached Murzuq, and his army was outside it, he pretended to be resting his men, before going on to Bornu. In that way he concealed his motives.
>
> The ruler's (*'amil*) nephew came to him and exposed to him how the population was suffering ... from his uncle's behavior. Al-Mukni enticed him to kill his uncle, and promised him that he could rule in his place: the nephew was attracted by that, fell on his uncle and killed him, informing al-Mukni, who entered the town with his army and held it without resistance, occupying the castle, and assembling the *'ulama* and the notables. He then called in the *'amil's* nephew, who, before them, admitted killing his uncle. They wanted revenge for him and asked al-Mukni to make an example... he killed him ...al-Mukni (now) took possession of the province.[72]

Such was the end of the Awlad Muhammad.

Feeling secure at Murzuq, al-Mukni did lead an expedition towards Bornu in 1816 and 1817 – alleged at the behest of Muhammad al-Amin al-Kanemi, then ruling at Kukawa – to suppress a revolt. With the fall of the Awlad Muhammad, the local economy had probably been feeling the loss of profits from the slave trade (in 1819, Lyon wrote that the commerce of Murzuq was still "chiefly in slaves"). Mukni now believed it imperative to obtain slaves from the neighborhood of Bornu (possibly from Baghirmi). Taking 1,800 slaves and prisoners, he drove them before his army towards the Fazzan.[73] Lyon states that every one of them perished along the route. It may be that the photograph in John Wright's *Libya*, of a skull, some scattered bones, and a metal bar with fetters attached is a reminder of the human cost of this extensive and vicious enterprise.

Al-Mukni and his overlord, Yusuf Pasha, having wiped out the Awlad Muhammad, now found a new threat to their control of the Fazzan. These were the numerous nomads of the Awlad Sulayman, composed of two factions, the Sayf al-Nasr and the Banu Bashir. Using his usual divisive techniques, Yusuf Pasha for a time succeeded in sowing dissension between the two groups and making them fight each other. Mukni helped this process along by attacking the Sayf al-Nasr whenever he could, hoping to weaken them, aided by the Maghariha, their neighbors and rivals. Eventually 'Abd al-Jalil, chief of the Sayf al-Nasr, fled to Egypt or the northwestern Sudan. About 1823, he returned to the Fazzan, and seems to have been on temporary good terms with Yusuf Pasha. In a letter of the same year to one of Yusuf's intimates, 'Abd al-Jalil declares:

> Were you to ask the news of the South (*Qibla*), all the Bornu and Sudan caravans have arrived at Murzuq: not a single one has failed to turn up. Praise to God, the Fazzan is in truly thriving condition.[74]

Ahmad Bey claims that Yusuf Pasha employed 'Abd al-Jalil to aid Muhammad al-Amin al-Kanemi a second time – on the occasion of a revolt in Bornu in 1826-27. Like al-Mukni, 'Abd al-Jalil set off with a contingent of Tripolitanian troops for Bornu, whence he returned shortly with large numbers of slaves and much loot.[75] Anticipating the fall of Yusuf Pasha, 'Abd al-Jalil assembled a new coalition of the Warfalla, the Maghariha, and the Qadadifa groups. When Yusuf Pasha abdicated in 1832 the Qaramanlis abandoned the Fazzan to the new tribal coalition, despite a last-ditch effort by al-Mukni to maintain control of the province. The now reunited Awlad Sulayman group and their allies were able to hold Murzuq and a strip of territory north of it until 1842, when Ottoman power was reestablished there.[76]

Towards the end of Qaramanli rule, a significant commercial report was compiled by the Swedish Consul at Tripoli, Gråberg de Hemsö, covering the years 1823-1828: it appeared in an Italian periodical of the time. From Gråberg's information, it is clear that Murzuq – as 'Abd al-Jalil had claimed – in these years maintained its excellent commercial position in trade to the "interior of Africa." Until c. 1835, it remained the largest point of exchange for goods going to and from Wadai, Bornu, Katsina, Sokoto in Hausaland, and Timbuktu. During this period (1823-28), European goods continued to enter Murzuq as usual, along with goods forwarded from Egypt or Tripoli. Among them was the famous "three moon" (*tre lune*) paper, made at Genoa or Livorno, in which so many contemporary Arabic mss. of the Western Sudan are written. Gråberg de Hemsö also observed that about 2,500 slaves per year were entering Tripoli from the Fazzan and Ghadamis, and about 10,000 *mithqals* of gold dust annually. They were accompanied by considerable amounts of *trona* (natron, calcium carbonate), senna leaves, ostrich plumes and feathers, and ivory. The Consul gives information about other goods as well, sometimes mentioning the quantities involved.[77]

Gråberg's description of the "southern trade" did not remain valid for long. If the fall of the Awlad Muhammad at Murzuq had created little confusion, the return of the Ottoman Turks was another matter. Here was a political change of great consequence, with many attendant uncertainties. Some elements in Libya now discovered that they had really preferred the Qaramanlis, and lent their support to several competing Qaramanli princes, who hoped to oust the Turks. Others supported the permanent rebel, Ghuma al-Mahmudi. Yet all of them realized after a time that Istanbul's control was solid and unlikely to be shaken off. By this time, too, a new sense of Muslim solidarity existed, intensified by the presence of French troops in Algeria. Another new factor was the settlement and growth of the Sanusi sufi order in eastern Libya, which soon became in many respects the allies, even the partners of the Turks.

In order to restore their rule, the Ottomans employed forceful, even tough policies, which temporarily disrupted and damaged trade. This went on for several decades after 1835, in some places into the 1850s. Hence the Turks had not scrupled to kill 'Abd al-Jalil of the Sayf al-Nasr branch of the Awlad Sulayman by treachery, his brother, and many of their followers in 1842. They also drove the survivors out of Libya towards Bornu and Lake Chad. In the same year, they despatched the man who had tricked and then murdered 'Abd al-Jalil, Hasan Bey al-Bel'azi, to Murzuq as the new Turkish administrator of the Fazzan. It was now made a *muteserriflik*, and Hasan Bey assumed the title of Pasha.[78]

From the start of the second Ottoman period in Libya, there is much evidence to suggest that the Turks first condoned the trade, as they had in the past. Yet by 1850, some higher Ottoman officials, at least, began to change their views and to set restrictions on slave dealing, trying to make it more humane. At the start, these attempts were ineffective and were generally disregarded: after 1860, however, they started to show results.

According to a document from the Tripoli Archives published by 'Umar 'Ali bin Isma'il, a group of local dealers in "slaves from the Sudan" complained to the Ottoman *Veli*, Mehmet Amin Pasha, on 1 January 1843, about the inequalities in the export taxes on slaves levied at Tripoli and other ports, such as Midilli (Mytilene), Izmir (Smyrna), and Istanbul. Hajj Muhammad Bu Humayra, his relative Hajj Ma'tuq Bu Humayra, 'Atiq 'Ali Pasha and four other merchants reminded the Pasha that for slave exports to Midilli, the export tax levied at Tripoli was less than at neighboring Izmir, or Istanbul. Sometimes the dealers had to pay one price at Tripoli, and sometimes additional tax at the point of sale. Arbitrarily, the rates varied from 3 to 9 per cent of the sale price of a slave: they wished to have these rates adjusted, so that as "loyal Ottoman subjects," whose livelihoods depended on the trade, they could avoid further losses. The Pasha's reply, if any, is not recorded: significantly, the entire matter is phrased as if it were a commonplace commercial transaction.[79]

Seven years later (in a document of 22 December 1850) al-Hajj Musa, then *Mudir* of Ghadamis, wrote to Ahmad 'Izzet Pasha at Tripoli to tell him that he had assembled the notables of the town, its merchants, and those who "dealt in captives from the Sudan," in response to the Pasha's order about the abuse, humiliation, and starving of slaves. They would now follow the Pasha's orders and give such captives better treatment, including more food, as well as riding animals to take them to the Tripoli slave market if needed![80]

Again, under Ahmad 'Izzet Pasha in 1859, an incident occurred which showed how little control the Turks had over their subjects, and to what extent a wish for profit was coupled with a wish to raid and obtain slaves for sale, whatever the Turkish élite at Tripoli had in mind. A colonel and some Ottoman officers led a group of about 3,500 Arab irregulars from Tripoli to Murzuq. At Sawknah on the road to the south, the Turkish colonel caught fever and died, but his troops swept on through the Fazzan into Tibesti where they took slaves. They pressed on to Ahir where they gathered some Tuareg captives, and even raided Ghadames merchants, subjects of the Sublime Porte. On the return journey, they were attacked and routed by Tuareg raiders. Most of their slaves died – not unlike the raids of Muhammad al-Mukni before 1820.[81]

However, the *velis* at Tripoli soon had some new orders. In August 1863, two separate decrees were sent out by the Pasha, one copy of which, addressed to 'Ali Bey, the *Qa'im Maqam* at Ghadamis, has been published by 'Umar 'Ali bin Isma'il. 'Ali Bey's reply promises obedience to the Sultan's imperial decree (*irade*) that the slave trade was now forbidden, that he would publish the order in Ghadames, and that he would read the text of the order to the local notables at his next council session. Another document of the same time amplified the details included in this decree: that whoever was found to be holding slaves would have them confiscated by the Ottoman authorities, and that the slaves' manumission would be compulsory. Violators of the order would be imprisoned for a year on their first offense, for two years on their second, etc.[82]

It may be assumed that similar orders were despatched to other places, to Murzuq, to Ghat, to Benghazi, and elsewhere.

Another account by Professor Adu Boahen mentions many of the same details. About the time of the Crimean War, the British put heavy pressure on the Ottomans to stop the Crimean, the Libyan, and particularly the Fazzan slave trade. Hence they placed British vice-consuls – such as the famous Gagliuffi – at Murzuq. Yet Boahen has much to say about an imperial decree, a *firman* of 1857.[83] What could account for a six-year delay in implementing the Sultan's order? Such deliberate postponement until 1863 – if such was the case – probably represents hard opposition to the decree by a Libyan slave-trading and slave-holding element, doubtless combined with administrative inertia and deliberate delay in announcing the prohibition of the trade. Ottoman officials were also aware of the economic disruption it would cause throughout their Libyan provinces: a parallel is the dislocation of the Sudanese economy – based largely on slaving – just before the start of the Mahdist period in the 1880s.

It is also noteworthy that these orders are concerned with Ghadamis. After 1860, Ghadamis (and Ghat as well), two towns west of Murzuq, seemed to be getting more trade than the old centre. This had to do with raiding across the caravan routes to the south by the Awlad Sulayman, wars among the Tubu of the Tibesti, and other disturbances. When the prohibition of slave trading took place, Murzuq became even less attractive as a "desert port." A 19th century Tunisian writer, al-Hasha'ishi, comments on this point:

> Murzuq was a stopping place for the travellers of the Sudan and Saharan caravans. It was the half-way point for persons going from Tripoli to Bornu (Kuka), and people went there from Waday, Egypt, Jalo, and Tuwat. Tuwati pilgrimage caravans used to go there, composed of thousands of people. They would stay for an interval of 25 days, buying and selling, then set off again. Trade grew to the point that Murzuq life reached a high degree of luxury. When one of the *Mutasarrifs* of the Fazzan banned the slave trade and freed all of them who lived in that place, and halted the entry of slaves, its traders withdrew. Caravans no longer came, and Ghat has been the place of commerce ever since.[84]

Another new factor in the slave trade was the opening of a new route from Waday to Tripoli via Benghazi. According to Hasha'ishi, an informal agreement existed before 1290/1873 among the Sudan and Saharan traders of Tunis, Ghadamis and Ghat, that no traders from Tripoli should be allowed into this profitable trade, at least the regions which they controlled, seemingly to the west and south of the Fazzan, and then to the southeast by various routes. But when Ghadamis and Ghat came under Ottoman rule in the mid-1870s, the situation changed. But already in 1868, a Tripoli merchant named Nasuf decided to open a direct route across the desert to Waday and other points. Nasuf first planned to take a Murzuq trader and his son as guides, but both of them died suddenly. Rather than abandon his plan, Nasuf made the hazardous journey from Benghazi to Waday by himself. He sold his goods and made a great deal of money. Many other Tripoli merchants followed him.[85] Within a few years, the new route was heavily travelled. Then, despite official Turkish efforts at Tripoli to prevent it, it was soon being used for the slave trade. The part played by the Sanusi order in maintaining this route is obscure. In any case, the new Waday road seems to have incurred official displeasure, because it was employed to bring slaves from Waday and the vicinity to the coast. Yet, as Benghazi was an independent *muteserriflik* administered directly from Istanbul for the last half of the 19th century, its history and trade is separate from that of Tripoli, and less well known. Hence conclusions about it must be tentative.

If the new route to Waday was an immediate success, that does not mean that trade over more traditional routes died out immediately. Despite the Sultan's order of 1863, the *Qa'im Maqam* of the Fazzan in 1864, one Halim Bey, was taking two *mahbubs* for each slave who passed through Murzuq. For that year Rossi records the passage of 4,408 persons.[86] Nevertheless, slave exports in the later 1860s and 1870s were diminishing at Tripoli, and doubtless at Benghazi as well. It continued unabated from minor ports and within the interior. In 1889, one estimate claims that slaves brought into Libya from the south had lessened to 500 to 1,000 a year. In 1889 also, Sultan 'Abd al-Hamid published yet another *firman* abolishing the slave trade.[87]

For the early 1870s, authentic information is available about the travels of a slave from Hausaland to Ghat and Ghadamis. It concerns a Hausa man named 'Uthman or "Atman," from Hadejia in northern Hausaland. Serving as an infantryman for "Hajji," (Mamman Hajji, 1868-1896), governor of Katagum, in a war against the Ambarkuri of Maradi, 'Uthman was taken prisoner at a battle near "Kassaoure" (doubtless Kazaure, about 45 miles NW of Kano). His captors immediately sent him to Zinder, where he was sold to Asben Touareg merchants and sent to Agades. At Agades, he was resold to other Tauregs, and crossed the desert to Ghat, a 25-day journey. His captors fed him three times a day, on a sort of gruel made of mixed corn and millet boiled with water. At Ghat, the slaves were given dates for the first time. 'Uthman was sold at the Ghadamis market once more, but escaped. For part of the way he was accompanied by two Hausa women from Zaria, Khadija and Zahira, who were both kidnapped from their village by 'Ali, ruler of the Bara of Genumbari. Taken from Zaria to Tassawa, they passed into the hands of the Bu Bakr Touareg at Agades, then crossed the desert to Ghadamis, where they made the acquaintance of 'Uthman. All three turned up in the middle of the night at a French military camp in the Wadi Suf in Southern Algeria, so that the author of an article about them, L. C. Féraud, was able to get his information at first hand.[88]

Ahmad Rasim Pasha and the Fazzan Slave Trade

At this point, it is useful to consider the efforts of Ahmad Rasim Pasha within Libya and to see what measures he took to cripple a declining slave trade.

III

Ahmad Rasim Pasha selected two principal avenues of attack on the slave trade. One of them was to prohibit and break up the trade wherever he could, including the import and export of captives. The other was to free slaves forcibly from their owners' control, and grant them documents of manumission, so that they could not be enslaved a second time. And since Ahmad Rasim proved to be an experienced and capable *veli* in the eyes of the Porte, and carried out some of the most progressive policies of Sultan 'Abd al-Hamid II, he was able to remain at Tripoli for a 15-year period. With this combination of a long period in office, and his active measures, Ahmad Rasim's procedures were highly effective. While it could not be honestly claimed that he halted the trade completely, there was little evidence of it in 1896, when he retired, compared to the uneasy situation on his arrival in Tripoli in 1881.

The Pasha continued to have his embarrassing moments, for occasionally the Porte itself would ask him to furnish black "servants" or guards – doubtless for *Töpkapi Sarayi* in Istanbul, where the presence of black slaves was an old tradition. Then too, African Muslim heads of state whom neither the *Veli* nor the Sublime Porte wished to offend – like Bornu and Damagaram – would send gifts of slaves or eunuchs to Tripoli for despatch to Turkey. This was a traditional kind of gesture of submission and friendship which was difficult for the Ottomans to refuse, particularly as 'Abd al-Hamid II was following his Pan-Islamic policies. Then, Ahmad Rasim Pasha had to contend with occasional interference by foreign consuls at Tripoli – sometimes with a troublemaking intent – over individual slaves. The Pasha had also to consider the economy of southern Libya. Here many aspects of local trade were geared to the northward passage of slaves. Unfortunately, Ahmad Rasim was unable to provide any substitute for this keystone in the arch of traditional commerce. This failure goes far to explain the angry complaints (usually sent to Istanbul by telegram) from a part of the Tripolitanian trading class in the 1890s, about Amhad Rasim's "tyranny."[90]

Ahmad Bey al-Na'ib, quoting a contemporary Ottoman *Salnameh*, sums up Ahmad Rasim's techniques as follows:

The importation of slaves from the lands of the Sudan to these parts by trading caravans is very old, likewise their sale. His Excellency the *Veli* has devoted strong measures (as laid down by the Government) against the trade in these Zanji (black) captives. He has given the strictest orders to those who require them, and the import of such slaves has been discontinued for a (long) time. Should any person be bold enough to import a slave or slaves in secret, he will be exposed to the appropriate punishment. Zanji slaves, sold or imported previously, will now be freed if they apply to the Government, and will be granted their manumission papers.[91]

In spite of his good intentions, Ahmad Rasim had hardly been in office a year (December 1882) when a request arrived from Istanbul for "20 well-proportioned blacks for service at the Sublime Porte," doubtless as bodyguards for 'Abd al-Hamid II, or as warders for his *harim*. The Pasha sent this request on to the *Qa'im Maqam* of Zawiya (Muhammad b. 'Ali Ku'bar). His deputy reminded him that they could only be made "to go in chains." If foreigners came to know of this, it would mean bad publicity. Should they be sent individually to avoid comment? Ahmad Rasim's answer to this letter remains unpublished, or is perhaps not extant.[92]

About April 1886, the Pasha sent a reply to the Amir of Zinder (or Damagaram), now in Niger Republic. In his letter he expressed his thanks to Amir Tinimu dan Sulayman for a previous communication, and for three black eunuchs. The three eunuchs were to be forwarded to Istanbul, except for one, "who is ours." Sultan 'Abd al-Hamid II had now replied, sending his thanks to the Amir of Zinder. Ahmad Rasim concludes with hopes that trade between Zinder and Tripoli would continue, along secure roads, and ends with the customary greetings and salutations.[93] Another very similar letter to Shaykh Hashim bin 'Umar al-Kanemi of Bornu (dated 10 May 1886) has much the same content. In it, the Pasha thanks Shaykh Hashim for the gift of two slaves, one of whom "is named Sulayman," and expatiates on the advantages to Bornu of diplomatic relations, trade, and friendship with the Ottoman "Caliphate."[94]

Hopefully, the Pasha liberated his eunuch and the slaves from Bornu immediately. Yet the importation of eunuchs from North Africa and the western Sudan was an old practice. N. M. Penzer claims that the use of black eunuchs – no doubt from West Africa – at the Ottoman *harim* dated to 1475. Penzer states: "Presents of slaves, both male and female, from conquered Emirs or princes wishing to gain the Sultan's favour and protection, would often include eunuchs . . . once the innovation had proved a success, the demand could easily be supplied." Penzer also claims that Baghirmi was a source of eunuchs, likewise Kordofan, Dongola, and Darfur. He also mentions "Kebabo and Marzuk in the Fazzan district" as sources of eunuchs.[95] To these he might have added the village of Ifara near Zinder. André Salifou observes that Damagaram eunuchs "étaient si appreciés qu'ils étaient demandés dans d'autres cours et envoyés à la Mecque, au Caire, et à Constantinople."[96]

From these matters, it is a far cry to the doings of foreign consuls in Tripoli. However, they made difficulties for the Pasha from time to time. In 1302/1884-85, some of them were claiming a right to manumit slaves who came to them and asked for this service. The *Muteserrif* of Khums, writing to the Pasha, commented sourly on this trend, saying that "slaves should not be permitted to go to foreign consuls: the (Ottoman) Government is quite able to give them their freedom.[97] On another occasion, an American Consul intervened on behalf of an old woman, a former slave, who was on occasion mistreated by her former master. In the "name of justice and humanity," he pleaded with the Pasha to aid her. This Ahmad Rasim apparently did, but he clearly disliked the way in which the Consul's request was expressed.[98]

In November 1893, the Pasha was found laying down the law to the *Qa'im Maqam* of Gharyan in western Libya. Rumours had reached him, he declared, that a clandestine caravan of black slaves from the Sudan had arrived there. The men and women in it were being sold off singly. He reminded the *Qa'im Maqam* and other government officials at Gharyan that to permit any such trade would be a violation of the law, and that they were not "to close their eyes to such matters." Caravans crossing district borders for such purposes were forbidden, and blacks being imported and sold in this way were to be liberated immediately.[99] And, in an older report (1306/1888-89), having been in office eight years, the Pasha could already claim, in a report to the Ottoman Interior Ministry, that he had liberated 1,420 slaves.[100]

These were no small achievements: and Ahmad Rasim Pasha could rightly be proud of them. By the time of the Italian occupation of Libya in 1911, the country was probably free of the slave trade, even if not all slaves had yet been manumitted. Ironically, the Ottoman administration in Libya was the target of a heavy press attack in 1905 by the Italian politician Giovanni Giolitti over the slave trade – part of a propagada war which terminated in an Italian invasion of Libya six years later. But that is another story.

NOTES

1. See the anonymous article, "Al-Wali Ahmad Rasim Basha wa islahatuhu fi Tarabulus al-Gharb," *Majallat al-Afkar*, Tripoli, no. 11, June 1957, pp. 21-22.
2. *Ibid.*, p.21.
3. Ahmad Bey al-Na'ib al-Ansari, *Al-Manhal al-'adhb fi ta'rikh Tarabulus al-Gharb*, ed. Tahir Ahmad al-Zawi, II, Cairo 1961, p.1.
4. Ahmad Sidqi al-Dajjani, *Libya qubayl al-Ihtilal al-Itali, aw Tarabulus al-Gharb fi akhir al-'Ahd al-'Uthmani al-thani (1882-1911)*, Cairo 1971, pp. 60-66.
5. Mahmud Naji (& Mehmet Nuri), *Ta'rikh Tarabulus al-Gharb*, trns. 'Abd al-Salam Adham and Muhammad al-Usta, Tripoli, 1970, p.168. There is another translation of this book, from Turkish to Arabic, by Akmal al-Din Muhammad Ihsan, Tripoli 1973, which seems to be a less careful job.
6. N. M. Penzer, *The Harem*, London 1936, pp. 189-191, etc.
7. Maurice Lombard, *The Golden Age of Islam*, London 1974, *passim.*
8. *Ibid., passim.*
9. Gernot Rotter, "Die Stellung des Negers" (thesis).
10. A. Teixeira da Morra, personal communication, May 1976.
11. Muhammad Sulayman Ayyub, *Jarma, min ta'rikh al-hadarat al-Libiya*, Tripoli, 1969.
12. Herodotus, *Histories*, ed. Godley, Book IV.
13. Muhammad Sulayman Ayyub, *Mukhtasar ta'rikh Fazzan, mundhu aqdam al-usur hatta 1811 miladiya*, Tripoli 1967, p.50, 54. See also A. J. Arkell, *Wanyanga, an archaeological reconnaissance of the southwest Libyan Desert*, Oxford 1964, p.18.
14. Ayyub, *Mukhtasar*, Chapter IV, *passim.*
15. Latin Anthology, *Codex Salmasiani*, 183.
16. Luxorius 43.
17. John of Biclar in Anno III Iustini Imp. (*MGH, AA*, XI, p.569).
18. Cosmas Indicopleustes, *Sources Chrétiennes*, vol. 141, III, 66.
19. Ayyub, *Mukhtasar*, p.73.
20. *Ibid*, pp. 70, 75.
21. Ibn 'Abd al-Hakam, *Futuh Misr wa Ifriqiya*, ed. C. Torrey, New Haven 1922, p.194.
22. Ettore Rossi, "Le Relazioni del Fezzan con Tripoli e la costa del Mediterraneo," in *Bolletino della Societa Geografica Italiana*, 85, Rome 1948, p.298.
23. Ayyub, *Mukhtasar*, pp. 74-75.
24. Ahmad ibn Abi Ya'qub al-Ya'qubi, *Kitab al-Buldan*, ed. de Goeje, Leiden 1892, p.245.
25. Ayyub, *Mukhtasar*, p.89-90.
26. Ayyub, *Mukhtasar*, p.85.
27. Rex O'Fahey.
28. Ayyub, *Mukhtasar*, p.90.
29. M. Breck.
30. Ibn Abi Dinar, *Kitab al-Mu'nis fi akhbar Ifriqiya wa Tunus*.
31. E. Rossi, *Relazioni*, p.298.
32. Ibrahim b. Muhammad b. Aydamur al-'Ala'i, known as Ibn Duqmaq, *Kitab al-Intisar li-wasita 'Aqd al-Amsar*, Beirut, n.d., Vol. I, p.17, Vol. II, p.15-37, and Evliya Chelebi, *Seyahatnamet*, X.
33. Abu 'Ubayd al-Bakri, *Al-Masalik wa'l-Mamalik*, ed. De Slane, Algiers, 1857, p.10.
34. Anon., *Kitab al-Ibtibsar*, ed. S. Z. 'Abd al-Hamid, Alexandria 1957, p.146.
35. 'Abdallah al-Tijani, *Taqyid al-Rihla*, Tunis 1958, p.243.

36. 'Imad al-Din Abu'l-Fida, *Taqwim al-Buldan*, ed. Reinaud & de Slane, Paris 1840, p.127.
37. Chapelle, *Nomades noirs du Sahara*, Paris 1957.
38. H. Duveyrier, *Les Touareg du Nord*, Paris 1864.
39. E. Rossi, *Relazioni*, p.299. The ms. in question is "Vat. Ar. 729."
40. H. Duveyrier, *Touareg*.
41. Ayyub, *Mukhtasar*, p.96-98: Rossi, *Relazioni*, p.298, note 8.
42. E. Rossi, "Storia del Medio Evo e dell'Eta Moderna," in *Il Sahara Italiano, I, Fazzan e Oasi di Ghat*, Rome 1937, p.337.
43. Ayyub, *Mukhtasar*, Chapter VII, esp. p.105.
44. Leo Africanus.
45. Ayyub, *Mukhtasar*, p.105.
46. For a provisional genealogy of the Awlad Muhammad, see G. A. Krause, "Zur Geschichte von Fesan und Tripoli in Afrika," *Zeitschrift der Gesellschaft fuer Erdkunde zu Berlin*, XIII, 1878, pp. 356-373. The chart is on p.371. Krause's article is based on a ms. history of Khoja Ahmad, the private secretary of 'Ali Pasha Qaramanli (dated c. 1763), from the Royal Library, Valetta, Malta. Khoja Ahmad derived much of his material from Ibn Ghalbun's *Tidhkar* (see below, note 50).
47. Ayyub, *Mukhtasar*, Chapter VII, *passim*, p.106.
48. Philip Ward, *Touring Libya, the southern Provinces*, has a map of the town of Murzuq which clarifies this description.
49. H. Duveyrier, *Les Touareg*.
50. Ibn Ghalbun, *Al-Tidhkar fiman malaka Tarabulus wa ma kana biha min al-akhyar*, ed. Tahir Ahmad al-Zawi, 2nd ed. Tripoli 1967, p.143.
51. Ibn Ghalbun, *Tidhkar*, p.144.
52. *Ibid*, p.144.
53. *Ibid*, p.144.
54. *Ibid*, pp. 147, 157, 158. The Turkish *'amil* in the first decades of the 17th century was Husayn al-Na' 'al (Ibn Ghalbun, pp. 147, 156).
55. Ibn Ghalbun, *Tidhkar*, p.156.
56. *Ibid*, p.160.
57. *Ibid*, pp. 193-195.
58. *Ibid*, p.193.
59. E. Rossi, *Storia*, pp. 340-341.
60. *Ibid*, p.193.
61. 'Umar 'Ali bin Ism'ail, *Inhiyar hukm al-usrat al-Qaramanliya fi Libiya, 1795-1835*, Tripoli 1966, p.39-40. See also Ahmad Bey al-Na'ib al-Ansari, *Al-Manhal al-'Adhb fi ta'rikh Tarabulus al-Gharb*, I, Tripoli, n.d., p.288, & Ibn Ghalbun, p.257.
62. Krause, *Geschichte*, p.370; E. Rossi, *Storia di Tripoli e della Tripolitania della conquista Araba al 1911*, Rome 1968, p.229 (abbreviated below as *Tripoli*).
63. *Ibid*.
64. G. F. Lyon, *A narrative of travels in northern Africa in 1818-1819 and 1820*, Frank Cass, London, 1966, p.278.
65. F. Hornemann, *Journal of travels from Cairo to Mourzouk*, London 1802, p.66.
66. Rossi, *Storia*, p.343.
67. L. C. Féraud, *Annales Tripolitaines*, Paris 1927, p.256.
68. *Ibid*, pp. 275-276.
69. Hornemann, *Travels*, p.64.
70. *Ibid*, p.65.
71. *Ibid*, pp. 67-68.
72. Ahmad Bey, *Manhal*, I, pp. 318-319.

73. *Ibid*, p.319; Lyon, *Narrative*, pp. 277, 129.
74. Rossi, *Storia*, p.345; also Taha Fawzi, Hasan Mahmud, and Kamal al-Din Kharputli, *Tarabulus taht hukm usrat al-Qaramanli*, Cairo 1961 (an Arabic translation, with useful additions to an Italian original by Rodolfo Michacchi) appendix, document 36, pp. 91-92.
75. Ahmad Bey, *Manhal*, p.330.
76. Rossi, *Storia*, p.345.
77. Rossi, *Tripoli*, pp. 291-293, Gråberg's original report is entitled "Prospetto di commercio di Tripoli d'Affrica e delle sue relazioni con quello dell' Italia," published in *Antologia* (Florence) in three sections, number 81, September 1827, pp. 37-99; number 88, April 1828, pp. 1-29; and number 111, for March 1830, pp. 75-97. This rare periodical is available in the Princeton University Library.
78. Rossi, *Storia*, p.346; Ahmad Bey, *Manhal* I, p.347.
79. 'Umar 'Ali b. Isma'il, *Inhiyar*, appendix, document 27, pp. 438-439.
80. *Ibid*, document 28, pp. 440-441.
81. Rossi, *Tripoli*, p.311.
82. 'Umar 'Ali b. Isma'il, *Inhiyar*, appendix, document 29, pp. 442-443.
83. A. A. Boahen, *Britain, the Sahara, and the western Sudan, 1788-1861*, Oxford 1964, pp. 155-158.
84. Muhammad b. 'Uthman al-Hasha'ishi, *Jala' al-karb 'an Tarabulus al-Gharb*, ed. 'Ali al-Misurati, Beirut 1965, p.82. This valuable book on the 19th century Saharan trade has barely been touched by researchers, and deserves to be much better known.
85. *Ibid*, p.113-114.
86. Rossi, *Tripoli*, p.317.
87. *Ibid*, p.318.
88. L. C. Féraud, "Délivrance d'esclaves nègres dans le sud de la province de Constantine," *Revue Africaine*, Algiers, XVI, 1872, pp. 167-179.
89. Ahmad Sidqi al-Dajjani, *Libiya qubayl al-Ihtilal al-Itali, aw Tarabulus al-Gharb fi akhir al-'Ahd al-'Uthmani al-thani, 1886-1911*, Tripoli 1971, pp. 60-80.
90. See the broad range of documents for the Libyan Archives presented by Ahmad Sidqi al-Dajjani and al-Hajj 'Adb al-Salam Adham in their joint *Wata'iq ta'rikh Libiya al-hadith: al-watha'iq al-'Uthmaniya, 1881-1911*, Benghazi 1974, and especially pp.83-93.
91. Ahmad Bey, *Manhal*, II, p.5. Slaves' manumission papers may be a useful sort of historical source. See E. Rossi's article on the manumission of a Christian slave at Tripoli in 1653, in *Jean Deny Armaghani*. Often called an *'itaqnameh* in Turkish, these papers occasionally give information about a slave's origin, and sometimes his former, as well as his present owners, and other useful details. See also Karl Jahn, *Ottomanische Freilassungsurkunden fuer Sklaven*, Naples 1968. Jahn points here to a new direction of investigations.
92. Dajjani & Adham, *Watha'iq*, p.22.
93. *Ibid*, pp. 49-50. See also Rossi, *Tripoli*, p.339, note 95, for another communication (of 1870) from the Amir of Zinder to the Pasha of Tripoli, about two eunuchs and a giraffe.
94. Dajjani & Adham, *Watha'iq*, pp. 50-51.
95. N. M. Penzer, *The Harem*, London 1936, p.140.
96. André Salifou, *Le Damagaram, ou le Sultanat de Zinder au XIXe Siècle*, Niamey 1971, (*Etudes Nigériennes*, no. 27), p.132.
97. Dajjani. *Libiya*, p.88.
98. *Ibid*, p.88.
99. *Ibid*, p.89.
100. *Ibid*, p.89.

V

Slavery and Society in Dar Fur

R.S. O'Fahey

'The Slave's Lot'

The slaves must do the work in the house; if they are unwilling to work, they must be beaten with the whip or must be beaten with the stick. Then they begin to cry (and) be willing to work. Their language is difficult; people don't understand them. If we find a girl among them, who pleases us, then she doesn't need to do any housework. I make her my wife, so that we can sleep together in bed and 'eat the skin,'[1] so that we will have children. Then she becomes pregnant and has a child. If it is a boy, then everything is fine.[2]

For approximately a hundred years, between 1750 and 1850, the Dar Fur Sultanate was probably the major supplier of slaves to the Egyptian market and the prosperity of its rulers was intimately bound up with the fluctuations of the slave trade.[3] The trade from Dar Fur to Egypt and North Africa has been described elsewhere,[4] here I wish to survey the nature and role of slavery within the sultanate. Since the material presented here derives largely from research on other topics, the survey is a tentative one, hopefully to be modified and corrected by research specifically directed towards slavery and related topics.

Much discussion, indeed controversy, has been devoted to the slave trade in the Sudan (used here and throughout for the Democratic Republic of the Sudan) and its attempted suppression by such stalwarts of nineteenth-century British public opinion as Sir Samuel Baker and Charles Gordon; more perhaps than for any other part of Muslim Africa.[5] Much less attention has been paid to slavery within the Sudan, despite growing evidence which suggests that the bulk of the slaves imported into the Northern Sudan were destined for the home market and that 'the heritage of slavery' has had profound political and economic consequences for the contemporary Sudan.[6] The use or misuse of the slavery issue in the propaganda of both sides of the North/South conflict is but one example of these consequences. Historically, Northern Sudanese Muslim society was a slave-owning society and the attitudes which arose from this fact, reinforced by what may be termed a 'frontier mentality', served to produce a complex of ideas and opinions, ethnic and religious prejudices, economic behaviour and expectations that pervaded all aspects of society and which survive in an attenuated form to this day.[7] In the nineteenth century and before, among the Northern Sudanese political and military elites of the Funj and Dar Fur Sultanates as well as later among the Khartoum traders in the south, there was an intimate connexion between horse warfare and chivalry (Ar. *furusiyya*), slave raiding, the nomadic ethos and disdain for physical labour, clientship and slavery.

A slave is a 'person who is the legal property of another or others and is bound to absolute obedience' *(Concise Oxford Dictionary)*: although the whole of Dar Fur society under the sultans was characterized by a complex hierarchy of dependancy and subordination, slaves were a distinct segment clearly marked off from the rest of society. Historians and anthropologists have been reluctant to use 'slave' – or 'serf' – too freely to describe servile or semi-servile status in African societies partly because of the American and West Indian images they conjure up,[8] but *riqq* is a precisely-defined status in the Shari'a, by which, with due allowance for local custom, slavery was largely regulated in Dar Fur;[9] everyone in Dar Fur knew (and knows) what 'slave' meant. Here I have used 'slave' as far as possible only when the sources, whether oral or written, talk of *'abd, raqiq*, or *khadim* (specifically a female slave or concubine) in Arabic, *koy* or *kurra* (pl. *abdiana*) in Fur.

Slave Origins and the Mechanics of Enslavement

The people who live in Dar Fartit are slaves and (yet) go free.[10]

The heart of the Dar Fur state were the Marra Mountains, its ethnic core the Fur people, whose ruling dynasty, the Keira, emerged as the dominant power in the region in the mid-seventeenth century. Rapid expansion soon gave the Keira control over a multi-ethnic empire, which by the end of the eighteenth century included Kordofan to the east, and with the disintegration of the Funj Sultanate of Sinnar, Dar Fur became Egypt's main African trading partner. However, by the middle of the following century Dar Fur's trading network had begun to be eroded by the penetration of the Khartoum traders into the regions south of the Sultanate, and it was the greatest of these traders, al-Zubayr Pasha Rahma, who overthrew the sultanate in

1874. The sultanate was briefly revived between 1898 and 1916 by Sultan 'Ali Dinar.

Although the slave trade was never the *raison d'être* of the state nor probably even the primary cause of its expansion, nonetheless slave raiding and trading loomed large in the activities of the ruling elite. The non-Muslim peoples whose enslavement was sanctioned both by religion (as interpreted in Dar Fur) and custom were collectively known as 'Fartit'. This was simply the Dar Fur term among a number of pejorative names used by the Muslims to describe those living to the south of them, who were by definition non-Muslim and suitable for enslavement; similar generic names included Shankalla below Sinnar, Nuba and Turuj below Kordofan, Janakhara below Wadai, and Kirdi or Kirdawi below Baqirmi.[11] To these may be added such terms as *jabalawiyyin* or *hajaray* – 'mountain people' – used to describe the pockets of semi-Muslim or pagan peoples within the Sudanic Belt proper.

Behind 'Fartit' lay a number of contradictory notions, not least of a vague sense of kinship between slaver and enslaved, symbolized by the Fur story that Fir 'the begetter of the Fur' had a brother, Firat, who was progenitor of the Fartit,[12] and the commonly-heard tradition that the Fartit were Fur who went south to avoid becoming Muslim. Nor are such ideas confined to the Fur; the Mileri, a small tribe in Dar Tama near the Chad/Sudan border, upon being Islamized took over Misiriyya (i.e. Arab) genealogies and now refer to the former inhabitants of their home (presumably their own ancestors) as 'Fartit' who went south upon the 'coming' of the Misiriyya Arabs. However, in the minds of the Mileri the transition is incomplete, since some Mileri clans are still regarded as 'more' Fartit than the others and as such the 'owners of the mountain' (*ashab al-jabal*).[13]

The inner hunting grounds of the slavers lay in an arc south and south-west of the sultanate, from the Western Bahr al-Ghazal, through the north-eastern corner of the Central African Empire to south-eastern Chad; here the Fartit included (going approximately from west to east) the Runga, Kara, Yulu, Kresh, Binga, Banda, Feroge, Shatt and a number of small groups around the copper mining area of Hufrat al-Nahas, the effective southern limit of the sultanate.[14] Within this inner arc relations between raided and raider were to become in some cases stabilized and formalized into tributary status. As the raiders ventured further south, and by the mid-eighteenth century they had reached the Mbomu River in what is now the Central African Empire, so Dar Fartit grew.[15] Not surprisingly the peoples of these regions have traditions of migration southwards, in some cases seemingly from southern Dar Fur, and of harassment by men on horseback, but it is not yet clear whether these movements were the result of raiding from Dar Fur as the traditions of horsemen would imply, or because of the later activities of the Khartoum traders.[16] The historical ethnography of Jabal Marra and southern Dar Fur, particularly the borderlands, has yet to be investigated and many of the clans of 'Fartit' now found among the Fur were undoubtedly slaves imported and settled by the sultans. But there is evidence to suggest a progressive southward extension of the Fur language and culture; thus the area called Dar Fongoro in the south-west appears to have been acculturated in very recent times.[17] Underlying the Fur traditions is the persistent belief or prejudice that slaves come from the south, freemen from the north.

Future research will, hopefully, throw more light and detail on these vague indications of the geographical and ethnic origins of the slaves;[18] one useful line of research would be the systematic accumulation of *awsaf* (sing. *wasf*) or the formal descriptions of slaves that appear for the purposes of identification in the various categories of legal documents arising from slavery, deeds-of-sale, certificates of manumission and the like. But they will need to be used with care since the ethnic label (*jins*) is often very imprecise. Nor should too great a stress be placed on the geographical 'slaveable/non-slaveable' distinction; unprotected persons, whether Muslim or not, could risk enslavement, although if they were lucky they could obtain legal redress.[19] Outside their homeland all were at risk, particularly in times of upheaval.[20]

Although the original impetus to the slave trade from the Dar Fur end came probably from the wars of the eighteenth century, particularly with neighbouring Wadai, the most characteristic means whereby slaves were captured was the *ghazwa* or *salatiyya* (lit. 'spear'), 'an armed expedition for the purpose of acquiring slaves'.[21] Muhammad al-Tunisi's vivid and detailed description of the structure, functioning and bureaucracy surrounding the *ghazwa* describes in fact a mobile Sudanic state using its mastery of cavalry warfare to exploit the acephalous peoples to the south, a theme fundamental to the history of the whole Sudanic Belt.[22] In a similar manner the cavalry-based *ghazwa* was to be transmuted in the mid-nineteenth century into the rifle-based *kubaniyya* of the Khartoum traders that could penetrate where horses could not go. The Dar Fur ruling elite were thus entrenched as suppliers to the merchants, who though they occasionally accompanied the *ghazwas* south were usually content to negotiate for their slaves in the commercial centres of the sultanate, pre-eminently Kobbei, a day's journey north-west of the political and administrative capital of al-Fashir.

Those slaves sold to merchants for transport to Egypt along the *darb al-arba'in* or 'forty days road' or to other parts of the Sudan do not concern us here except insofar as their sale provided the means whereby the sultan and the notables could purchase the luxury goods from Egypt whose 'conspicuous consumption' was an integral part of their style. Naturally the sultan took the lion's share, a tenth of those taken by the *ghazwas* and a number as tribute from those Fartit tribes who preferred to pay than be raided.[23]

Most slaves were sold at Kobbei or al-Fashir privately, which tended to facilitate the sale of stolen slaves.[24] Public sales were rare, although as late as 1914 the slave girl, Sallamth (possibly for *salamathu* 'his well-being'),[25] was sold by public auction (*bi'l-mazad al-'alani*) in al-Fashir for 72 dollars.[26] Prices naturally fluctuated,[27] but the fragmentary data we do have, given here in tabular form, suggests that there was price-inflation throughout the nineteenth century and that horses were consistently and markedly more expensive.

SLAVE AND HORSE PRICES IN DAR FUR

No attempt has been made to standardize the prices.

Year	Item	Price	Source
1793	'One slave, which is commonly purchaseable ... for the value of fifteen piastres in Egyptian commodities'		Browne, *Travels*, 220.
c.1805	*sudasi* [male]	10 dollars	Al-Tunisi, 315-6
1837	'good slave' horse	5-6 dollars 10-30 dollars	Abdin Archives, box 262: 25 Safar 1253/31 May 1837
1862	male slave	8 cows	170.18/30
1874	*sudasi* good horse	30 dollars 150 dollars	Nachtigal, iv, 37 *ibid.*, iv, 254.
1879	horse good horse	50-60 dollars 300-400 dollars	R. W. Felkin, 'Note on the For tribe' *Proceedings of the Royal Society of Edinburgh*, xiii (1884-5) 251
c.1900	concubines	50-150 dollars	Muhammad 'Abd al-Rahim, *Muhadara*, 86
1910	slave woman	12 *majidi* dollars	77.10/2, 25 Rabi' II 1328/6 May 1910
1914	slave woman	72 dollars	76-10/1,21 Ramadan 1332/13 August 1914

Royal Slaves and Confidants

The employment of slaves as a counterweight to an hereditary tribal or territorial nobility is common in the administration of Muslim states and beyond. The lack of 'new men' or an independently-based commercial class (although merchants did take on administrative functions in some Sudanic states) made the development of a bureaucracy to administer an increasingly centralized state difficult without slaves. Dar Fur was no exception and career opportunities, albeit involuntary, for slaves were varied. Within the *fashir* or palace complex (whence al-Fashir, the capital from 1206/1791-2) they functioned as soldiers, bureaucrats, concubines, domestics, guards and attendants organized in a complex hierarchy of groups and titles. Outside the *fashir* they were employed by the sultans and notables as labourers, herders and soldiers on estates and settlements throughout the sultanate. This widespread horizontal and vertical use of slaves by the elite is well documented; what is still unknown is the proportion of ordinary households owning slaves. It may have been relatively circumscribed, although nomads may have made greater use of slaves, to whom in any case they had easier access. In general it is probable that slaves were the prerogative of the great, the rich and the holy, indeed that they were a symbol of power, wealth or sanctity.

The *fashir* was an enormous complex of buildings and courtyards housing the sultan, his family and *harim*, stores of food, weapons and trade goods and a host of palace officials and their retinues; at a reasonable guess its personnel cannot have numbered much under three to four thousand.[28] Physically it was divided into two sectors, male and female, entered by the male (*ɔrrɛ de*) and female (*ɔrrɛ baya*, literally 'narrow entrance') entrances respectively. Within the male sector lay the *somiŋ dogala* (literally 'the children of the school' [or 'palace', *som* can bear both meanings]), a species of school where both young slaves and freemen were trained for the sultan's service.[29] Although nothing has been recorded on what was taught, it is reasonable to assume that it included reading and writing.

Among the slaves who served in the *fashir* were the *korayat* or grooms to the royal horses, the *kɔrkwa* or guards and attendants upon the sultan and the great officers of state, the *falaqna* or royal heralds as well as various other groups; each group had its own area within the male sector and chiefs who were not themselves necessarily slaves.[30] Within the female sector the number of concubines and serving women who worked to prepare food, always the most laborious of women's work, must have been very great; Sultan 'Ali

Dinar is said to have employed five hundred women simply to bring water to his palace.[31] The female area and the *harim* were administered by eunuchs, most of whom came from Dar Runga, a kingdom within Wadai's sphere of influence south-west of Dar Fur. Al-Tunisi recounts with gusto various anecdotes of *harim* intrigue and of the power of the eunuchs, who he said numbered more than a thousand.[32]

It was an eunuch who held the greatest office of state, that of *ab shaykh dali*, governor of the Eastern Province and controller of the palace.[33] Although the *ab shaykh* had to be an eunuch in order that he might enter all parts of the *fashir*, not all who held the office were slaves, 'whether they had been castrated as a punishment for some crime, or because of illness, or had done it themselves out of ambition'.[34] Ambition undoubtedly determined the career of the greatest of the *ab shaykhs*, Muhammad Kurra.

Kurra, born either a slave or freeman,[35] joined the *kɔrkwa* of Sultan Muhammad Tayrab (1166-1200/1752-3-1785). He soon won the sultan's favour and was promoted an overseer in the *somiŋ dogala*. Accused of interfering with one of Tayrab's numerous concubines, he demonstrated his innocence by castrating himself; nevertheless the sultan gave him to the Fur notable, 'Ali b. Jami'. However, his abilities won him promotion as one of the *muluk al korayat* or masters of the royal grooms and as such he accompanied 'Ali to Kordofan when Tayrab conquered that province in 1200/1785.

The succession crisis that followed Tayrab's death in Kordofan first brought Kurra to the fore politically. A state of deadlock had arisen in which none of the 'sons of the sultans' (*awlad al-salatin*) were able to mobilize enough support to seize power. Kurra, as an eunuch, had access to the *harim*, which was with the army, where he negotiated between one of the claimants, 'Abd al-Rahman, and the late sultan's premier wife. In return for his support Kurra was promised the office of *ab shaykh*. Although it seems that 'Abd al-Rahman emerged as sultan mainly through the intervention of the *faqih*s, Kurra helped by neutralizing the Fur notables led by his erstwhile master 'Ali b. Jami'. After a civil war in Dar Fur and various conspiracies, 'Abd al-Rahman, now undisputed sultan, was able to instal Kurra as *ab shaykh*.

Kurra's governorship of Eastern Dar Fur was extended to take in the newly-conquered and still rebellious Kordofan, whither he went probably in 1206/1791-2.[36] Five years later relations between Kurra and the sultan had become strained, the former being accused of wishing to make himself independent in Kordofan. Finally the *wazir*

Muhammad b. 'Ali Dokkumi, son of Kurra's former master and his bitter enemy because of the eunuch's betrayal of his father, was sent to bring him back. Although publicly disgraced, he was soon restored to favour and office.

In 1215/1801 Kurra engineered the accession of 'Abd al-Rahman's fourteen-year-old son, Muhammad al-Fadl (1215-54/1801-38), despite the opposition of the Fur notables and the other 'sons of the sultans'. Nicknamed *jabir al-dar*, 'tyrant of the land', Kurra was now supreme throughout the state, but within a few years the notables were able to turn the growing rift between the young sultan and his over-mighty servant to their advantage; in Rajab 1219/October-November 1804 Kurra was forced by his enemies into rebellion and killed.

Kurra was the only slave in Dar Fur's history to achieve a quasi-independent position of power, the brevity of his hold upon it demonstrated the inherent fragility of the slave's position. Free notables held and inherited office by right, slaves at the pleasure of their masters; once Muhammad al-Fadl was old enough to utilize the strength of his office Kurra was probably doomed.[37] He was succeeded by a line of slave confidants Adam Bosh, Bakhit b. Adam Bosh and Khayr Qarib, who dominated court politics and manipulated the succession, but their power never equalled his and was circumscribed and sustained by the sultans.[38] And just before the sultanate was overthrown by al-Zubayr in 1874, the notables had seemingly begun to react against slave domination; Sultan Ibrahim Qarad was installed as sultan in April 1873 by Bakhit b. Adam and Khayr Qarib in the face of determined opposition from the notables.[39] Neither benign treatment nor great power altered legal or social status; slaves remained essentially tools to be taken up and discarded at the will of their masters. Gifted individuals from the slave caste were raised up by the sultans precisely because they were more tractable than the powerful hereditary nobility, which drew its strength from ethnic loyalties and the posession of great estates. The Dar Fur sultans had particular cause to be wary of the notables, since two early rulers had met their deaths indirectly at the hands of the chiefs.[40]

The difference between status and power may be illustrated by another way in which the sultans used slaves. Gifts fueled intercourse among the great, denoting the giving or seeking of favour, and slaves and horses were very acceptable marks of favour. The literature abounds in examples; the great *wazir* Adam Bosh began his career as a present sent at the orders of Sultan Muhammad al-Husayn (1254-

90/1838-73) to a merchant who had presented the sultan with a particularly fine *tarbush*. Dislike caused the overseer of the *somiŋ dogala* to choose Adam as the present; he was recalled by the sultan but but was ever after sensitive to his nickname, *Tarbush*.[41] 'Ali Dinar reciprocated some presents from a Majabra merchant with a slave girl, 'pleasing of looks', and some cloth,[42] while the progress of the Tunisian travellers, 'Umar al-Tunisi and his son Muhammad, through Sinnar, Dar Fur and Wadai was marked, as befitted the father's status as an al-Azhar *'alim*, by gifts of slaves.[43]

One such gift had consequences; as a poor and unimportant member of the royal family the future sultan 'Abd al-Rahman was once given a Beigo slave girl. She became the mother of Sultan Muhammad al-Fadl, upon whose accession the Beigo, a despised 'Fartit' tribe living on the southern margins of the sultanate, came into their own, symbolized by the story of Fazari, the slave girl Umm Busa's brother. When a messenger came to tell Fazari of his nephew's accession, he was watering his animals; in a gesture he broke the mud walls around the well, letting the water run into the ground, and rode off to al-Fashir, where he was given the revenues of an Arab tribe.[44] The Beigo were freed from their semi-servile status, their chief entitled 'sultan' and various Beigo achieved positions at court, of whom one, 'Abd al-Bari, became *wazir* to the new sultan.[45]

Estate Slavery

Dar Fur is a sparsely-peopled land (2,000,000 [1973 estimate] for an area of 140,000 square miles) with few concentrations of population apart from Jabal Marra and its foothills. Rainland agriculture involved movement and resettlement and the agricultural cycle was seasonally labour intensive, weeding being a particularly crucial time.[46] Scarcity of people made man-power a pressing need for both the sultans and notables, one solution to which was the settlement of captives and slaves within the state. Wars of expansion and slave-raids were probably intended as much to supply the home market as the export trade; difficulties of supply were to cause 'Ali Dinar to have the illegitimate children of Jabal Marra rounded up and brought to al-Fashir as slaves.[47] The centralizing policies of the sultans (increasing proliferation of offices, concentration of the elite at the capital, the more systematic collection of taxes, etc.) made the demand for people more acute and led to a shift from a tribally-based system of administration to a more direct and perhaps exploitative relation between ruler and subject. By no means all immigrants were slaves,[48] but they must have formed a very substantial majority. Tayrab and 'Abd al-Rahman were particularly assiduous; the former, who had earlier settled slaves around his first capital at Shoba, later brought in the Turuj Nuba from the Daju Hills in Kordofan. They were settled anew among those Daju living near Tayrab's later capital at Ril.[49] 'Abd al-Rahman also brought back with him Nuba slaves from Kordofan.[50]

The royal slaves, known collectively as *'abidiyya*, were dispersed in greater or smaller communities throughout the sultanate, administered by the *malik al-'abidiyya*, a high-ranking official.[51] The origin of one small *'abidiyya* community may serve as an example; in 1924 a community of forty men in five villages living at Fashil in the northwest described themselves as of Shatt origin from the Western Bahr al-Ghazal, their ancestors having been settled there by Muhammad al-Fadl.[52] In function these *'abidiyya* settlements were similar to the Fulani *rumada* described by M. G. Smith and the princely estates of Songhay, permanent servile communities living a village life whose purpose was to provide soldiers when needed and to produce food and more slaves.[53] Some had specialised functions; the *kuuriŋa* (literally, 'the king's people') settled near al-Fashir made padded horse armour in Muhammad al-Husayn's time, while the *saariŋa* ('swordsmen', from the Fur *saar* 'sword') and *daadiŋa* (followers of the title-holder, the dadinqawi) were primarily soldiers also settled near the capital.[54]

These royal slave communities not only lay outside local authority but in some sense partook of the royal prestige; the Turuj settled among the Daju by Tayrab are said to have taken over the chieftainship from the latter precisely because they were royal slaves, while by a form of inverse snobbery the Kara community of Dar Iŋa (north-central Dar Fur) are so-called not because they descend from Kara from Dar Fartit, but because their first chief was a Kara slave put over them by one of the sultans.[55] Unlike other slave-owners, the sultan combined both sovereign and property rights over his slaves. The Shatt community of Fashil 'paid no dues on land or anything else except to the sultans. [The ruler of] Kobbe (where their settlement lay) was obliged to accept them as the sultan's personal following and could not come down on them for anything'.[56] Not surprisingly the *'abidiyya* could be tiresome neighbours; in a court case of 1261/1845-6 the defendant, a *faqih*, complained of trespass by a gang of *'abidiyya* and later received an injunction from the sultan restraining the slaves' leader.[57]

Until local studies are made, the wider economic significance of these slave estates and the similar royal domains in Jabal Marra and Dar Fongoro remains difficult to evaluate. Recently-photographed correspondence between 'Ali Dinar and several district chiefs in the al-Fashir region reveals a constant outward flow of demands for grain, money, cloth and soldiers and a tendency to pre-empt revenues for particular purposes or persons. The demands have yet to be related to any estimates of yields and the circumstances under 'Ali Dinar were in any case exceptional, but it may be reasonably assumed that the slave estates were an integral part of the general move towards centralization and the erosion of local interests.[58]

The sultans held no monopoly of slaves or land; the shift from a tribal to a court elite (in the sense of where they generally lived and where their primary loyalties lay) was accompanied by the division of much of the sultanate into estates (Ar. *hakura*, pl. *hawakir*) granted by the sultans to members of his family, court officials, military leaders, great merchants and *faqihs*.[59] There is some evidence for the presence of slaves upon these estates; one rather doubtful source alleges that some notables had between five and six hundred slaves on their estates, a more certain example is the charter issued by Muhammad al-Husayn in 1263/1846-7 granting a son-in-law an estate 'with its slaves who number fifty'.[60] Unlike those of the sultan, the slaves of others were subject to local administrative and judicial authority; thus a group of *jallaba* or merchants held an estate in Dar Konyir in western Dar Fur. Their slaves on the estate were obligated to subscribe to *diya* or blood-compensation collections made by the Konyir district chief, although the *jallaba* were themselves exempt.[61]

This brief account of estate slavery must be seen within the context of the evolution of the estate system. When the sultans granted estates they appear to have given them in fertile and populated districts (for example, in south-western Dar Fur) or to have confirmed rights over pre-existing settlements. The rights thus granted and promulgated in written charters were rights to exact revenue from the people on the estate or, less often, rights to the service of a group of nomads as herders. This being the case, references to slaves on estates probably refer to slaves working the 'home fields' of the estate-holder rather than to any notion of a vast estate being worked by gangs of slave labourers. The estate-holders were thus only doing on a grander scale what the less exalted also aspired to, namely to possess and use slaves to supplement domestic or kin labour. Nevertheless greater wealth and above all participation in the *ghazwas* must have given the elite the incentive and opportunity both to acquire slaves in considerable numbers and to set them to work on their lands.

Domestic and Pastoral Slavery

We have very little direct evidence as to how far below the elite slave-ownership went, nor can we go much beyond the obvious generalization that slave-owning was pyramidal in structure. The elite, which broadly defined may have numbered between five and six hundred people,[62] were substantial slave-holders, but how broad the base of the pyramid was is, in the absence of any local studies, a matter for speculation. Generalized estimates that slaves formed between 20 and 30 per cent of the total population of the Northern Sudan are, for the moment, neither securely documented nor do they indicate how the slaves were distributed within the social order.[63]

Domestic slaves were concentrated in urban areas, essentially al-Fashir and Kobbei, since below the elite it was the middle-ranking merchants and *faqihs* (closely-allied professions in Dar Fur) who would be most likely to own slaves.[64] Merchants not only dealt in slaves, they used them as porters and as a form of 'traveller's cheque'; Nachtigal's travelling companion, al-hajj Ahmad Tangatanga, had with him thirty to forty slaves when they travelled from Abéché to Kobbei, while three merchants going to Kordofan from al-Fashir in 1906 took with them '90 cattle, including 10 calves, 9 camels carrying tobacco and 7 male slaves'.[65] Given the great market in slaves in Dar Fur and their relative cheapness, domestic slavery was undoubtedly very common, a view supported by the numerous casual references throughout the works of Browne, al-Tunisi and Nachtigal.[66]

Furthermore, the rainland agricultural cycle would have made it useful to have had one or two domestic slaves in households of above-average prosperity to help with weeding, harvesting and the local herding and watering of animals, but probably not so profitable as for example in the irrigated agriculture practised along the Nile, where the loss of slaves in the Mahdiyya led to land going out of use.[67] The Arabic documents increasingly coming to light in Dar Fur largely describe the granting of land and privileges and land disputes among middle-ranking rural communities of *faqihs* in and around al-Fashir. They contain relatively few references to slavery, but these are so casual as to suggest that slaves formed an integral if unnoticed part of these communities. To give two examples: in 1279/1862-3 a case came before the deputy judge Muhammad Ishaq in which the slave Bakhit, jointly owned by four women, had injured the son of the *faqih*

Ibrahim. The details are unclear, but the judge ordered that a settlement (*sulh*) be made, in which the slave was valued by the elders of the court at eight cows and handed over to the *faqih*.[68] In a later example, the young sons of the late al-Nur Adam al-Jami had inherited a male slave, Marjan, from their father; in 1893 permission was given by the judicial authorities in al-Fashir for Marjan to be exchanged for 'Khayr, a Baya woman, black (*zurqa*) by colour and of medium height'.[69]

On his way to al-Fahir in 1874 Nachtigal met a seemingly impoverished youth who was buying a horse for two slaves, 'a young Jenge (Dinka) deaf-mute and a small girl'.[70] The youth was a nomad, from the Baqqara or cattle-nomads of southern Dar Fur; they were assiduous slave raiders although not on the organized scale of the *ghazwas* sent south from the sultanate. Rather 'they lie in ambush, and as soon as one of the children is within reach, they seize it, mount their horses and ride away with their prize at full gallop.'[71] The nomads used their slaves both as herders and to produce food as a 'cushion' against want within the nomadic cycle; indeed, although it is difficult to document, it is probable that the cattle and camel nomads of Dar Fur and Kordofan were more nomadic in the nineteenth century and before than in recent years and that slavery was a crucial factor in this change. 'Ideally the Hababin [of central Kordofan] would prefer to return to their pre-Mahdiya system of animal husbandry with cultivation mainly by slaves';[72] agricultural labour was and is regarded by the nomads as degrading work, fit only for slaves. The use of slaves among the Baqqara of Dar Fur was highly developed; not only did they have a constant inflow of new domestic slaves but they also controlled servile or semi-servile communities of Mandala or Bandala. The Mandala were old-established 'Fartit' colonies, who cultivated for their owners but otherwise lived quite separately; they identified themselves closely with their masters in their names, dress and customs and, on occasion, fought alongside them, a relationship which continued when numbers of them fled south to the northern fringes of the Western Bahr al-Ghazal during the Mahdiyya.[73] Two of the Mahdi's greatest generals, Hamdan Abu 'Anja and al-Zaki Tamal, were Mandala.[74] The importance of slavery to the nomads may be gauged by the tenacity with which they resisted the anti-slavery measures of the first years of Condominium rule.[75]

This brief survey of slavery within the Dar Fur Sultanate, although admittedly written from the perspective of the slave-owners, has tried to show how fundamental slaves were to the middle and upper groups within the state. Further research is needed, particularly among the nomads, before any attempt can be made to evaluate the economic significance of slavery or its consequences for contemporary social attitudes.

NOTES

1. I.e. 'consummate the union'.
2. From a nineteenth-century Fur song given in E. Zyhlarz, 'Eine auslese aus Max Müller's Kondjara-werk', *Zeitschrift für Eingeborenen-Sprachen*, xxxii (1941-2) 174-5.
3. For a survey of the sultanate's history, see R. S. O'Fahey and J. L. Spaulding, *Kingdoms of the Sudan* (London, 1974) 107-84.
4. In my 'Religion and trade in the Kayra Sultanate of Dar Fur', in *Sudan in Africa*, ed. Yusuf Fadl Hasan (Khartoum, 1971) 87-97, and 'Slavery and the slave trade in Dar Fur', *Journal of African History*, xiv/1 (1973) 29-43.
5. See the critical evaluation in Abbas Ibrahim Muhammad Ali, *The British, the Slave Trade and Slavery in the Sudan, 1820-1881* (Khartoum, 1972).
6. See further Peter F. M. McLoughlin, 'Economic development and the heritage of slavery in the Sudan Republic', *Africa*, xxxii (1962) 355-89.
7. On attitudes towards the descendants of slaves, and *vice versa*, see Ahmed S. al-Shahi, 'Proverbs and social values in a northern Sudanese village', in *Essays in Sudan Ethnography*, ed. I. Cunnison and W. James (London, 1972) 87-104.
8. Meillassoux's comment that it is American and West Indian slavery that should be regarded as aberrant within a typology of slavery is relevant, *L'Esclavage en Afrique Précoloniale*, ed. C. Meillassoux (Paris, 1975) 19-20; however, Abbas Ibrahim's conclusion that 'by the standards of Western slavery, most slaves, if not all, in the Sudan who were categorised by British writers as slaves were not slaves', is far too disingenuous, *op cit.*, 130.
9. On Shari'i and Customary Law, see my 'The office of *qadi* in Dar Fur: a preliminary enquiry', *Bulletin of the School of Oriental and African Studies*, xi/1 (1977) 110-24.
10. Zyhlarz, *op cit.*, 177.
11. Mohammed ibn-Omar El-Tounsy, *Voyage au Ouaday*, transl. N. Perron (Paris, 1851) 273.
12. G. D. Lampen, 'History of Darfur', *Sudan Notes and Records*, xxxi/2 (1950) 181.
13. Hasan Imam Hasan and R. S. O'Fahey, 'Notes on the Mileri of Jabal Mun', *Sudan Notes and Records*, li (1970) 152-61.
14. F. Mengin, *Histoire de l'Egypte sous le Gouvernement de Mohammed-Aly* (2 vols., Paris, 1823) ii, 234 lists the tribes from whom slaves were captured; Rong (Runga), Befeg (?), Chal (Shala), Feroukah (Feroge), el-Hofrah (the people around Hufrat al-Nahas ?), Dang (Dango), Kar (Kara), Youl (Yulu), el-Nabeh (?) and Bonoud (Ar. pl. form of Banda?). See further, S. Santandrea, *A Tribal History of the Western Bahr el Ghazal* (Bologna, 1964).
15. There are a number of references to expeditions venturing very far south from the sultanate (i.e. journeys of 30 to 40 days): El Tounsy, *Ouaday*, 274-6; W. G. Browne, *Travels in Egypt, Syria and Africa* (second ed., London, 1806) xv; E. de Cadalvène and J. de Breuvery, *L'Egypte et la Nubie* (second ed., Paris, 1841) ii, 236; M. Brun-Rollet, *Le Nil Blanc et le Soudan* (Paris, 1855) 131-32; H. Barth, 'Account of two expeditions in Central Africa by the Furanys', *Journal of the Royal Geographical Society*, xxxii (1853) 120-22; letter of H. de Bizemont in *Bulletin de la Société de*

Géographie, 63 série, i (1871) 120-30. The extent of these journeys is discussed in E. De Dampierre, *Un Ancien Royaume Bandia du Haut-Oubangui* (Paris, 1967) 59-60.

16. An attempt needs to be made to investigate the effect of slave-raiding on population movements on both sides of the Muslim/non-Muslim divide.

    On the traditions from the Central African Empire region, see J. Leyder, 'Note préliminaire à l'étude des grandes migrations de l'Afrique centrale', *Revue de l'Institut de Sociologie d'Université Bruxelles*, xiii/1 (1932) 44-7; *idem*, 'De l'origine des Bwaka (Ubangi)', *Bulletin de la Société Belge de Géographie*, lx (1936) 49-71; B. O. Tanghe, 'Histoire générale des migrations des peuples de l'Ubangui', *Congo: Revue Générale de la Colonie Belge*, ii/4 (novembre 1938) 361-91; *idem*, 'Pages d'histoire africaine', *Aequatoria*, vi/1 (1943) 1-7; *idem*, 'Pages d'histoire africaine', *Aequatoria*, vii (1944) 35-41.

17. The Rev. Dr A. J. Arkell's Papers now deposited in two batches at the School of Oriental and African Studies, University of London, provide the ethnographic data that would serve as a starting point for such an investigation from the Dar Fur side (hereafter the papers will be cited as AP[1] or [2], box no./file no., folio no.) See also H. A. MacMichael, *A History of the Arabs in the Sudan* (2 vols., Cambridge, 1922) i, 94 & 97.

18. We have some examples of the slave biography *genre* from the Dar Fur region: T. H. B. Mynors, 'The adventures of a Darfur slave', *Sudan Notes and Records*, xxx/2 (1949) 273-5 (a Kara enslaved by al-Zubayr's men, c. 1865); C. Meinhof, 'Sprachproben von der Sprache in Darfur von Karl Tutschek', *Zeitschrift für Eingeborenen-Sprachen*, xvi (1925-6) 162 (three ex-slave women at Aswan), 165-96 (the autobiography of Musalam Motekutu). On Musalam, see P. E. H. Hair, 'The brothers Tutschek and their Sudanese informants', *Sudan Notes and Records*, L (1969) 53-62

19. See the examples given in T. Walz (Chapter VIII of this volume). To which may be added the case of a wrongfully enslaved girl from Dongola who was liberated by the Dar Fur Sultan, Browne, *Travels*, 259-60.

20. Among examples of 'Northerners' enslaved we have Halima bint 'Abdallah al-Furiyya, who had a brideprice settled upon her in Cairo in 1120/1708-9 (T. Walz, personal communication, 27 November 1973); another Fur woman, Zayn Sayyida bint 'Abdallah (in both cases the patronymic is presumably fictitious), who was manumitted in Kordofan on 29 Rajab 1294/9 August 1877 (her deed of manumission is given in Husayn Sid Ahmad al-Mufti, *Tatawwur nizam al-qada' fi'l-Sudan* [Khartoum, 1387/1959]i, 88); for a Rizayqat soldier enslaved and sold during the Mahdiyya by the Kababish in Kordofan, see A. C. Hope, 'The adventurous life of Faraj Sadik', *Sudan Notes and Records*, xxxii/1 (1951) 154-58.

21. Browne, *Travels*, 219.

22. El Tounsy, *Ouaday*, 467-95, and my commentary in 'Slavery and the slave trade', *op cit.*, 32-34.

23. Browne, *Travels*, 343; G. Nachtigal, *Sahara and Sudan*, transl. A. G. B. and H. J. Fisher (London, 1971-) iv, 359, and El Tounsy, *Ouaday*, 474.

24. Browne, *Travels*, 274. Runaway or stolen slaves were always a problem: Sa'id b. al-hajj Adam bought in good faith a slave woman at Tinat, who turned out to have run away two months earlier from the *malik* Tutir; similarly in 1290/1873-4 Jum'a was sued by the *malik* Abbakr for the return of the runaway Sa'da. Perhaps it is more than coincidence that in both cases the girls ran away from *maliks* to *faqih*s (Field catalogue nos. 122.13/7 and 175.18/35: from a photographic collection of Arabic documents made by the author, now deposited in the Central Records Office, Khartoum, and the Department of History, University of Bergen; hereafter documents are cited solely by their field catalogue number).

25. A suggestion I owe to Dr T. Walz.

26. 76.10/1 21 Ramadan 1332/13 August 1914: she is described as a *jabalawiyya*, either from Jabal Marra or, more probably from the mountainous regions between Dar Fur and Wadai.
27. War naturally depressed prices by flooding the market: 'Karamallah Kurkusawi [Kurqusawi], the Mahdist *amir*, when he occupied the Bahr al-Ghazal in 1303 [1885-6] sold 300 slaves by public auction and they were knocked down for 25 dollars to a man called Muhammad Salih al-Ja'fari', Muhammad 'Abd al-Rahim, *Muhadara 'an al-'aruba fi'l-Sudan* (Khartoum, 1935) 86.
28. See the diagram in O'Fahey and Spaulding, *Kingdoms of the Sudan*, 147.
29. Muhammad b. 'Umar al-Tunisi, *Tashhidh al-adhhan bi-sirat bilad al-'arab wa'l-sudan*, ed. Khalil Mahmud 'Asakir and Mustafa Muhammad Mus'ad (Cairo, 1965) 206, and *Voyage au Darfour*, transl. N. Perron (Paris, 1845) 199 (hereafter the page reference for the French translation will be given in brackets after the Arabic); Nachtigal, *Sahara and Sudan*, iv, 329 and 335.
30. On the *korayat*, al-Tunisi, *Tashhidh*, 182 (174); Nachtigal, iv, 335-6: on the *korkwa*, al-Tunisi, 79-80, 169, 178 and 183 (62, 161, 169 and 174) and Nachtigal, iv, 333: on the *falaqna*, Browne, *Travels*, 226-8; al-Tunisi, 153-4 (139-40) and Nachtigal, iv, 335.
31. P. J. Sandison's Papers [uncatalogued], Sudan Archive, School of Oriental Studies, University of Durham.
32. Al-Tunisi, *Tashhidh*, (250-70).
33. Al-Tunisi, 95, 116, 152 and 182 (78, 105, 137-8 and 173) and Nachtigal, iv, 324-5 and 328-9.
34. Nachtigal, iv, 329.
35. The main written sources for Kurra are al-Tunisi, 63-72 and 93-116 (45-54 and 77-105) and Nachtigal, iv, 294-301; both assert that Kurra was born a freeman, but Abu Adam 'Abdallahi (interview, Nyala, June 1969) called him a Tarjawi (i.e. from the Turuj) and a slave. Perhaps the act of castration made one a slave.
36. On Kurra in Kordofan, see R. S. O'Fahey and J. L. Spaulding, 'Hashim and the Musabba'at', *Bulletin of the School of Oriental and African Studies*, xxxv/2 (1972) 316-33.
37. Compare L. Brenner, *The Shehus of Kukawa* (Oxford, 1973), 89-103.
38. On Adam Bosh, see Nachtigal, iv, 307-8 and 311-15, and C. Cuny, 'Observations générales sur le Mémoire sur le Soudan de M. le Comte D'Escayrac de Lauture', *Nouvelles Annales des Voyages* (mars, 1858) 3-28. In two documents Bosh is entitled *al-wazir ala-a'zam*, reminiscent of Ottoman usage (206.22/2 dated 18 Rabi'II 1262/15 April 1846, and 63.8/7 dated 25 Rajab 1267/7 June 1851). On his son Bakhit, Nachtigal, iv, 319-20 and 370-1 (an eye-witness account of Bakhit's investiture as *wazir*). On Khayr Qarib, described as a Fartit slave and *amin al-khaziniyya*, see Na'um Shuqayr, *Ta'rikh al-Sudan al-qadim wa'l-hadith wa-jughrafiyatuhu* (3 vols., Cairo, n.d. [1903]), ii, 133-34.
39. This was how the succession crisis was interpreted to Nachtigal in Wadai (iv, 70-7, 88 and 319-20).
40. 'Umar Lel (c. 1730-39) and Abu'l-Qasim (c. 1739-52); the 18th century history of the sultanate was marked by tribal and clan conflicts, see O'Fahey and Spaulding, *Kingdoms of the Sudan*, 125-34.
41. Nachtigal, iv, 307-8.
42. 82.10/7 dated Muharram 1323/April 1905. See also Nachtigal, iv, 247, 365 and 367.
43. To give just the first examples: Muhammad al-Tunisi is given an Ethiopian slave girl by the ruler of Sinnar; Muhammad Kurra gives the young al-Tunisi two slave girls and a male slave and Malik al-Futawi, the Fulani *wazir*, adds another female slave, *Tashhidh*, 31 and 65-6 (13 and 47-8).

44. Shuqayr, ii, 123-4.
45. Al-Tunisi, 99-100 (88-9); Nachtigal, iv, 301 and 333; R. Slatin, *Fire and Sword in the Sudan* (London, 1896) 44-5. Muhammad al-Fadl's favour to his maternal kin is echoed in two charters, one from the *amin* 'Abd al-Bari and dated Dhu'l-hijja 1231/December 1815-January 1816, the other from 'Abd al-Bari's son, Muhammad al-Fadl, who was probably named after the sultan (179.18/39 and 152.18/12). The Beigo recovered their position under 'Ali Dinar; one of his confidants was Muhammad Kebkebe, a Beigo for whom he revived the title of 'sultan'.
46. L. Holý, *Neighbours and Kinsmen: a Study of the Berti People of Darfur* (London, 1974) 24-6 and 83-4. Weeding is important because the more effectively it is done the greater the subsequent yield; among the Berti it is the main agricultural task to require labour from outside the domestic group.
47. AP², 10/48, 23.
48. There is a continuum of policy ranging from the encouragement given by the sultans to itinerant *faqihs* to settle through grants of land and tax-privileges to the forcible immigration of whole servile communities; the objective was the recruitment of labour, whether skilled or unskilled. On the former, see my 'Saints and sultans: the role of Muslim holymen in the Keira Sultanate of Dar Fur', in *Northern Africa: Islamization and Modernization*, ed. M. Brett (London, 1973) 49-56 and 'The Awlad 'Ali: a Fulani holy family in Dar Fur', *Veröffentlichungen aus dem Übersee-Museum: Deutsche Geographische Blätter*, li (forthcoming).
49. AP¹, 3/13, 186 and 6/25, 5; AP², 10/48, 115. See also MacMichael, *History*, i, 89-90.
50. Al-Tunisi, 93-8 (76-85).
51. *ibid.*, 175 (183), and *Ouaday*, 439-40.
52. Northern Darfur District Archives (Kutum) NDD/66. B. 4/3 Tribal: Magdumate Area: Dar Sereif; letter dated 12 March 1924; and NDD/66 B. 7/3/6 Tribal: Zaghawa: Dar Galla: boundaries, evidence from Sultan Dosa [of Dar Zaghawa Kobe], April 1935.
53. *The Economy of the Hausa Communities of Zaria* (London, 1955) 102-3, and M. Tymowski, 'Domaines princiers au Songhay', *Annales*, 25/6 (1970) 1637-58.
54. AP², 10/48, 86 and interviews with Rihaymtallah Mahmud al-Dadinqawi, al-Fashir June 1970.
55. AP², 10/48, 114: the close identity between master and slave led in a number of cases to slaves taking their royal or chiefly owners' clan names; thus the slaves of the Berti chiefs were like their masters called *Basang'a*, Holý, *Neighbours and Kinsmen*, 54.
56. Evidence of Sultan Dosa cited in n.52.
57. 99.12/7 and 98.12/6.
58. On a comparative note, the royal estates around Abéché in Wadai yielded 30,000 dollars annually, or approximately 10% of the sultan's total estimated revenues in 1903, Capt. Julien, 'Le Dar-Ouadaï', *Bulletin du Comité de L'Afrique Française: Renseignments Coloniaux*, xiv (mars, 1904) 140-1. See further Anders Bjørkelo, *State and Society in Three Central Sudanic Kingdoms: Kanem-Bornu, Bagirmi and Wadai*, unpublished 'hovedfag' thesis, University of Bergen 1976.
59. Some fifty charters and other documents relating to this topic are given, together with an introduction, in R. S. O'Fahey and M. I. Abu Salim, *Land in Dar Fur*, to be published as vol. iii of the *Fontes Historiae Africanae: series arabica*.
60. The doubtful source is a Tunisian traveller: his travels, if that is what they are, have been recently published (in mimeograph) as, Chaykh Muhammad, fils d'Ali, fils de Zayn al-'Abidin de Tunis, *Le Livre du Soudan*, translated from the Turkish translation of the untraced Arabic original by Marcel Crisard and J.-L. Bacqué-Grammont (Laboratoire d'ethnologie et d'archéologie tchadiennes et camerounaises,

CNRS, Paris, 1975) 10-11. The only previous translation is Zein el-Abdin, *Das Buch des Sudan*, transl. E. Rosen (Leipzig, 1847). The charter is given in Shuqayr, *Ta'rikh*, ii, 139.

61. Northern Darfur District Archives (Kutum) NDD/66 B. 8/2 Tribal: Dar Fia: Fur, note on Gelli, 23 April 1931.
62. Included in this definition are first and second generation members (male and female) of the royal family; court officials; provincial, tribal and district chiefs; *imam*s, *'ulama'* and *faqih*s at court and other major centres of the sultanate, and the long-distance merchants or *khabir*s (of whom there were about 25 operating out of Kobbei in the 1860s).
63. Compare McLoughlin, 'Economic development and the heritage of slavery', *op cit.*, 361.
64. There are no reliable estimates of the population of al-Fashir in the nineteenth century (the figure given in al-Tunisi, transl. 154, namely 30,000 males is greatly exaggerated). In 1911 it was estimated that half the population of Abéché, a town comparable to al-Fashir, were slaves, J. A. Works Jr., *Pilgrims in a Strange Land: Hausa Communities in Chad* (New York, 1976) 72. Works also comments that following the French occupation of Abéché in 1909 many of the slaves emigrated since 'the aristocracy could no longer support the large number of domestic slaves . . .' without a continuation of a commerce which in turn was heavily dependent upon the export of slaves' (p.72).
65. Nachtigal, iv, 236 and 79.10/4 Safar 1324/17 April 1906.
66. The same impression comes from the much more substantial travel literature on Kordofan, even if A. E. Brehm exaggerates with his comment, 'Die Frauen Kordofahns haben ebensogut ihre Sklavinnen als die Männer ihre Sklaven', *Reisen im Sudan 1847 bis 1852* (Tübingen, 1975) 206.
67. See G. Warburg, 'Slavery and Labour in the Anglo-Egyptian Sudan' [Princeton Slavery Conference Paper].
68. 170.18/30.
69. 36.7/9, 37.7/10 and 38.7/11: Khayr was probably from the Gbaya people.
70. Nachtigal, iv, 243.
71. I. Pallme, *Travels in Kordofan* (London, 1846) 125, a description of *Baqqara* slave-raiding in Kordofan.
72. L. G. Hill, 'Hababin village economy', *Sudan Notes and Records*, xlix (1968) 58-70. See also I. Cunnison, *Baggara Arabs* (London, 1966) 40, 66 and 80.
73. G. K. C. Hebbert, 'The Bandala of the Bahr el Ghazal', *Sudan Notes and Records*, viii (1925) 187-94, and Nachtigal, iv, 165.
74. R. Hill, *A Biographical Dictionary of the Sudan* (second ed., Frank Cass, London, 1967) 147-8 and 389.
75. McLoughlin, 'Economic development', *op cit.* Equally, the nomad's mobility made it that much harder to suppress slavery among them.

VI

Al-Zubayr Pasha and the Zariba Based Slave Trade in the Bahr al-Ghazal 1855-1879

Lawrence Mire

Al-Zubayr Pasha Rahma Mansur (1830-1913) is a particularly sinister figure in the English literature dealing with the nineteenth century Sudan. He has been execrated as "Sultan and Slaver"[1] and the "greatest slaver who ever lived"[2] while being credited with being "practically the ruler of the Bahr al-Ghazal"[3] or even "the absolute ruler of an area larger than France."[4] More recent scholarship has reduced the scale of his grandeur to that of a merchant prince[5] without, however, clarifying the source and extent of his power in the Bahr al-Ghazal. What follows is neither a biography nor a political history. Rather, it will describe the society and institutions which nourished al-Zubayr and in which he flourished, with particular emphasis upon the *zariba* system. For al-Zubayr was not acting in a vacuum, he was part of a larger movement of numerous independent Khartoum based predominantly Muslim merchants entering the Bahr al-Ghazal in the 1850s in search of ivory.[6] As the profits from ivory dwindled, these same merchants turned to the slave trade in the 1860s and 1870s.

Al-Zubayr's meteoric rise to predominance among these Khartoumers was due not to his individual daring and intelligence alone, for there were many daring and clever men in the Bahr al-Ghazal then. His success was largely due to his fortuitous geographical location in the region and the important services he was able to render the Khartoumers as a whole from this position. These crucial services were: securing an overland trade route as the Nile was being closed to the slave trade through the actions of Sir Samuel Baker and others; opening new territories in the southern and western Bahr al-Ghazal as the Muslim advance was checked elsewhere; defending the rights of the slave traders against corrupt representatives of the central government. This study will therefore address itself primarily to the structure and mechanics of the slave trade in the Bahr al-Ghazal. To accomplish this, I have divided the study into four parts: the first is a short introduction describing indigenous slavery in the Bahr al-Ghazal; the second discusses the Muslim slave trade in the region before the advent of the Khartoumers in the 1850s; the third describes the new system established by the Khartoumers; and the final part discusses the crises leading to al-Zubayr's great successes.

I. Introduction

The institution of slavery was widespread among the indigenous peoples of the Bahr al-Ghazal. It was found in all societies, among the pastoral and nomadic Dinka of the northern areas, among the scattered, politically divided agricultural communities of the various peoples in the central regions, and among the centralized, agricultural based kingdoms of the Azande in the southern regions. All of these societies had a low level of technology, and domestic animals were not exploited for their labor potential. Consequently human labor was the only source of power available. This placed a high premium on securing human labor, and slavery was one means of accomplishing this. The most common sources of slaves were captives taken in intercommunal wars and cattle raids. In some communities, criminals were enslaved as well. Such slaves were used both in production (e.g. farming and herding) and as domestic servants, usually female slaves employed in the arduous and time consuming task of grinding eleusine flour (finger millet). One woman working all day could grind enough flour to satisfy the daily needs of five or six people. In general, they were well treated and considered almost as a family member. Even before the advent of the Khartoumers some of these slaves were sold to wandering *jallaba* (itinerant Muslim merchants).[7]

The Azande are the best documented of the indigenous peoples; they were also the most powerful of the agricultural peoples. The term Azande encompasses a number of different peoples in various stages of "zande-ization" under the leadership of the Avungara clan, the ruling dynasty of the Azande people. The nineteenth century was a period of aggressive expansion by the Azande. This warlike and cannibalistic people pushed northward across the Wele River early in the nineteenth century following a bloody path to the north. The conflict between the northward expanding Azande and the southward expanding Khartoumers provides much of the drama of this period, for these people were active in the slave trade both as slavers and as slaves.[8]

There were four sources of slaves in Azande society: captives taken in war; fugitives from other groups without a blood relative in the village; criminals reprieved from a death sentence (or the cooking pot); and women paid to the king as tribute or for damages. The social status of these slaves was not particularly onerous. They lived in the various homesteads much like another member of the family, with the exception that the hardest, dirtiest and more menial jobs were assigned to them.[9] They were free to marry. Female slaves were automatically freed upon marriage, and a married male slave with several children was treated almost as a free man. More significantly, all children of slaves were free and adopted into the clan of whoever paid the brideprice. Even while still a slave, although not formally accepted socially into the clan, the bridewealth duties frequently fulfilled by the owners constituted a *de facto* assumption of a clan relationship.

Azande slaves performed a variety of functions in daily life. Commoners used them in farming and grinding the eleusine. The kings had numerous slave concubines as well. One Azande king even had a eunuch officiating in his numerous households.[10] Moreover, slaves were employed in the king's bodyguard, a prestigious position. Azande kings who found themselves near Muslim areas were willing and eager to trade slaves for firearms, copper bars, and beads from *jallaba* merchants. One king in the western Bahr al-Ghazal, Mofio, actively raided for slaves and collected them as tribute from subject peoples for the jallaba trade amassing an arsenal of three hundred guns in the process.[11]

II. *Muslim slave trade before the Khartoumers (pre 1850s)*

The Muslim area with the oldest trade relations with the Bahr al-Ghazal was Dar Fur, whose activities were concentrated in the northwestern region which they called Dar Fartit. The Dar Fur state originated in the Jabal Marra mountains, the only agricultural base available for state building in the desert regions between the Nile and Lake Chad. The Fur organized themselves under a sacred king at a fairly early period and the state expanded to include non-Fur peoples and regions along with the expansion of trade. The sacral kings became sultans in the course of the eighteenth century as the long and complex process of Islamization began.[12] Slave owning was quite extensive in Dar Fur, and played an important role in the social, economic and political life of the country. They were found at all levels of society, from the Sultan to the Baggara nomads. Since the latter half of the eighteenth century, the Sultan had been using slaves on a large scale to strengthen his position vis-à-vis the Furwa nobility. Consequently slaves were to be found at all levels of government in a system of political and military slavery strikingly similar to that found in the central Islamic lands.

There was a large eunuch establishment at the palace. The most powerful position in the Dar Fur state was that of the Abu Shaykh Dali, the virtual ruler of the eastern half of the state. This position was usually reserved for eunuchs of the Sultan.[13] Slaves filled other offices at the palace, up to and including that of the *wazir*. Slaves were also used as inspector generals, sent secretly to observe the workings of provincial government.[14] At the bottom rung of government service, eunuchs staffed the prisons.[15] Such slave officials played an even more important political role by controlling access to the Sultan and serving as his confidants and advisers to the exclusion of the *Furwa* nobility. Such slaves received high honors from the Sultan, and those in the upper ranks of government lived in luxury. Their behavior in office, especially that of the eunuchs, was by no means servile. The population at large considered them haughty, extortionate and avaricious, and provide many anecdotes of their behavior.[16]

Slave soldiers were also utilized in large numbers by the Sultan to buttress his power. All of the archers in the Dar Fur army were slaves from Dar Fartit, and they were regarded as effective and loyal troops.[17] They served as spearmen also, and the Sultan had a special bodyguard of two thousand slave spearmen. There were, however, very few slave cavalry troops, which was the preserve of the Furwa nobility. The few slaves mentioned as armoured cavalrymen were high officials, whose horse, armour and equipment were signs of honor.

Slaves were important to the state economically as well. Colonies of slaves were settled upon the land by the Sultan both to develop the state economically and to increase his personal wealth.[18] They were actively involved in and beneficial to the general economy. They were used in the agricultural and the pastoral sectors of the economy. In contrast, slaves played no significant role as artisans in Dar Fur. This was probably due to the low level of artisanal development in Dar Fur as a whole rather than to any lack of accomplishment among the peoples of Dar Fartit, whose industrial accomplishments are compared favorably to those of the English in some respects.[19] Newly-captured slaves were used as a medium of exchange in the marketplace, and some tribes paid their taxes in slaves.[20] More importantly, the proceeds from the slave trade both within Dar Fur and with neighboring Muslim areas was of crucial importance to the Dar Fur economy. The loss of Dar Fartit to al-Zubayr and to the Khartoumers was an almost crippling blow to Dar Fur. The loss of revenue from the slave trade forced the state to increase taxation which caused widespread discontent among the people.[21] Many of the Furwa nobility who had supplemented their income by slave raiding in Dar Fartit were impoverished.[22]

The slave trade in Dar Fartit was pursued in three ways: small scale, unofficial raiding (actually little more than organized kidnapping) by the Baggara tribesmen in the fringe areas; jallaba based trade in which itinerant Muslim merchants bartered beads, copper, tin, cloth and sometimes guns for captives held by local peoples; and a highly organized series of large scale raids undertaken by enterprising individuals under contract to the state.

The official slave raids were very remunerative to the state and the economy as a whole. The applicant for *Sultan al-Ghazwa* (leader of the raid) obtained his letter of commission and his salativa (a broad bladed spearhead symbolic of his office) by virtue of distributing the potential fruits of his endeavors among the court notables in the form of bribes. Another large proportion of the potential profits was promised to the men recruited for the raid in the form of a stipulated share of the slaves captured by force. Anyone who surrendered voluntarily fell to the *Sultan al-Ghazwa*. This portion could amount to a sizable proportion of the captives, because certain communities near the frontier areas were in a tributary status with Dar Fur, which, if the *Sultan al-Ghazwa* chose to recognize it, gave them the option to volunteer captives rather than be raided for them. Indeed, one such community was exempted from raids altogether, because the Dar Fur Sultan's mother was of that community. Upon the return of the raiders, those merchants who had advanced the sums to finance the raid but chose not to accompany it received their share, as did the Dar Fur Sultan. From sixty to seventy raids were commissioned each year, each with its own routes and raiding area. No attempt was made to call the local peoples to Islam during these raids, and local society in the Bahr al-Ghazal seems to have been but little disrupted.[23]

Parallel to these raids was the thriving jallaba trade. There were large numbers of these predominantly Dongalawi and Ja'alyn merchants in Dar Fur and Kordofan (formerly the eastern province of the Dar Fur state until its conquest by Muhammad Ali's Egypt). There were some five thousand jallaba households in Dar Fur alone.[24] These men, many of whom were religious scholars, played an important role in the economy of the geographical Sudan as a whole. They were active in both the internal and external caravan trade of Baqirmi, Wada'i, Dar Fur, Dar Fartit, Kordofan as well as the Nilotic

Sudan. They ventured as far west as the Hausa states of Nigeria. In Dar Fur and Kordofan they had their own separate communities.

Individual jallaba, sometimes with a small, armed escort would travel among the pagan peoples of Dar Fartit buying captives and criminals for beads, copper, tin, cloth, and guns. Throughout their travels they were subject to local tolls and the exactions of the local communities. Unlike the raiders, they thus traded with the indigenous, pagan peoples on a basis of equality. They also did a brisk trade with the Baggara who had their own captives for sale. Some of the more prosperous jallaba remained the entire year in Dar Fartit under the protection of influential local leaders. They founded permanent encampments, called *dayms*, which served as depots for slaves and ivory. The captives were often used to grow food for the daym while awaiting transhipment. This system was particularly well developed in the western regions of Dar Fartit, where a large establishment was created at Daym Gudyoo to trade with the aforementioned Azande king Mofio. Another important daym was located near Delgauna, which was an important center for the ivory trade of the jallaba.

This was the situation prevailing before the onslaught of the Khartoumers. Sudd, an heretofore impassable barrier of floating vegetation, had protected all except the Dar Fartit region of the Bahr al-Ghazal from any significant interaction with the Muslims to the north. Indigenous society was fairly stable. There was some disruption in Dar Fartit resulting from the slave raids, but no mention is made of widespread devastation or depopulation. In the south, the various Azande kingdoms were expanding at the expense of the politically fragmented and scattered agricultural communities in the south. The bulk of the Bahr al-Ghazal was left undisturbed. In the northern Nilotic Sudan, however, great events were happening which were soon to throw the Bahr al-Ghazal into turmoil.

III. *The Khartoumers and the advent of the zariba system*

One of the products of Muhammad Ali's violent conquest of the Sudan (1820-1826) was a great increase in the demand for slaves. One of the primary reasons for the conquest was his desire to equip himself with a large slave army composed of Sudanese blacks. Towards this end, the newly established government undertook huge slave raids. Such official and semi-official raids continued to the early 1850s. During this period, although the proposed slave army failed to materialize, slaves continued to be sought to pay the heavy taxes imposed upon the Sudan.

Events further afield also played their part in opening the Bahr al-Ghazal. The first of these was the increasing demand for ivory in Europe, which spurred trade explorations along the Nile. As for the slave trade itself, the Russian conquests in the Caucasus cut off the supply of Circassian concubines, leading to an increased demand for African slave girls.[26] More importantly, there was an increasing prosperity in Egypt resulting from the spread of cotton cultivation. This too strengthened the demand for domestic slaves. This demand reached a peak during the cotton boom caused by the American Civil War during which Egyptian cotton was at a premium in the mills of Manchester. The profits were so high that even the fellahin were able to purchase slaves, both as servants and as workers to help them increase production.

In 1839, the Sudd barrier had been penetrated by steamships. The first beneficiary of this enterprise was a flourishing ivory trade on the White Nile, which was dominated by Europeans at first. The various peoples living along the White Nile had little or no trade experience. Their lack of discrimination between what appeared to the Khartoum based traders as gifts, tolls, theft, and extortion on the one hand and a rational exchange of goods on the other, soon led to escalating violence on both sides. The traders soon felt compelled to arm themselves to the teeth, and established themselves in zaribas (fortified, armed camps). Once again, the Europeans were in the lead. Many of the groups, especially the Dinka, had few needs which traders could fulfill. Therefore, when people in a community had what they considered to be an adequate number of beads, they refused to cooperate or exert themselves on behalf of the traders. Faced with this new impasse, the traders resorted to large scale cattle raiding to acquire a commodity for which the local peoples would exert themselves. The different zaribas involved themselves in the many intercommunal wars by forming alliances with certain communities for their mutual benefit. Cattle raiding soon degenerated into brutal slave raiding as the profits from ivory declined.[28] Therefore, by the time the first ivory traders entered the Bahr al-Ghazal, the ivory trade was already transforming itself into the slave trade. The merchant warriors entered the area in heavily armed, bellicose groups.

The first Khartoum based trader to reach the Bahr al-Ghazal was John Petherick, a former British consul and mining engineer. He arrived in the region in 1835 with armed Nubian retainers. At first the trade was hazardous and not very profitable.[29] The local people had little or no trading traditions. Petherick had to pay bribes and gifts to each village through which he passed. The people here preferred plunder to trade and some of the Muslim expeditions following him were massacred.[30] Even under the best conditions, the bearers refused to go beyond their community's territory, causing additional trouble and expense for the traders.

Despite these drawbacks, trade increased rapidly in the area because the ivory stores were largely untouched. Within two years some twenty-four zaribas were built between the rivers Rohl and Biri among the Dinka, Jur, Bongo and Golo peoples.[31] The Dinka bead market was soon glutted, and the Khartoumers turned to cattle raiding. The most productive of the resulting alliances was that made by 'Ali Amuri with Shol, a Dinka queen living near Meshra' al-Req, the main port of entry into the Bahr al-Ghazal. This partnership guaranteed the security of this vital position and gained a valuable ally for all cattle raids.[32]

Soon however, the problem of diminishing ivory stores came to the fore. As profits declined, the Khartoumers began to make more efficient use of their cattle raids to reduce their overhead and increase their profits. In addition to cattle, they began seizing grain supplies and large numbers of captives, who were used to carry the ivory to Meshra' al-Req where they themselves became merchants. At this point, the European merchants withdrew. This process initiated a period of increasingly widespread devastation. This process was accelerated by the continued growth in the numbers of zaribas. Within the first ten years (1853-1863) over eighty zaribas appeared between the Biri and the Rohl. The local inhabitants were enslaved by the thousands, entire villages were wiped out, and in only three years the area between the Tondy and the Dyoor rivers was desolated.[33] A point of rapidly diminishing returns was slowly being approached which was only averted by continued expansion, seeking new sources of ivory and slaves. This expansion was to have two unforeseen results.

Expansion westward brought the Khartoumers into Dar Fartit and contact with the jallabas and the state raiders of Dar Fur. The latter were gradually squeezed out of the area. The former welcomed the Khartoumers. The imposition of the zariba system freed the jallaba from paying tolls and being subject to control by the indigenous communities and their trade barriers.[34] Moreover, as the area was pacified by the proliferating zaribas, the jallaba were also largely freed from the necessity of maintaining their own armed retainers. The balance of power had shifted decisively in their favor.

The new system did, however, place some restrictions on their activities. With the exception of the trade with Mofio in the far west, whose arsenal was a deterrant to the Khartoumers, the jallaba soon found themselves reduced to middle men, fully incorporated into the zariba system. Nevertheless, both sides benefited from the new arrangements. The zariba owners gained new marketing facilities, and the jallaba could expand into areas newly opened up by the Khartoumers. The Khartoumers could barter their newly acquired captives on the spot for needed supplies and luxury items (but not cash). More importantly, they were introduced to the overland caravan route through Dar Fur and Kordofan which bypassed the increasingly well patrolled Nile route. The White Nile at this time was being effectively closed to the slave boats in the 1860s due to the efforts of Sir Samuel Baker and other functionaries of the Egyptian government. Egypt was smarting under the verbal and diplomatic lashing of European governments which were acting in response to a large and vocal lobby of abolitionists and missionary groups.

Expansion toward the south brought the Khartoumers into direct contact with the centralized, expansionary Azande kingdoms. By the 1860s, the Azande territories were the only regions which still had large, untouched stores of ivory. The Azande were eager for trade, especially for copper. In the beginning, they actively sought out the traders, and were eager to meet them.[35] The leaders, in order to cement their new trading relationships, would offer their daughters and granddaughters in marriage to the Khartoumers. Nevertheless, they were wary of the newcomers and took pains to preserve their independence. The Azande refused to allow the traders to penetrate their territories to trade with the lands beyond them, partially to monopolize the copper trade with their more remote rivals, and partially to keep these dangerous newcomers at a distance. More significantly the Azande would not tolerate slave raids by Khartoumers in territories they considered their own although they were quite willing to sell their non-Azande captives to the newcomers. The Khartoumers, forced to trade on more equal terms, were obliged to reform their rapacious trading practices in order to conserve the manpower resources left to them. The resolution of this problem provided the finishing touches to the zariba system of the Bahr al-Ghazal.

The rapid expansion of the zariba based ivory and slave trade was not totally haphazard. It was governed by a gentlemen's agreement whereby the Bahr al-Ghazal was divided into spheres of influence by the six great trading houses in Khartoum and the half dozen lesser trading groups associated with them. Although some companies had obtained concessions for certain areas from the government in Khartoum, on the whole it was a first come first served operation.

When a group founded a zariba and entered into trade relationships with the local communities, it automatically had a monopoly in the area. This parcelling out of routes was due not so much to geographical considerations as to the problem of supplies to support the expeditions using these routes. It was actually access to the food supplies in these areas which was monopolized. Different companies could, and did, mount joint operations using the same routes, but this had to be agreed upon beforehand.[36]

Such agreements were effected in order to avoid conflict and were not a result of conflict. There was a strong sense of solidarity among the traders, both Coptic and Muslim, resulting from their common origins vis-à-vis the pagans. The Nubian *askar* (the Muslim and Arab soldiers of the zaribas) would refuse to fight their fellow askar. When one station was in trouble, the others would send aid. Fighting between zaribas, though rare, did occur, but recourse to locally levied auxiliary troops was necessary.

This first come first serve method led to a rather confusing intermingling of the resulting spheres of influence. Each company had a number of zaribas scattered over a wide area, interspersed among the zaribas of other companies. A map depicting this would resemble a checkerboard of some twelve or so different colors, with the squares of different sizes and the number per color different also. Each sphere of influence had one main zariba of from two to three hundred armed men (half of whom were usually armed slaves taken from the peoples of the Bahr al-Ghazal), and a thousand or so personal slaves belonging to the personnel of the zariba.[37] There would be from four to six subsidiary zaribas scattered throughout the monopolized area. Each sphere of influence was linked through the headquarter zariba to Meshra al-Raq by a series of subsidiary zaribas of various sizes which secured the routes and supplied the expeditions travelling them. By far the greatest number of zaribas were involved in supplying such routes.[38] A bearer could only carry fifty pounds, so that without these supply depots the expeditions would be unable to transport a profitable amount of ivory and trade goods.

These subsidiary zaribas were under the command of *wakils* (agents) of the owners. Owing to the great difficulties in communication in the Bahr al-Ghazal, the wakils were on their own much of the time. The owners therefore needed to have confidence in the loyalty of their agents. Thus, these wakils were often personal slaves of the company owner's household in Khartoum, raised since childhood with his family. Relatives were also employed in such positions. In the very small zaribas, wakils were chosen as much for ability as for loyalty, and a wider variety of men headed these establishments (for example, converted slaves from the local communities or deserters from Sudanese regiments of the Egyptian army).

The functioning of the zariba system was scarcely less complex than its distribution and leadership. The individual zaribas were not only forts, they were communities as well, with a welter of relationships with the surrounding indigenous peoples. Each one surrounded itself with a community of the local people which was in a state of virtual vassalage to the zariba.[39] These people cultivated the land, supplying the zariba with food, and acted as bearers on the annual expeditions. In return, they were protected from the slave trade. Most wakils were quite insistent upon this latter point. Khalil, a wakil of a Turkish zariba owner, refused to allow the jallaba to purchase any of his zariba's people, in order to assure himself of future bearers and cultivators.[40] It was not unknown, however, for avaricious wakils in the more remote zaribas to sell orphans to jallaba for quick profits. All in all, a main zariba and its immediate subsidiaries could control an area of two hundred square miles with some twelve thousand associated vassals.

There were numerous rights and duties on both sides. A new type of political community came into being with the indigenous peoples being ruled by a caste of at least nominally Muslim traders and soldiers. By 1870, conditions had stabilized to the extent that many of the local peoples who had fled the earlier depredations of the Khartoumers were returning. Two thousand five hundred people returned to Ghattas, the Copt's main zariba in the north eastern Bahr al-Ghazal, alone.[41] The pagan peoples were organized under their own village headmen, who now had new powers vis-à-vis their fellow villagers because they were backed by the power of the Khartoumers. Some villages, at a considerable distance from their zariba were less effectively on their own. The headmen were responsible for maintaining order and assigning the tasks related to the traders. The Khartoumers found themselves forced to treat the remoter headmen with a certain amount of respect if they wanted his villagers to remain.[42]

The local people directly associated with the zaribas thus became partners of a sort with the Khartoumers. The bearers on an expedition had a right to a share of the proceeds and to protection. In all raids undertaken by an expedition, the bearers had a right to a portion of the booty. Moreover, in cattle raids, not only the actual participants, but all the associated headmen as well, received a share from the captured cattle. Nevertheless, all of these rights and duties were subordinated to the overiding concern of the Khartoumers of realizing a profit.

The pagan peoples were never treated as equals in this partnership. A striking example of this occurred during an expedition led by Abu Sumat, a former servant of Petherick who had gone into business for himself. During his absence, the pagan bearers complained that three of their number had been eaten by the local Azande confederates.[43] Although the Azande overseer was arrested, he was released upon Abu Sumat's return because the need for Azande cooperation in a planned raid was deemed more important than the rights of the bearers to protection. Nevertheless certain of the pagan peoples came to play an important part in the life of the zariba as trackers, interpreters and craftsmen. In the eastern Bahr al-Ghazal, the Bongo blacksmiths made the manacles and chains used in the slave trade, did minor repairs for the Khartoumers, and accompanied the expeditions to work the bars of trade copper into smaller, more valuable ornaments for the Azande trade.[44] Such individuals received better treatment than did their companions.

The Khartoumers were intimately involved in the problems of crime and punishment. The wakil adjudicated cases of murder and theft. The general rule was that the criminal was enslaved, often with his wife and children. During the pacification stage, whole villages were devastated, the women and children sold into slavery if the village refused to give up a criminal.[45] The harshness and severity of such matters of course varied from one wakil to the next. Some zariba owners, such as al-Zubayr himself, even claimed to be guided in the judicial decisions by the Shari'a.

There seems to have been little or no religious interaction between the Khartoumers and the indigenous pagans. There was no apparent proselytizing by and of the large numbers of 'ulama' jallaba wandering through the region. In general, there were only two ways in which people were brought into the fold of Islam. The first was through slavery, including the personal slaves and concubines of the Khartoumers themselves (this must be qualified by saying that many of the slave soldiers of the Khartoumers were actually free-born Azande who had volunteered for this job). The other avenue of conversion was by disappointed Azande dynasts who sought Khartoumer support for their cause by this means. The little interaction which did take place was imitative in nature. For example, some pagans, like Shol's husband, wore amulets similar to those made by the religious scholars of Dar Fur. Although he adopted the form, he did not quite grasp the content, and he was quite willing to substitute some German phrases supplied by Schweinfurth for verses from the Qur'an.[46] Moreover, some of the local headmen took to wearing clothes while dealing with the Khartoumers, which they promptly discarded afterwards. Although these incidents bear some resemblance to the process of popular Islamization noted elsewhere in Africa (e.g. Trimingham's observations in his *Islam in Ethiopia*), the process was cut short by the ultimate expulsion of the Muslim traders.

The Khartoumers themselves were mostly young men from the region between Berber and Khartoum, although the owners could be Egyptian Muslims, Copts, Sudanese or even Turks. Like the jallaba, the majority of the Khartoumer askar had fled the Nile valley to escape the ruinous taxation, and the insults of poverty. As Abu Sumat himself put it, "They were accustomed at home to carry mud, but here they carry a gun instead."[47] Although all found adventure, very few found fortunes amidst the hardships of life in the Bahr al-Ghazal.

The most numerous element among the Khartoumers were of course, the askar. These young men were hired on yearly contracts. They were paid roughly six pounds a month, from which they had to feed and clothe themselves. The pay was seldom in cash, usually being in the form of cloth, cattle, slaves and other goods. The askar did have some say in the proportion of each, however. These goods were bartered with the jallaba for the necessities of life. The most profitable undertakings, from their point of view, were the razzias, from which they received a third of the booty outright. Nevertheless, the askar were almost continuously in debt to the wakil, who overcharged them for the goods he sold them.[48] Their greatest hope for profit would be to have their slave booty marketed in their own behalf in Khartoum, for cash. From the numbers involved, this may have been the primary source for that part of the slave trade still transported down the Nile after Sir Samuel Baker's arrival. An additional source of revenue for the askar was to enroll their slaves as soldiers and so pocket their pay for themselves.

In this manner, up to one half of the zariba's armed force came to consist of slaves. These pagan, slave soldiers were not called askar. Rather, they were called *narakik* (elephant gun), *bazinear* and *farukh*. They were generally regarded as being the better troops, but most wakils avoided having too great a dependence upon them because they frequently deserted while the askar remained constant in their loyalty. On an expedition, the local troops acted as flankers, and scouts, the more difficult and dangerous tasks being assigned to them in general. The Islamization and arabization of these troops were imperfect at best. In addition to their military duties, they kept order among the pagan vassals of the zaribas, helped out at harvest time, and supervised the bearers while marching. Although strictly speaking slaves, they were allowed to marry, own their own land and even to acquire their own slaves.[49]

The askar married very quickly, soon acquiring families wherever they settled. At any one time, they usually had ten to twenty slaves on hand, the bulk of which were to be sold. Each askar had two or three personal slaves and some concubines who were not for immediate sale. Among these personal slaves, a small boy was always to be found who accompanied his master on expeditions as a gun bearer and, when grown, was signed on as a slave soldier. Other personal slaves would be used to grow food, but this practice was more common among wakils, resident jallaba, translators and other zariba officials than among the askar.

During their tour of duty in the Bahr al-Ghazal, the askar were under the constant threat of hunger and violent death. Food production in the region had been greatly decreased by the early depredations of the Khartoumers. The indigenous peoples had ceased to store food, attempting to consume what they produced as fast as possible, as usually occurs in areas under oppressive taxation or exploitation. Now, however, there was a large population of non-productive elements to be fed. Approximately fifty-five thousand askar, jallaba, concubines and children had to be supported by some one hundred and ninety-five thousand pagan cultivators. Consequently, there was widespread hunger every year prior to the harvest. The problem of hunger was compounded by the faulty distribution of the available food, and the disruption of cultivation caused by porter duties.

Violent death, while omnipresent as a threat, was relatively rare. Areas near the Dinka were constantly under the threat of attack in reprisal for cattle raids. Far into the 1860s the regions beyond the Rohl were still unpacified, and the Babuckers could still overrun and destroy isolated zaribas. As the ivory stores in Azande territories dried up, they too posed a threat to the Khartoumers who tried to penetrate farther in search of new ivory.

The next most numerous Muslim element in a zariba were the jallaba, either transient or resident. Although the jallaba came from every direction, they were generally Dongalawi or Ja'alyn by origin. Most, however, had emigrated from the Nile valley some time before and were residents of Dar Fur and Kordofan. The resident jallaba played an important role in the life of the zariba. In addition to being representatives of large slave trading firms, they were also active in the religious life of the zariba. They acted as *faqhis, imams, qadis, katibs* and in some cases ran Qur'an schools for the children of the askar and wakil. They were the representatives of Islam in the zaribas.

Islam, though pervasive, was not a significant motivating force for the zariba system. The zariba system, although an enterprise undertaken by Muslims, was not an Islamic movement like the state-building activities arising from the slave trade in other parts of the Sudan. Each company, even that of Ghattas the Copt, had a banner replete with crescent and verses from the Qur'an exhorting jihad against the unbelievers. These banners were regarded as talismans by the askar and were treated with respect. The feast of Ramadan was observed in the zaribas, and the Khartoumers in the Bahr al-Ghazal were regarded as more fanatical than their brethren elsewhere by the Europeans. A few in fact did believe they were involved in jihad. Nevertheless, this was more *esprit de corps* than religious fervor. The loudest prayers were said by the jallaba, not the askar; stills and alcohol were abundant; morality was not particularly lofty; syphilis common; belief in witchcraft widespread and no attempts at proselytizing were made.[51] Al-Zubayr himself said that the pagans there were not yet ready for Islam.[52]

IV. *Al-Zubayr's role in the zariba system*

This then was the zariba system which was assuming its final shape as al-Zubayr was entering the Bahr al-Ghazal. Al-Zubayr Pasha Rahma Mansur was born in 1831, attended a *maktub* school in Khartoum at age seven, married a cousin at age fifteen, and became a petty trader in the Nilotic Sudan. His family was neither rich nor poor. He first entered the Bahr al-Ghazal in 1856 by mistake while trying to dissuade his cousin from joining 'Ali Abu' Amuri's company. Al-Zubayr soon found himself a lowly askar, and he was treated poorly at first until he distinguished himself in combat. After saving 'Amuri's zariba from being overrun, al-Zubayr was made wakil with a promise of a ten percent share in the profits during 'Amuri's absence in Khartoum. Through hard work he was able to quadruple the expected profits. Preferring to strike out on his own, al-Zubayr refused a subsequent offer of a fifty percent partnership in the zariba. Al-Zubayr returned to Khartoum, bought trade goods, hired and armed some askar and together with several cousins began operations on his own in the Bahr al-Ghazal. He himself provides a lively account of his adventures in a series of interviews printed in the *Contemporary Review*, vol. 52 (1887 pp. 333-49; 568-85; 658-82).

By 1859 he had reached Azande territory, entering into a trade agreement with Tikima, a king of the Anunga branch of the Azande. Al-Zubayr received a daughter of Tikima as a wife. He then began buying criminals who he claimed were destined for the cooking pot, and proceeded to arm them. After amassing four hundred armed retainers in this fashion, Tikima became alarmed, and eventually forced al-Zubayr to flee. He fled to Dar Fartit and conquered the Kreish. Soon afterwards, he constructed his principal zariba, Daym Zubayr, near Delguana, the former entrepot of the Dar Fur ivory trade. At this time, al-Zubayr was just one trader among many. He was neither the richest nor the one with the most extensive territories. The one thing which did distinguish him from other merchants was that he reinvested a large percentage of his profits into guns and men.

During the late 1860s, the ivory trade in the Bahr al-Ghazal was faced with two crises in which al-Zubayr played an important role. The first of these was precipitated by the Egyptian government's attempts to halt the slave trade. This attempt was in two forms. The first was the closure of the White Nile. The second was through attempts to extend direct government control into the Bahr al-Ghazal. The second crisis which they faced sprang from the rapidly declining stores in Azande trading areas.

As ivory stores declined, tensions between the Khartoumers and the Azande increased. The former attempted pushes further south, and the latter attempted to resist these. As their expansion was thwarted, tensions arose among the Khartoumers themselves in the eastern Bahr al-Ghazal. Armed strife broke out between Abu Sumat and Sharifi, ostensibly over an escaped slave girl. A more plausible explanation might be found in Sharifi's resentment at Abu Sumat's bypassing and outflanking of his sphere of influence, thereby preempting much of the remaining area at what Sharifi felt to be his expense.

The Khartoumers had some success surmounting their problems with the northernmost Azande, by manipulating their dynastic struggles to their own benefit, and installing puppet rulers at the heads of some communities. The most successful of these endeavors was that of Abu Sumat, with his Azande protégé Surur (formerly Mbagahli), who had been a royal spearman of a hostile chief killed by Abu Sumat. Although Surur had been Arabised somewhat, his Islamization left much to be desired (e.g. he had far more than the canonical four wives). Nevertheless, he was given the use of forty askar, and controlled an area of seven hundred square miles virtually on his own. His Azande were to assemble upon command for raiding, hunting labor and portage. He even moved entire villages to act as supply depots. The local village headmen received shares of ivory and the burdens imposed upon them by the Khartoumers were lighter than those imposed upon others.

Al-Zubayr Pasha and the Zariba Based Slave Trade

Unfortunately for the Khartoumers, this process could not be repeated elsewhere in the eastern Bahr al-Ghazal. The next tier of Azande, that of the Ambomu, were more determined to resist the Khartoumers. During the closing years of the 1860s, various Azande leaders began attacking trading expeditions which sought to pass through their lands. More importantly, they began combining their forces to attack the Khartoumers, both in their zaribas and while on march.

The climax of this struggle was reached in 1870 when a large expedition of two thousand two hundred and fifty people from the combined forces of three zariba owners attempted to break through the Azande barrier. They attempted to sweep through Ndoromo's territory. He, however, had secretly accumulated an arsenal of firearms seized from overrun zaribas, together with instructors in their use in the form of Azande deserters from the Khartoumer forces. With his troop of armed men, Ndoromo inflicted a great defeat on the Khartoumers. One hundred and fifty askar were killed. Subsequently, the askar began refusing to enter Azande territory, claiming they had been hired to fight savages, not armed men. A similar, but less dramatic situation prevailed in the western Bahr al-Ghazal when the Anunga Azande expelled al-Zubayr earlier.

Al-Zubayr was able to provide solutions to both of these problems. As the Nile route was closed, he began to secure and organize the overland route through Dar Fur and Kordofan. He made Daym Zubayr into a vast entrepot and port of entry for the jallaba. All the jallaba entering and leaving the Bahr al-Ghazal passed through Daym Zubayr, and the jallaba caravans leaving the region passed through it also. Daym Zubayr also became the largest market place for slaves in the Bahr al-Ghazal, and grew into a small town with hundreds of huts and a large area of cultivated land. Al-Zubayr himself began to live in splendor. He had a virtual palace, replete with a richly-carpeted reception hall and chained lions.[53]

There were two factors which aided al-Zubayr in securing this route. The first was geographical. Daym Zubayr was astride the traditional jallaba trade routes, and located a few days march south of the Dar Fur frontier, providing a convenient resting place and assembly point for the caravans and individual jallaba. The second factor was al-Zubayr's relatively large military force. This was first used in pacifying the area around Daym Zubayr totally, and then the Dar Fur frontier, thus securing that portion of the trade route as well. His armed might also enabled al-Zubayr to make a favorable treaty in 1866 with the Rizqayat Arabs who controlled the deserts between Dar

Fur and Kordofan. By this treaty, he was able to guarantee safe passage for the jallaba merchants upon payment of an agreed toll.[54]

The jallaba prospered under this system. Shakka, a town in Rizqayat territory near the Dar Fartit frontier, grew into a large entrepot in its own right, as an assembly point for caravans entering the Bahr al-Ghazal. Here, the jallaba could also purchase trade and pack animals (which themselves were sold prior to leaving the Bahr al-Ghazal), and butter, a rare delicacy in the Bahr al-Ghazal. The majority of them were small merchants, who with one or two donkeyloads of trade goods managed a precarious living. Although the profits were good, the loss of a single donkey or the escape of a slave could spell disaster. The chief media of exchange were copper bars, calico, guns, cattle grain and luxury items (e.g. pipes). They catered to the everyday needs of the zariba personnel and their fellow jallaba as well. In 1870, a good year, over three thousand jallaba travelled through Daym Zubayr.[55]

A few years after the Rizqayat treaty, al-Zubayr was able to thwart the extension of direct government control into the region. A man named al-Hilali (or Bulali or Belali) was expelled from Dar Fur under mysterious circumstances. He then made his way to the Egyptian Sudan where he made extravagant claims to the copper rich region of Hofrat al-Nahhas, just north of Dar Fartit. He was given a number of Nizzam troops (Sudanese levies) and some irregular cavalry under the command of the Turkish zariba owner, Kuchuk Ali, and dispatched to the Bahr al-Ghazal to establish Egyptian control in the area. He immediately imposed a burdensome grain tax upon arrival in which more grain was consumed in delivering the tax than was actually demanded.

Al-Hilali's subsequent behavior was open to question. Kuchuk Ali, his erstwhile ally, soon died suddenly in mysterious circumstances, and al-Hilali seized his zariba before the heir could arrive. He then began making threats and confiscating other zaribas in the area one by one. The Khartoumers were alarmed and looked to al-Zubayr for guidance because he had the most troops in the immediate area. After desultory and inconclusive attempts at negotiations on both sides, al-Zubayr was compelled to fight and defeat al-Hilali after sending a letter to the governor of the Sudan complaining of al-Hilali's irregularities.

Ismail, the ruler of Egypt, soon realized that al-Zubayr had more troops on the spot than Egypt could afford to bring to bear and acceded gracefully to the *fait accompli*. Al-Zubayr was made a bey and appointed the governor of the Bahr al-Ghazal. The new title appears to have made little difference in al-Zubayr's relations with the other zariba owners, with the exception that he now found it easier to requisition troops from the other zariba owners for large scale ventures to their joint benefit.

Parallel to these political events, al-Zubayr continued to pursue his own trade, operating from some thirty zaribas. Soon after the defeat and death of al-Hilali, war broke out between al-Zubayr and Tikima. The immediate causes of the war are unclear but Tikima and his Anunga allies were defeated after a hard fought thirteen month campaign. As a consequence of the victory, he and the other Khartoumers were able to continue their expansion south as far as the Wele River. The Khartoumers were thus able to outflank the Amboru Azande. This too built up the prestige of al-Zubayr among the other Khartoumers. In 1872, he was to boast of making over twelve thousand pounds a month, disposing of tens of thousands of slaves annually, and possessing a private army of twelve thousand troops.

While al-Zubayr and his forces were involved in the Azande war, the Rizqayat broke their treaty with him and began pillaging the caravans crossing their territories. In one of these raids, several members of al-Zubayr's family were thought to have been killed. He demanded reparations from the Sultan of Dar Fur, the nominal overlord of Rizqayat. When he refused, al-Zubayr undertook to chastise them himself. He called upon the other zaribas for help and after another hard fought campaign he managed to defeat the Rizqayat despite his lack of cavalry. This placed Shakka too under his control, giving him an even greater grip upon the overland slave route. The defeated tribesmen appealed to their nominal suzerain for aid.

The new development was not unwelcomed by al-Zubayr, for he was inclined toward war with Dar Fur himself. In the east, the Egyptian government was consolidating its hold over Kordofan, thus posing a threat to the caravan routes through the desert. Moreover, the Egyptians themselves were contemplating the conquest of Dar Fur, which would have given them potential control of all the overland routes. The Sultan of Dar Fur began making threatening motions against al-Zubayr in response to the demands of the fugitive tribesmen and the unruly Furwa nobility suffering from the loss of Dar Fartit to al-Zubayr. The first step taken by the Sultan was to cut off all grain shipments to al-Zubayr's lands, shipments which were vital to the well being of the Khartoumers in the Bahr al-Ghazal. Al-Zubayr therefore called for reinforcements from the other zariba owners to launch an invasion.

The Sultan was the first to act, sending an army of forty thousand men against al-Zubayr's forces of five thousand men. Al-Zubayr crushed his opponents, his Azande levies eating many of the dead, thus further demoralizing the Furwa warriors. Two more huge armies were sent against them, and they too were defeated. The Egyptian government hastily prepared a small expeditionary force of its own, alarmed at the specter of Dar Fur too becoming part of al-Zubayr's growing domain. Al-Zubayr pressed his attacks across the Dar Fur frontier into Wada'i before returning to al-Fashir at the request of the Egyptian commandant. Unfortunately, dispute soon arose between al-Zubayr and the Egyptian commandant whom al-Zubayr suspected of trying to deprive him of the fruits of his victories.

Although the Egyptian government made him a pasha, al-Zubayr felt compelled, nevertheless, to travel to Cairo and plead his case personally before the Khedive. Al-Zubayr set out for Cairo in 1876 taking with him prodigious bribes for the Khedive and his pashas. Ismail was quick to take advantage of this windfall, politely informing the redoubtable conqueror of Dar Fur that he was to consider himself a permanent guest of the Khedive, never to return to the Sudan. Although his son Sulayman continued his father's aggressive policies in the southern Bahr al-Ghazal, the era of the slave traders was coming to a close. Under the leadership of Europeans like Gordon and Gessi, the Egyptian government began to make real progress toward extirpating the slave trade. Exploiting rivalries between the Khartoumers, arming the pagans and inciting the Rizqayat against the jallaba, Gessi was able to defeat, expel and massacre the Khartoumers and the jallaba. The zariba system was at an end.

Al-Zubayr, however, continued to live in secluded splendor in Cairo, remaining a power in his own right. He served with distinction in the Russo-Turkish war of 1878, adding further laurels to his military honors, and achieving the rank of general in the Egyptian army. Al-Zubayr had one more brush with history when Gordon was recalled to evacuate the Sudan after the outbreak of the Mahdist revolt in the Sudan. The two former enemies met and Gordon was impressed with al-Zubayr's iron will and tireless energy. Gordon became convinced that only al-Zubayr could stop the Mahdi. Gordon was even able to convince the pragmatic future Lord Cromer, but neither of the two Englishmen were able to convince their government to overlook al-Zubayr's bloody and notorious past. After a brief incarceration on Gibraltar for alleged dealings with the rebels in the Sudan, al-Zubayr was to spend the rest of his days in Cairo.

NOTES

1. As shown in the title page of H. C. Jackson's *Black Ivory and White: The Story of El-Zubeir Pasha Slaver and Sultan*, B. H. Blackwell, Oxford, 1913. This work is based on interviews with al-Zubayr conducted by the author and his predecessors.
2. Hake, A. E., "Zebehr, Slavery and the Sudan," *Illustrated London News*, vol. 84 (1884) p.462.
3. Slatin-Pasha, R., *Fire and Sword in the Sudan*, Harper & Brothers, New York, 1896, p.47; a colorful account of the author's adventures as governor of Dar Fur under Gordon and later as prisoner of the Mahdi. Contains many useful observations.
4. Jackson, H. C., *Black Ivory*, p.102.
5. Holt, P. M., *Modern History of the Sudan* (Oxford University Press), London, 1962. The best work on the Sudan as a whole.
6. Gray, R., *A History of the Southern Sudan 1839-1889*, Oxford University Press, e.g. p.45 and *in passim*. Gives a very good account of the evolution of the ivory and slave trade along the White Nile, and provides some material on the Bahr al-Ghazal as well.

    Schweinfurth, G., *The Heart of Africa: Three Years' Travel in the Unexplored Regions of Central Africa*, Harper & Brothers, New York, 1874, vol. 2, p.55, 396, vol. 1, *in passim*. By far the best and most detailed first person account of the Bahr al-Ghazal during the heyday of the zariba system. Unfortunately, he had a peculiar blind spot as to the actual capture of slaves, an oversight extending to his personal servants who were caught red handed attempting to smuggle fifteen slaves past the river patrol on his return.
7. Schweinfurth, G., *The Heart*, vol. 1, p.156.
8. For more information on the Azande see: Evans Pritchard, E. E., *The Azande* (Oxford University Press), 1961, and Thuriaux-Hennebert, A., *Les Zande dans l'Histoire du Bahr al-Ghazal et de l'Equitoria*, Editions de l'Institut de Sociologie de l'Université Libre de Bruxelles, 1964.
9. Evans-Pritchard, E. E., *The Azande*, pp. 51-2.
10. Schweinfurth, G., *The Heart* vol. 2, p.50.
11. Baxter, P. T. W., Butt, Audrey, "The Azande and related People," *Ethnographic Survey of Africa*, ed. Daryl Ford, part IX, East Central Africa, p.51. Contains the most thorough account of slavery within Azande society.
12. Arkell, A. J., *A History of the Sudan from Earliest Times to 1821*, University of London, 1955. See pages 213-24 for Keira dynasty, the contemporary of al-Zubayr.
13. Nachtigal, G., *Sahara and Sudan*, vol. iv. Hurst & Co., London, 1971, p.294. Provides a detailed account of the position of slaves in the Dar Fur state prior to al-Zubayr's conquest.
14. *Ibid.*, p.326.
15. El Tounsy, Mohammad ibn Omar, *Voyage au Ouddday*, Chez Benjamin Duprat, Paris, 1855, p.65. A lively, anecdotal travel account which nevertheless contains useful information.
16. For examples, see Nachtigal, *Sahara and Sudan*, p.256, and el-Tounsy, *Voyage*, pp. 253-4.
17. El-Tounsy, *Voyage*, pp. 434-5.
18. O'Fahey, R. S., "Slavery and the Slave Trade in Dar Fur," *Journal of African History*, XIV, I (1973), pp. 30-1.
19. Nachtigal, G., *Sahara and Sudan*, p.355.
20. *Ibid.*, p.359.
21. Slatin-Pasha, R., *Fire*, p.47; Nachtigal, G., *Sahara and Sudan*, p.365.

22. Nachtigal, *Sahara and Sudan*, pp. 355-6.
23. El-Tounsy, *Voyage*, p. 486. For a more detailed account of these raids see O'Fahey's article mentioned above.
24. Nachtigal, *Sahara and Sudan*, p.365.
25. *Ibid.*, p.354.
26. Baer, Gabriel, *Studies in the Social History of Egypt*, University of Chicago Press, 1969, p.169.
27. *Ibid.*, p.165.
28. For a more detailed account of events along the Nile see Gray's *A History*.
29. Petherick, J., *Egypt, the Sudan and Central Africa*, William Blackwood & Sons, London, 1861, p.368. Although not as systematic as some other observers, as a principal actor in these events his testimony is still valuable.
30. *Ibid.*, pp. 418-19.
31. Thuriaux-Hennebert, *Les Zande*, p.20.
32. *Ibid.*, p.20.
33. Schweinfurth, *The Heart*, vol. 1, p.343, for example.
34. *Ibid.*, vol. 2, p.366.
35. *Ibid.*, vol. 2, p.37, p.56.
36. *Ibid.*, vol. 2, p.484.
37. *Ibid.*, vol. 1, p.175.
38. *Ibid.*, vol. 2, p.305.
39. *Ibid.*, vol. 2, p.47.
40. *Ibid.*, vol. 1, p.306.
41. *Ibid.*, vol. 2, p.270.
42. *Ibid.*, vol. 1, p.238.
43. *Ibid.*, vol. 1, pp.220-2.
44. *Ibid.*, vol. 1, p.280, p.485.
45. Jackson, *Black Ivory*, p.49.
46. Schweinfurth, *The Heart*, vol. 1, pp. 141-2.
47. *Ibid.*, vol. 1, pp. 351-2.
48. *Ibid.*, vol. 1, p.176.
49. *Ibid.*, vol. 2, p.421.
50. *Ibid.*, vol. 2, p.427, p.322
51. *Ibid.*, vol. 2, p.322.
52. Shaw, F. L., "The Story of Zebehr Pasha as Told by Himself," *Contemporary Review*, vol. 252 (1887), pp. 568-85.
53. Schweinfurth, *The Heart*, vol. 1, p.341.
54. Jackson, *Black Ivory*, p.26.
55. Schweinfurth, *The Heart*, vol. 2, p.357.
56. Schweinfurth, *The Heart*, vol. 2 p.266; Slatin Pasha, *Fire*, pp.48-9; Jackson, *Black Ivory*, p.33-43; Nachtigal, *Sahara and Sudan*, pp. 316-17. All four provide slightly different versions of the event.

VII

The Ethiopian Slave Trade and its Relation to the Islamic World

Mordechai Abir

Ethiopia's traditional exports, gold, ivory, musk, incense and slaves, were known to the people of the Mediterranean civilization from ancient times. Colonies of foreign merchants, Greek, Egyptian, Arab and possibly Indian, prospered on the Ethiopian coast as early as the first millenium B.C. while caravans originating in Egypt reached the Ethiopian plateau still earlier. Most of Ethiopia's luxury products were produced in the southern and western part of the plateau, and caravan trade between these areas and the north must have developed at an early date. To some extent the growth and development of the city-states in northern Ethiopia and later of the Axumite empire are due to their having been centres of caravan trade and to their domination of the routes connecting the coast and the interior.

The Arab trading communities on the Ethiopian coast adopted Islam shortly after its inception in Arabia in the seventh century. Yet, the expansion of Islam in the north was slow at first, mainly because of Christian political hegemony, accompanied by the unique local culture. The situation in the south was, however, very different. At first, the Muslim trading communities of the coast joined forces with immigrants from southern Arabia to establish new strongholds on the Harari plateau. This important step facilitated the development of caravan trade to the southern and southwestern parts of the plateau, the sources of Ethiopia's luxury trade. It also served as a springboard for the expansion of Islam among the ruling classes of the multitude of weakly-organized Cushitic Sidama principalities which lacked a clear cultural orientation.

Following the rise of the new Solomonic dynasty in 1270, the expansionism of the Christian kingdom was directed towards the rich southern and southwestern provinces. It was not long before the politico-commercial interests of the new Solomonic dynasty clashed with the interests of the Muslim principalities of the southeastern part of the Horn of Africa and their Cushitic satellites in central and southern Ethiopia. Due primarily to the continuous successes of the Christians, this rivalry gradually adopted the characteristics of a religious war. During the fifteenth century, individual Muslims from Arabia and elsewhere joined the unofficial Jihad against the Christian kingdom. Moreover, in addition to the tacit support of the mamelukes of Egypt, some rulers of Yemen and the Hijaz gave active help to the Muslim leaders in the Horn. Religious motivation was probably strengthened, *inter alia*, by the need to ensure the uninterrupted flow of Ethiopian trade and slaves to the Yemeni ports. Young Ethiopian female slaves were in high demand in the markets of the Muslim world, but the supply of young Ethiopian males was even more important to the Arabian rulers, whose power depended on private armies composed largely of Ethiopian slaves.[1]

The relations between the Muslim world and the Horn of Africa underwent a dramatic change in the sixteenth century. As a result of the appearance of the Portuguese in the region, followed by the Ottomans and the temporary conquest of Christian Ethiopia by the coastal Muslim elements, tens of thousands of slaves, it is claimed, were exported from the plateau following the Muslim victories. However, the inclusion of the countries of the Red Sea Basin within the Ottoman Empire had a more permanent impact on the Horn. New horizons were opened for Ethiopian trade in general and for the exportation of "red" Ethiopian slaves in particular. In addition to the traditional markets in Arabia, Egypt and the Indian Ocean, these new markets triggered an insatiable demand for Ethiopian slave girls and male slaves considered "prime merchandise". The former were renowned for their beauty and sexual temperament, and the latter, for their honesty and belligerent character. It is impossible to estimate the average number of slaves exported annually from Ethiopia. Yet, it could be safely said that, excluding periods of unusual circumstances, several thousand slaves, at least the majority of whom were young females and males, were sent annually from Ethiopia to Muslim countries by way of Sennar in Sudan or the ports of Massawa, Zayla and Berbera. However, Abyssinian (Ethiopian) slaves were not only shipped to the markets of the Ottoman Empire, but to Persia, India and the Far East.[2]

The decline of Muslim power in the Horn of Africa, beginning at the end of the sixteenth century, only fostered closer relations between Ethiopia and its Muslim neighbours, especially in the field of trade. Notwithstanding their bitter experience with the Jesuit missionaries, Ethiopian kings in the seventeenth century attempted to expand trade relations with the Dutch in Batavia and the British authorities in India, not to mention with the Ottoman Empire. Special missions were sent to Persia and other far away countries. More important, *wakils* (agents, who were Ethiopian ex-slaves or trusted servants of merchants or rulers) of the Ethiopian "Emperors" could be found in every important trading centre in Arabia, Egypt and the Persian Gulf.

Thereafter, many Ethiopians were to be found in Constantinople and other major centres of the Ottoman Empire, in Persia and India, holding in some instances exceedingly important positions. Emancipated *Habasha* joined the ranks of the *Jabartis* and some engaged in theological studies in the Jabarti college (*riwak*) of al-Azhar, in al-Medina and in Damascus. A few even rose to prominence in the world of Islamic learning. Others excelled in government service, society and above all in trade. After many generations of intermarriage with Ethiopian slave-girls, a large segment of the population of Hijaz, Yemen, Southern Arabia and the Persian Gulf possessed Ethiopian blood, and Ethiopian customs somewhat influenced the mannerisms of these areas.[3] This, however, was not a one-sided affair, and there was strong interaction between the Muslim world and the Horn of Africa, primarily through the slave trade.

Emancipated Habasha, as well as Ethiopians who had grown up and were educated in the Arab provinces, returned to the Horn and strengthened Islam and its expansion in the coastal areas, the North and Harari. Others became the backbone of Ethiopian trade, especially the caravan trade, which traversed the plateau from North to South and from East to West. These caravans later became the primary vehicle for the peaceful expansion of Islam throughout the plateau and into the most remote areas. This development stimulated in turn the gradual Islamization of parts of the Cushitic Sidama agriculturalists but, more important, of Galla pastoralists, whose migration to the plateau, starting in the sixteenth century, was to change the demographic map and the politics of the region in the ensuing centuries.

The reappearance of Europeans in the Red Sea area, as well as the spread of the coffee-drinking habit from the Muslim countries to Europe in the seventeenth century, also poured new blood into the veins of the Red Sea trade. Because the Europeans had little to offer beyond the traditional wares imported from southeast Asia, they paid handsomely for local merchandise, principally with silver and gold coins. Such transactions had a thoroughly positive effect on trade in the region.[4]

The revival of the Red Sea trade had an immediate effect on

Ethiopian trade in general and on the slave trade in particular. Demand for slaves was temporarily met by the numerous slaves reaching the markets of the plateau; these were the victims of incessant wars, caused by the decline of the power of the central authorities. This decline of law, order and authority created a state of insecurity that diminished commercial activity, particularly the caravan trade, and invariably such a situation eventually led to complete anarchy and the stagnation of the plateau's economy and trade. The rapid decline of the Ottoman Empire, during the close of the seventeenth century and the beginning of the eighteenth century, also exerted a strong adverse effect on Ethiopian trade in general, the slave trade included.[5]

As elsewhere, slavery as an institution had existed in Ethiopia from time immemorial and slavery and slaves could be considered to have been an integral and important part of Ethiopian society and economy. It was not an unknown phenomenon among the pastoralists to adopt young slaves, captured in warfare or purchased, into the clan or tribe in order to strenghten its position. Among the sedentary agriculturalists, slaves could be found in every household that could afford one. Slaves, especially those belonging to the military-traditional nobility, were used as field-hands or to perform manual work around the house. Moreover, the use of slaves in private armies, and as the bodyguards of war-lords, was not uncommon.

The biggest slave owner in Ethiopia was the "King of Kings". In addition to slave labour utilized in the extensive crown properties, hundreds of slaves were used to perform all the manual labour in and around the palace. Many slaves became important functionaries in the palace and some gained tremendous influence. The royal bodyguard, which played an important role in the history of the country, was partly composed of slaves; its importance and strength did, however, fluctuate according to circumstances and times.[6] It is evident, in short, that the life of the slaves in Ethiopia in general could be considered happier and more secure than that of Ethiopia's lower classes. Although slaves were considered to be at the bottom of the social ladder, the average serf (*gabar*), for instance, was cruelly exploited, had no security of life and property and was not even assured of minimal subsistence. The slaves, on the other hand, as the property of their masters, were protected by them and were ensured of the household food.

Ethiopian society, composed of ruler-aristocrats, soldiers, clergymen and agriculturalists, always looked down upon trade as a profession and the people engaged in it (this did not include everyday intercommunal activities). Possibly because they were excluded from the ruling society and possibly because of their better relations with the Muslim world, Ethiopian Jabartis[7] gained a near-monopoly over trade in the highlands. They also had an important edge over the handful of Christians who engaged in medium or large-scale trade because Christians were, at least theoretically, forbidden by ecclesiastical law from indulging in the slave trade (although not from possessing slaves). Since slaves were the most common "commodity" in the markets of the interior and brought handsome profits on the coast or in nearby countries, Muslim merchants who were not inhibited from trading in slaves, were in a better bargaining position in those markets and were more enthusiastically welcomed by the local inhabitants.[8] Ironically, because of the service they performed and the taxes they paid to their connections abroad, the Jabartis were also preferred by the Christian lords. Consequently, Ethiopia's trade, and especially its caravan trade, was monopolized by Muslims, a fact that was to play a most important role in the future of the country.[9]

The revival of Islam in the Arabian peninsula, during the second half of the eighteenth century, had an immediate impact on the opposite coast of the Red Sea. This period of renewed Islamic zeal coincided with a period of growing frustration among the Galla chiefs of the north who found themselves repeatedly rejected and despised by the Christian semiticized society. Paradoxically, the reappearance of Christian power and merchants in the Red Sea, in the latter part of the eighteenth century, served as another stimulus to the expansion of Islam through trade. The Anglo-French rivalry, the cheap European manufactured goods, the missionaries and political missions which introduced more cash and many more firearms to the region, paved the way for and accelerated the spread of the caravan trade throughout the Ethiopian plateau. The substantial growth in the demand for Ethiopian merchandise and slaves encouraged Muslim merchants from Arabia, Sudan, and the Ethiopian and Somali coasts to penetrate deeper and deeper into the interior. This time, the trade caravans were accompanied by zealous *'ulama'* who were determined to spread the teaching of Islam among the heathens. Intentionally, or unintentionally, the numerous caravans and merchants arriving from the coast also sparked wars aimed at gaining control over the sources of trade, its centres and the trade routes. Ethiopia's exotic products were still welcomed on the coast, but, as the demand for "red" Ethiopian slaves grew by leaps and bounds in the markets of the Muslim world, slaves received the highest priority.

The Caucasus, the traditional source of the best grade female and male slaves for the Muslim world, was finally conquered by the

Russians at the end of the eighteenth century and, as a result, this source dried up. Thus, the demand and the value of Abyssinian slaves increased substantially. Due to political developments in nearby countries and especially in Arabia, more Ethiopian slaves were needed for the private armies of local rulers, not to mention the demand resulting from the new prosperity in the region. Partly because of European activity and partly because of the innovations and better security established by Muhammad Ali, the ruler of Egypt, the nineteenth century economic revival in the Red Sea Basin caused a substantial expansion of the *Hajj* caravans. Consequently, the demand for slaves, especially of a better grade, on the markets of Hijaz, Egypt and Yemen became nearly insatiable. Finally, due to British intervention, the attention of many slave merchants from the Persian Gulf and southern Arabia was diverted from East Africa to the Ethiopian markets.[10]

Although the "red" (so called because of their light brownish colour) Ethiopian slaves (Habasha) were generally classified as "Enarean" (after a principality-kingdom in southwestern Ethiopia) or "Guraguen" (after a district in south Ethiopia beyond Showa), these slaves were not Ethiopians in the true sense, nor were they Enarean or Guraguen. With few exceptions, slavers were careful not to purchase Christian-Amhara or Tigrean slaves, nor did they purchase Muslim ones. Caravans going to northern Ethiopia brought, from the southwest, slaves belonging to the multitude of pagan Galla tribes or animist Sidama (southern) or Agew (northern) Cushitic peoples. These were called "Enarean" slaves, only because Enarea was formerly the centre of commerce and especially of the slave trade in the southwest and was still an important trading centre in the nineteenth century.[11] A good number of Negroid (*Shanqalla*) slaves from peripheral areas were also purchased by the northern caravans, but these always remained in Ethiopia and served as plantation and field hands and performed all the hard manual labour in the household of the wealthy farmers and the nobility.

Ethiopian slaves reaching the markets of Yemen and the Persian Gulf by way of the southern Dankali (Afar) ports, Zayla and Berbera, were commonly called Guraguen. This name was used because Gurague was historically a centre of the slave trade in the south. In the nineteenth century, most of the slave caravans coming from the south still reached markets in Gurague or marched through Gurague to markets in southern Showa. Again, the true origin of the slaves was basically the multitude of pagan Galla tribes and Sidama Cushitic sedentary peoples in the southern plateau.[12] The majority of the so-called Enarean and Guraguen slaves were youngsters up to the age of sixteen. The most favoured were young girls, followed by boys in their early teens. However, caravan merchants also carried with them older slaves who fetched a lower price, since they were considered beyond the training age and suitable only for manual labour.

A clear distinction must be made between Ethiopian-Jabarti merchants and the Jalaba of the Sudan, the Dankali, Somali and Arab merchants who participated in the long-range caravan trade. The Jabarti merchants, being Ethiopian Muslims, had the freedom of the whole country, had good contacts throughout the plateau and therefore had a distinct advantage over the foreign merchants. As long as they refrained from kidnapping or acquiring slaves belonging to the peoples with whom they dealt or through whose countries they passed, the fact that they dealt in human flesh was not a hindrance, but rather an advantage. Naturally, they were always targets for extortion and their safety depended on their wits, number and on the goodwill of the population; at best, they were repeatedly forced to pay numerous taxes and dues along the road.[13] Nevertheless, taking this into consideration, they, or their masters, were handsomely rewarded when they reached the markets in the north or the coast with their merchandise.

Because the demand for slaves during the first half of the nineteenth century could no longer keep pace with the supply, the Jabarti caravans penetrated further than ever before into the interior. Merchants of consequence would stay for an entire "season" in an important market-village (*mander*) allotted to them by the local ruler or the population, and in some instances, they remained in these villages for a longer period in order to exchange all their merchandise for slaves and other luxury products. Only rarely did the merchants join with local adventurers to cross the boundaries of the southwestern and western principalities in order to participate in slave raiding among Negroid elements and peripheral disorganized Cushitic peoples. In most cases, they patiently awaited the arrival of the caravans from the surrounding areas, which descended upon the village-markets in order to trade with, or to join, the long-range caravan merchants.[14]

The expansion of the Ethiopian trade, beginning at the turn of the eighteenth century, gave rise to a new social phenomenon – a class of Galla merchants satisfied with small-scale trade and quick return, usually travelling between the more remote markets and the larger markets in the south and southwest. The services of such merchants, as well as those of the middlemen in every important market, were essential to the substantial expansion of Ethiopian trade and especially of the slave trade in the nineteenth century.[15]

In addition to authentic Jabartis many merchants who travelled into the interior with the Jabarti caravans were ex-slaves, emancipated by their Muslim owner, who traded on their own account or who were the agents (wakil) of their ex-master. Their knowledge of the country, its language, customs and sometimes of its people was an important advantage, and contributed to their success. These ex-slaves, the new Muslims and the *'alims* (Muslim scholars) who travelled with the caravans from Arabia played a most important role in the dispersion of Islam among the Galla and the pagan Cushitic agriculturalists of the plateau, and in the transformation of the traditional societies in western and southern Ethiopia.

Notwithstanding the impact of the Jabarti merchants on the culture, economics and politics of the plateau, Islamization was their most important long range effect. The Jabarti merchants and their caravans provided the main vehicle through which Islam and cultural influences were introduced to the most remote parts of the plateau. Directly, or indirectly, they were also responsible for substantial changes in the socio-economic spheres. They contributed, for instance, to the transformation of the majority of Galla society from pastoralism to agriculturalism. In the area of the Gibe river in southwestern Ethiopia, moreover, the Jabarti merchants and a handful of Arab 'alims who arrived in their caravans were no doubt a significant factor in the formation of Galla monarchies.[16] This political-social framework was a revolutionary change from the traditional Galla social organization which was based on the tribal and the age group system. The introduction of small quantities of firearms into the south and southwest by the Jabartis was no doubt an important factor in the struggle for power in the plateau and for control over the trade centres and routes.

Foreign Muslim merchants, Sudanese Jalaba, Dankalis, Arabs and Somalis were prominent in Ethiopian commerce and actively participated in its caravan and slave trade. Although generally not permitted beyond the major markets on the peripheries of the plateau, their impact on the emergence of trade, cultural, social and political changes in the Horn of Africa should not be underestimated. Some Jalaba merchants obtained Ethiopian luxury merchandise and slaves directly by travelling the dangerous routes to the edge of Wollega or as far as the border of Kaffa in the west.[17] However, these were the exception. The majority of the Sudanese merchants reached Ethiopia's capital, Gondar, and other important markets in the north by way of

The Ethiopian Slave Trade

Massawa or of Sennar and Gallabat. Here the Jalaba lived and mingled with their Jabarti coreligionists. Here they acquired Ethiopian merchandise, including approximately one thousand slaves annually from caravan merchants arriving from the south or from the greater resident merchants whose wakils accompanied the long-range caravans.[18] Because their time of residence in Gondar and nearby centres was prolonged, their religious, cultural and political influence was an important factor in developments in the north. On the return leg of their journey, they were generally accompanied by pilgrims, Jabarti-Christian merchants and others who disposed of their merchandise in the major Sudanese markets or in Egypt, thus serving as an important link between the latter country and Ethiopia.

The trade route to Massawa by way of Wello or northern Ethiopia was virtually monopolized by Jabarti highlanders or by coastal elements who lived in and around the port of Massawa. These merchants and the wakils of Arab or Ethiopian merchants formed many caravans and were extremely active in the trade with the interior. The Massawa route was considered the most important outlet for the Ethiopian trade. It was estimated that in the nineteenth century some two to three thousand Ethiopian slaves were shipped in a normal year from Massawa and nearby ports to Arabia and Egypt.[19] Disregarding the social and commercial impact of the foreign merchants and 'ulama' who reached the heart of Ethiopia by this route, it may be said that the Islamic influences generated by the revivalist movement in Arabia, starting in the eighteenth century, found their way to Ethiopia mainly through the Massawa route and to a lesser degree through Sudan and Gondar. The mass Islamization of the Galla of northern Ethiopia and later of the southwest could be attributed to the activities of "missionary" merchants, who penetrated the plateau from this direction. Their important cultural-political impact was observed by many western travellers who reached Ethiopia in the nineteenth century and was even mentioned in the royal chronicles of Ethiopia.[20] In any case, slaves were the major catalyst for the expansion of the caravan trade. Indirectly, they paid for the imported European merchandise needed by the northern aristocracy to build its power and for the firearms which provided an important advantage to the Christian rulers over their Muslim Galla rivals.

The rise of the kingdom of Showa in central Ethiopia, starting at the end of the eighteenth century, played an important role in changing the pattern of trade of southern Ethiopia. As a result, it made an outstanding contribution to the political change in the region and to the future of Ethiopia in general. Once they had consolidated their position in Showa-proper, the Showan rulers, motivated to a large extent by the wish to control the sources of Ethiopia's trade, major markets and trade routes, directed their expansionism particularly towards the south and southwest. In turn, as soon as they had established their hegemony in the area they benefited greatly from trade. Caravans reaching Showa's southern markets brought gold, ivory and musk, which fell within the framework of royal monopolies, as well as an assortment of other goods and above all slaves.

The expansion of the Showan kingdom prevented Somali and Harari merchants from reaching the south.[21] Caravans coming from the southern Somali coast never travelled beyond the rift valley lakes,[22] while the more important merchants of the north Somali coast and Harar were no longer able directly to tap the trade of southern Ethiopia. Therefore, the amir of Harar found it prudent to reach an agreement with the Showan rulers which enabled his subjects, as well as merchants, to live and trade in the market-villages on the borders of Showa. Showan Jabartis and the king's wakils were now officially permitted to travel to the port of Zayla and to the annual market at Berbera by way of Harar.[23] Thus, it is estimated that during the nineteenth century more than two thousand slaves were shipped annually from the northern Somali coast to the Persian Gulf. The British conquest of Aden in 1839 did not hinder this branch of the Ethiopian slave trade, but rather caused its expansion. In an attempt to purchase food for their garrison, gain the goodwill of the inhabitants of the opposite coast and to reach the kingdom of Showa, the British in Aden became the source of cash, manufactured goods and firearms, all of which facilitated an expansion in the volume of trade by the southern routes.

Encouraged by the revival of the Red Sea trade and the developments in the plateau, Afar (Dankali) merchants built up, from the end of the eighteenth century, a direct route from their petty coastal sultanates (mainly Tajura) to Showa and Wello which successfully competed with the ancient Zayla-Harar route. Salt was always in demand on the plateau; therefore, the salt deposits located in the southern Afar coast undoubtedly stimulated this development. Salt from this source and the manufactured goods acquired in Berbera or the Yemeni ports, were later bartered in the markets of eastern Showa, mainly against slaves. The volume of the Afar slave trade in the nineteenth century was between one thousand and two thousand in normal years.[24] Very rarely did Dankali merchants travel to Hijaz and Egypt. In most cases, they sold their slaves either in Tajura or Berbera or in the Yemeni ports, preferably Mukha. Strangely enough the Afar slave route and slave caravans assisted European penetration into Ethiopia's heartland, and thus it may have seemed to undermine the interests of the Afars themselves. In effect, cash and trade goods obtained from the Europeans helped the Afar merchants to consolidate and expand their slave trade irrespective of British protest.

Keenly aware of the benefits of the development of trade in their kingdom, the Showan kings also realized that it would be foolhardy, if not dangerous, to allow foreign Muslim merchants to traverse their country or travel freely in it while their Galla, Sidama and Amhara subjects, many of them Muslims or animists, were still not fully integrated into the kingdom. Hence, coastal and Harari merchants were rarely allowed to travel beyond the kingdom's eastern markets, while merchants coming from the south were generally not permitted to travel to the coast. Consequently, Showa's market-villages became a beehive of activity and many stories circulated about the bulging treasuries of the ruler of Showa. While the royal monopoly on luxury items such as gold, ivory and musk further enriched the rulers, the right of pre-emption which the Showan kings preserved concerning incoming slaves provided suitable manpower for their bodyguards, for the cultivation of their estates and for their households.[25] But the cultural and social impact of the foreign Muslim merchants here was less noticeable than in the north.

The flourishing trade of their country was the source of quantities of firearms, which greatly contributed to the success of the Showan army. In fact, coastal merchants were encouraged to bring firearms to Showa, and the Europeans, who were first to reach this kingdom in the nineteenth century, soon realized that the presents that pleased the rulers above anything else were such weapons. The Showan rulers, unknowingly at first, even exploited the Anglo-French rivalry to strengthen further their position by acquiring from their visitors more modern firearms and trade goods. The firearms thus accumulated enabled the Showan dynasty to become the most powerful and stable political entity in the Ethiopian plateau, in the first half of the nineteenth century.[26] As a result, Showa attracted still more merchants and trade and continued to prosper. Slaves were undoubtedly the backbone of the Showan trade and the main reason for its success. Even the British, who tried to suppress the slave trade in this period, soon realized that Showa's kings, as well as the coastal population, were hostile to any attempt to tamper with this trade.[27]

Although it greatly accelerated the Islamization in the plateau and facilitated Islamic propagation, the revival of Muslim caravan and slave trade beginning in the eighteenth century, was either insufficient in itself, or did not last sufficiently long to create a true cultural and socio-political upheaval. New centres of learning did not emerge in the Horn, nor did old ones, such as the one in Harar, begin to flourish. The expansion of trade did not produce a Jabarti aristocracy or middle class, since Muslim merchants and landowners were on the whole not permitted to integrate themselves into the traditional society or ruling classes. Despite their new power and wealth the Jabartis were still considered inferior or even despised by the non-Muslim population.

The rapid increase in caravan trade based primarily on slaves throughout the plateau, no doubt enhanced the considerable expansion of Islamization, especially among the Galla. The northern Muslim Galla rulers played an increasingly important role in the political and social changes which occurred in the region. Nonetheless, as soon as they realized that they were unacceptable to the traditional semiticized society, they became determined to destroy the framework of the Christian kingdom. Hence, the fusion of Galla frustration, Islamic zeal and the ambitions of Muhammad Ali in the first decades of the nineteenth century nearly changed the history of the Horn.

The reaction of the Christian semiticized population to Galla-Muslim predominance and the revival of the Christian kingdom were made possible through the renewed activities of western powers in the region and through the quantities of firearms that the Christian warlords were able to acquire. Ironically, these weapons, utilized to counterbalance the superiority of the Galla cavalry, were acquired with revenues from the slave trade and through the activities of Muslim merchants. The export by the Jabarti, Jalaba, Afar, Somali and Arab merchants of some seven to eight thousand slaves from Ethiopia in normal years was the source of new wealth for the ruling classes in Ethiopia and indirectly paid for the imported luxuries they consumed. Unwillingly, these merchants made an important contribution to the reestablishment of the hegemony of the Christian semiticized element within the framework of the heterogeneous Ethiopian society, as well as to the emergence of the new united Christian kingdom. Although this new framework adopted the traditional foundations of the Solomonic kingdom and its Christian orientation, the fact remained that a good part of its inhabitants were now Muslim. This factor, which had influenced the character of the kingdom of Showa in the first half of the nineteenth century, continues to influence Ethiopia's society, politics and orientation to the present day and is a major factor in the Erithrean secessionist movement and the development of the Ethiopian revolution.

NOTES

1. Francisco Alvarez, *The Prester John of the Indies* (rev. and ed. C.F. Beckingham and G.W.B. Huntingford), Cambridge University Press 1961 (The Hakluyt Society, series II, Vol. CXIV), Vol. II, pp. 205, 408, 455; Ibn Fadl Allah al-Umari, *Masalik al-Absar* (trans. Gaudefroy-Demombynes), 1927, pp. 15-17; G. Viet, "Les Relations Egypto-Abyssines sous les sultans Mamlouks", *Bulletin de l'association des amis des Eglises et de l'art Coptes*, Le Caire 1938, pp. 115-40; John Winter Jones (ed.), *The Travels of Ludovico di Varthema*, Hakluyt Society 1863, pp. 64-4, 83-4, 86.
2. *Purchas His Pilgrims*, Hakluyt Society, Glasgow, 1905-1907, Vols. III, IV, on Europeans in Red Sea end of 16th century and beginning of 17th century; *Ibid.*, Vol. III, p.459; R. B. Serjeant, *The Portuguese off the South Arabian Coast*, Oxford 1963, pp. 114-29; R. R. Madden, *Travels in Turkey, Egypt, Nubia and Palestine in 1824-1827*, London 1829, Vol. I, p.6; C. Beccari, *Rerum Aethiopicarum scriptores occidentales inediti a saeculo XVI ad XIX*, Rome 1914, Vol. XIII, pp. 36-55, 134-5; J. Lodulphus, *A New History of Ethiopia*, London 1864, pp. 231, 337, 397; R. Basset, "Études sur l'histoire d'Éthiopie", *Journal Asiatique*, 1881, ser, 7, 17 and 18, 292-3; Thevenot, *The Travels of Monsieur de Thevenot*, London 1687, Vol. I, p.238; A. Kammerer, *La Mer Rouge, l'Abyssinie et l'Arabie depuis l'Antiquité. Essai d'histoire et de géographie historique*, Cairo 1949, pp. 422-3, 426.
3. J. L. Burckhardt, *Travels in Arabia*, London 1829, reprinted Frank Cass, 1968, pp. 180, 182, 186-8; Ministère des Affaires Etrangères - Correspondance Commerciale (et Consulaire), Djeddah, Vol. I. Fresnel, p.3, 1840; Bibliotèque Nationale Paris - d'Abbadie papers. Catalogue France Nouvelle Acquisition No. 21301, p. 150; India Office - Bombay Proceedings. Range Series 385, Vol. 49, p.3340, Dr. Finlay, October 1823; E. Combes et M. Tamisier, *Voyage en Abyssinie*, Paris 1838, Vol. I, p.72.
4. M. Abir, *Ethiopia and the Horn of Africa*. A chapter in R. Gray (ed.), *The Cambridge History of Africa*, Vol. 4, Cambridge 1975, pp. 550-1; Viscount G. Valentia, *Voyages and Travels in India, Ceylon, the Red Sea, Abyssinia and Egypt in the Years 1802, 1803, 1804, 1805 and 1806*, London 1809, Vol. III, p.268; J. de la Roque, "An account of the captivity of Sir Henry Middleton at Mokha by the Turks in the year 1612", in *A Voyage to Arabia Felix . . . in the Years 1708, 1709, 1710, 1711, 1712 and 1713*, London 1732, pp. 1-2, 107, 135-6, 234-6; A. Hamilton, *A New Account of the East Indies*, Edinburgh 1727, pp. 3-7.
5. India Office Archives, Marine Miscellaneous, Vol. 891, report from 15.8.1790; India Office Archives, Factory Records, Egypt and Red Sea, Vol. VI, No. 393, 'A sketch', etc.; *Ibid.*, Murray report from 6.10.1799.
6. C. J. Poncet, *A Voyage to Aethiopia made in the year 1698, 1699 and 1700*, Hakluyt Society, London 1949, pp. 47, 69; Beccari, Vol. XIV, No. 14, p.3; J. Bruce, *Travels to Discover the Source of the Nile in the Years 1768, 1769, 1770, 1771, 1772 and 1773*, Edinburgh MDCCXC, Vol. III, pp. 475-6; Basset, *Etudes*, p.339.
7. Jabart, a district in eastern Showa, gave its name to all the highland Muslims. 'Jabarti' gradually became a synonym for Muslim-Ethiopian merchants.
8. M. Abir, *Ethiopia: The Era of the Princes*, London 1968, p.54.
9. M. Abir, *Ethiopia*, chapter III, pp. 44-73.
10. Burckhardt, *Arabia*, pp. 120, 132, 188; G. L. Sulivan, *Dhow Chasing in Zanzibar Waters and on the Eastern Coast of Arabia*, London 1873, reprinted Frank Cass, 1968, pp. 399-408, 410-11; Abbadie F.N.A. 21301, pp. 25, 150; Ministère des Affaires Etrangères - Correspondance Commerciale (et Consulaire), Djeddah, Vol. 1, Fresnel Report, 9.3.1840; Public Records Office - Foreign Office 1/1, p.61, Valentia, 8/5/1810.

11. Abir, *Ethiopia*, pp. 53-70 on Ethiopian slave trade.
12. Antoine d'Abbadie, *Bulletin de la Société de Géographie*, Paris, Vol. 17, 1859, p.174; Sir William Cornwallis Harris, *The Highland of Aethiopia*, London 1844, Vol. I., p.228.
13. Abir, *Ethiopia*, p.54.
14. Abbadie, F.N.A., 21300, pp. 219-20, 236, 797; Antoine d'Abbadie, *Géographie de l'Éthiopie*, Paris 1890, pp. 79-80; A.E. – Correspondance Commerciale (et Consulaire), Massawa, Vol. I, Degoutin, 10.9.1844; Krapf, *Travels and Missionary Labour in East Africa*, London 1860, p.51; India Office – Bombay Secret Proceedings. Lantern Gallery. Vol. 196. No. 3491, Harris Slave Report, 20.7.1842, para. 21.
15. M. Abir, "Southern Ethiopia", a chapter in R. Gray & D. Birmingham, *Pre-Colonial African Trade*, O.U.P. 1970, pp. 126-8.
16. Abir, *Ethiopia*, chapter IV, pp. 73-94.
17. C. T. Beke, *On the Countries South of Abyssinia*, London 1843, pp. 11-12; M. Abir, "The Emergence and Consolidation of the Monarchies of Enarea and Jimma", *Journal of African History*, Vol. 2, 1965, p.205.
18. A. Von Katte, *Reise in Abyssinien im Jahre 1836*, Stuttgart 1838, pp. 130-1; A.E. – Mémoires et Documents Afrique, Vol. 61, p.404, Lejean, 15.5.1863; P. Matteucci, *In Abisinia viaggio di . . .*, Milan 1880, p.270; Combes et Tamisier, Vol. I, pp. 110-11.
19. A.E. C & C Massawa, Vol. I, Report 10.9.1844; *Ibid.*, Rochet, 10.11.1848; J. L. Burckhardt *Travels in Nubia*, London 1819, p.399; T. W. Arnold, "Notes on Islam in North Abyssinia", *The Moslem World*, Vol. I, 1911, pp. 183-4.
20. Bruce, Vol. IV, p.206; H. Weld Blondel (ed.), *Royal Chronicles of Abyssinia*, Cambridge 1922, p.286; 'Abdul Majid al-Abadin, *Bayna al-Habasha wa'l-'Arab*, Cairo (no date), pp. 199-201; India Office – Political & Secret Records. Letters from Aden 1842, Vol. 26, Christopher Report, 1.4.1842.
21. Harris, Vol. 1, p.384; C. Johnston, *Travels in Southern Abyssinia*, London 1844, Vol. II, pp. 18-19, Abir, "Southern Ethiopia", pp. 131-2.
22. Abbadie, F.N.A. 21300, pp. 419-20, para. 277, Sakka September 1845; E. Cecchi, *Da Zeila alle frontiere del Caffa*, Rome 1886, Vol. I, pp. 490, 539; *Ibid.*, Vol. II, p.60; Public Records Office – Foreign Office Abyssinia 1/3, p.54, Krapf, 3.7.1840; L.G. Vol. 189, No. 2060 G, paras 23, 24, Harris 5.1.1842.
23. Each group of merchants was allotted a village in which the merchants were to live while in Showa. Harris, Vol. I, p.484; Johnston, Vol. II, pp. 18-19; India Office Archives – Bombay Secret Proceedings, Lantern Gallery, Vol. 185, No. 1440, Barker, 7.1.1842; Abir, *Ethiopia*, p.173.
24. Abir, *Ethiopia*, pp. 155, 172.
25. Church Missionary Records, London, Vol. 1841, pp. 3-4, Isenberg; L.G. 145, No. 4618, Haines, 28.8.1840, Morsely (probably Moresby) report; A.E. – Mémoires et Documents Afrique, Vol. 13, p.225, Combes, 26.4.1841.
26. Abir, *Ethiopia*, chapter VIII, pp. 114-182.
27. L.G. 164, No. 2141, Instructions of Board, 5.6.1841; L.G. 182, No. 837, Minutes governors of Board, 6.2.1842.

VIII

Black Slavery in Egypt During the Nineteenth Century As Reflected in the Mahkama Archives of Cairo

Terence Walz

The condition of servitude by black Africans in Egypt is hardly known. The few personal histories of enslaved blacks, virtually all of which have been published in European languages,[1] concentrate on the mechanics of the slave trade in Sudanic states and the traumatic experience slaves endured in order to reach markets in Egypt.[2] In the nineteenth century, short stories about slaves became a popular literary form among Europeans who visited the Nile Valley, but the heavy dose of romance in the retelling has made it difficult to separate fact from fiction.[3] The best evidence, first-hand accounts written by slaves or former slaves – such as have been written in this country by former slaves – is missing from modern Arabic literature. For a portrait of slave life, however, recourse may be made to the archive of the religious courts of Cairo, the Mahkama al-Shar'iyya, which contains a mass of information about slave market conditions, servitude, freedom, marriage, inheritance and estate. The following study is based largely on documents culled from that archive in the course of research on a different but related subject, the trans-Saharan trade of Egypt in the eighteenth century.[4] The Mahkama archive holdings show that an in-depth study of slavery in Egypt can be – and deserves to be – written.[5]

Slaves in Markets

Every important town in nineteenth-century Egypt had a slave market, the largest of which was located in Cairo. This market, known as Wakalat al-Jallaba, the Travelling Merchants' Caravanserai, was situated in the heart of "Grand Cairo", near the al-Azhar mosque and Khan al-Khalili, the city's richest and most famous market where the luxurious textiles, carpets and manufactures of Turkey were sold. Wakalat al-Jallaba also served as the main distribution point for all Sudan goods brought to Cairo, such as ivory, feathers, tamarind, ebony, gum and rhinoceros horn, and in its heyday it was one of the liveliest and largest markets in the city.[6]

The commercial importance of Wakalat al-Jallaba was undermined, however, in 1843 when the Egyptian Government, under abolitionist pressure from European powers, banned the sale of slaves in the heart of Cairo and forced merchants to transfer the public sale of slaves to the outskirts of the city. This order marked the beginning, albeit a reluctant one, of the Government's efforts to suppress the slave trade, and from this time onwards the sale of slaves was largely conducted in the privacy of slave merchants' homes. The sale of slaves was officially prohibited in 1855 and orders were given forbidding the importation of slaves from the Sudan. This new decree had little actual effect beyond the regulation that slave sales no longer be recorded in official court registers,[7] but in 1877 a new convention between Egypt and Great Britain put teeth into existing anti-slavery measures and a more visible decline in the slave trade resulted. A surreptitious trade nonetheless continued to function until the beginning of the present century.[8]

Until abolished, public markets remained bustling foci of the slave trade and from accounts of the slave market in Cairo, they appear to have been great public spectacles. Drawings of Wakalat al-Jallaba in the 1830s and early 1840s picture a dilapidated two-storey structure bursting with activity. Small groups of slaves sit in circles in the central courtyard, viewed by merchants and clients in baggy trousers and ornamental daggers, while about them move a procession of passers-by, including veiled women on donkeys led by small boys. Boxes, bundles and crates are piled high everywhere. The slave market in Cairo was in fact cut through by a public alley, linking al-Sanadiqiyya Street and Khan al-Khalili, and passengers through the market, Lane commented, were "amused" by "observing and quizzing" slaves who waited there patiently to be sold. Considering the public aspect of the market, it is not surprising that for the sake of decency female slaves were removed from public scrutiny and cloistered in second-floor rooms. Many were removed altogether from the market and quartered in the homes of slave merchants.[9]

Wakalat al-Jallaba obtained its slaves from several sources. New slaves from black Africa, three-quarters of whom were female, were brought in by merchants coming from the Sudan, known as *jallaba*, or by merchants from "up country" who purchased them from jallaba soon after the latter arrived in Upper Egypt. Some slaves were then sold to merchants attached to the market, but most probably passed from jallaba to private individuals through market brokers. Brokers received a one or two percent commission on each slave sold and saw to it that a sales tax levied on black slaves was paid to the proper authority. At least 1,500 slaves were sold annually at Wakalat al-Jallaba at the turn of the nineteenth century, a figure that rose substantially after Muhammad 'Ali's conquest of the Sudan in 1820-21. According to Dr Bowring, the number of slaves on sale at the market was never less than between one and two hundred.[10]

There were also important local sources. Slaves came onto the market from disgruntled owners who wished to exchange them or resell them and from slave-owning households whose belongings were auctioned off upon the death of the master. (In the eighteenth century household slaves were resold in a separate market.) In some instances, slaves may have become resalable at their own wish, as they were guaranteed this right by law if unhappy with their present owner. Elsewhere, slaves were furnished to the market by the Government which could not employ those they captured in the Sudan in the army or vice-regal establishments, and some slaves on sale may have been picked up by local governors and provincial police who found them lacking suitable papers indicating their status.[11]

Slaves were given clothes by their owners, be they merchants or private individuals. Men were dressed in a sort of loin cloth or longer *'abaq'*; women in a flowing robe of white or blue cloth. Some may still have been wearing a *rahat*, or leather-thong fringe skirt, brought from the Sudan. Merchants were not allowed to take away these articles of clothing when a slave was sold. Some women were decorated with beads and silver trinkets; others had accumulated wardrobes of head-dresses, vests, veils and kerchiefs. They were allowed to anoint themselves with butter to protect their skins from the harsh Cairene sun.[12]

Dr Bowring examined the diet given to slaves during his visit in 1837-8. With the exception of meat, fish and beverages, it resembled the usual Egyptian fare of lentils, lupines or millet, maize bread and vegetables, dates and sugar. The cost of the food was borne by the sellers (or owners if the slave were merely consigned to the seller) and were entered in account books of merchants under the heading *masarif ma'kal wa mashrab ar-raqiq*. Costs ran between 20 and 25 piasters per slave per month in the nineteenth century, and as a continuing drain on merchant balances they were no doubt an incitement for sellers to come to an agreement with prospective buyers as soon as possible. It seems unlikely – except during exceptional times, such as epidemics of plague – that slaves stayed for more than a month in the market.[13]

Wakalat al-Jallaba seems to have been open every day. At night the great doors were closed and locked, as was the case in every khan in the city. Despite the openness of the market during daytime, slaves were rarely shackled. Handcuffs or leg-irons do not appear in slave merchants' inventories and in any event would probably not have been necessary for slaves just arrived from the Sudan since they were total strangers to Cairo. They may nonetheless have been needed for recalcitrant slaves who had been sent to the market for resale. A case in point is a dispute dated 1797 referring to a slave named Nasr, consigned by his owner Amir Muhammad Agha to Furat al-Ruman, the nickname of a slave merchant whom the historian al-Jabarti called "the vilest of the Greeks in Cairo". His owner admitted he had bound Nasr with leg-irons "for fear of his escaping" before he had been delivered to Furat, and charged that the merchant had been negligent by leaving open the door of the room in which Nasr had been kept so that when he broke his shackles he could easily escape.[14] There are, nonetheless, relatively few cases in the Mahkama archive referring to slaves escaping from the market, and it seems likely that those who desired to run away waited to do so until they were lodged in private houses. This subject will be resumed later.

Slaves were treated as common merchandise in the market, the sale of them falling under contract laws regulating general commercial practice. The term *raqaba*, *'azm* or *ra's*, "neck", "bones" or "head" was applied to them as to chickens, donkeys, cows or sheep. Though drawn from many nations in black Africa, enslaved Africans were categorized by color rather than by nationality. In earlier times legal deeds describe them by using many colors, including such odd ones as red, yellow, green and blue – all reflecting varying shades of darkness – but by the nineteenth century three colors became standard: black (*aswad*), brown (*asmar*) and *habashi*. *Habashi* denotes, of course, a native of Ethiopia, but in Egypt the term is also applied to Egyptians who become sunburnt, much to the confusion of genealogists.[15] There seems to have been a market perference for Ethiopian slaves, who were considered exceptionally handsome and intelligent, so that many "brown" slaves, though lighter and therefore handsomer by local standards of beauty, may have passed for *habashi*. Merchants were prohibited, however, from advertising their goods fraudulently, and if a buyer discovered his newly-purchased slave were black and not habashi, as stipulated in bargaining procedures, then he could sue for annulment of the transaction.[16]

Slaves were also sold according to size and age-grade, the sizes ranging from three-span to seven-span, each of which carried an age equivalency. Five-span slaves were believed to be between nine and eleven years old; six-span slaves, the most sought after, were aged between fourteen and fifteen. Egyptians are said to have preferred six-span slaves in the belief they were old enough to be trained and young enough not to have developed bad habits. Newly-arrived slaves, moreover, could be expected to develop a loyalty to their new masters while older slaves, most often taken from auctioned-off estates, were thought to retain a loyalty to members of the old household.[17]

Despite this particular predilection, slaves offered for sale at Wakalat al-Jallaba were often on consignment there from previous owners. It is reckoned that of those slaves in the possession of al-Hajj 'Abd al-Karim "al-Bghl", shaykh of the market 1836-43, at the time of his sudden death, about 20 percent came from private sources in Cairo, having been given him "on consignment" (*'ala sabil al-amana*).[18] (In calculating numbers of slaves annually imported into Egypt, little account has been taken of this phenomenon.[19]) The history of Zulaykha bint Hamad al-Malik Jawish, an unjustly enslaved Shaqiyya woman who sued for her freedom in 1852, exemplifies the situation. She recounted in court her marriage in 1838-9 to a man from her home country in the Sudan who subsequently brought her to Cairo and sold her to a slave merchant. The merchant sold her to a Turkish lady, Jantamikan, daughter of Ibrahim pasha Yagen, who subsequently sold her to Mustafa Agha al-Shami; he then sold her to Isma'il bey, a police officer, who sold her to Isma'il Radi, shaykh of Wakalat al-Jallaba (after the death of 'Abd al-Karim), who sold her to Nasir Agha, a merchant in that market. Thereafter, her testimony continued, she was sold eight times until coming into the possession of her present master, Sa'id Agha al-Habashi. She had had, in short, fifteen owners in as many years and had been on sale in the slave market at least twice. Zulaykha's story may have been extreme, but there is little doubt that many slaves passed through the market several times in their lifetime.[20]

Names given black slaves by merchants and owners appear so often on Mahkama documents that certain of them must have been synonymous with servitude. The commonest names for women may have been Fatima and Zaynab, names generally popular among all classes of Egyptian women, but Bakhita, Mahbuba, Sa'ida, Zahra, Za'faran and Halima appear to have been reserved for female slaves in Cairo. Za'faran, meaning saffron, was almost always given to Ethiopian women because of their light skin; names such as Khudra (ashen black), Nila (indigo), Hulkiyya (pitch black) or Hibra (ink) were obviously adopted for darker women. Those just arrived from the Sudan often bore unfamiliar "Sudanese" names which were doubtless changed after being taken into private Egyptian households.[21] Among men, the most popular names were 'Abd Allah, Murjan, Sa'id and Bakhit, masculine equivalents in many cases to female slave names. Slaves tended to be named after scents, fruits or flowers, jewels, animals or Qur'anic personalities, or were given names suggesting a happy or pleasing servile disposition or an alluring physical appearance. Certain names were affected by changes in fashion. Maryam and Bilal, popular female and male names in the eighteenth century, proved far less common in the nineteenth.

Since all people have fathers, even slaves whose fathers were pagan, it was conventional to identify slaves as sons and daughters of 'Abd Allah, the name of the Prophet's (pagan) father.

Servitude

A buyer was usually given three days to discover any "legal defect" in a newly-purchased slave, after which the sale was considered complete and the final instalment of the purchase price paid. As a matter of fact, "defects" were often not recognized until several weeks and even months after the slave had been purchased, and owners went to court to prove they had been defrauded by the slave's seller. The nature of alleged "defects" in such cases gives startling insights into individual slave conditions.

Black slaves were usually assigned heavier household duties. These would have included washing, cleaning, cooking, preparing coffee – a tedious task rather than a difficult one – and running errands.[22] Slaves were used as nannies and nursemaids,[23] and were asked to run messages between households.[24] Cooking skills were especially prized, and slaves carrying the title *'usta* sold for high prices.[25]

In such circumstances, the health of slaves was important. Those listed as "unwell" (*mutawa'ik*) or "invalid" (*saqat*) in merchant inventories are valued far below the average since owners would not want to take on slaves who could not perform common household work.[26] One purchaser complained his slave "could not lift a decanter filled with water"; another declared his slave was crippled in the left leg. Blindness or impaired vision, sometimes caused by trachoma, was an obvious impediment.[27]

Yet it seems true that the health generally enjoyed by slaves was, to use the nineteenth-century term, "delicate."[28] Dr Frank, who studied the physical condition of slaves in the Cairo slave market at the end of the eighteenth century, found they were particularly susceptible to bronchial infections and smallpox, often with direst consequences, and suffered from diarrhea, venereal diseases, worms and scabies.[29] Plague and cholera affected them apparently more than the indigenous population. Burckhardt claimed that eight thousand slaves died during the 1815 plague season in Cairo alone, possibly as much as two-thirds of the existing slave population.[30] From Dr Colucci's published statistics of mortality from the cholera epidemics of 1850 and 1855, it is evident that the combined groups of "Nubians", "Ethiopians" and "Blacks" accounted for 11 percent and 13.6 percent of victims during those two epidemics while they numbered no more than 4 percent of the population of Cairo.[31] The dangers of what might be thought the most ordinary illnesses were underlined in a common saying, "A blow that scarcely makes an Arab stagger knocks down a slave."[32]

Mahkama records show that slaves suffered from "cough and shivers", diarrhea and other intestinal disorders, fevers, headaches and incontinence. Slave sales could be annulled on the basis of recurrent fevers and incontinence, but medical evidence submitted to the court indicates these illnesses generally occurred after the slave was purchased. Certain disorders, such as "heart-throbbing and diarrhea", "loose bowels and shivers" and "fits" may even be construed as neurological in origin, brought upon by the strain of adapting to new and difficult circumstances.[33]

The health of slaves seems also central to another aspect of their exploitation, the legal right of a slave owner to exploit sexually his female slaves. The degree that this kind of exploitation occurred must be weighed against at least two inhibiting factors: the consent required from a man's wife if she were the slave's owner; and the hostility which would have been provoked in a man's household if the slave were found pregnant. In the first instance, it is interesting to note that of 58 inventories of deceased freed slaves dating from the nineteenth century, 28 percent are identified as former slaves of Egyptian or freed black and white women. Their consent allowing their husbands to abuse their slaves was, according to Lane, "very seldom" given.[34] Second, it seems probable that the majority of slaves were housed in small households where spatial distances between its members were minimal. The introduction of an "outside" female into such compact structures would cause interminable uproar as the wife feared for her own sexual rights while she and her family feared for her children's inheritance.[35] On the other hand, the inability of some Egyptian women to bear children seemed sometimes to justify their husbands' use of slaves to generate an heir.

Whatever the particular tension, the master's sexual exploitation of his own slaves was a right which brought him no "blame" in the eyes of God and the Law.[36] Mahkama records are occasionally explicit about the exercise of that right, though a master had disturbing second thoughts when his slave was found pregnant and he was unsure of the child's paternity. The key evidence presented in cases involving pregnant slaves was based on the timing of the slave's menses and whether or not it occurred within days – and certainly within a month – of her purchase. Mahmud efendi, for example, a tailor's workshop director, sought to return Za'faran al-Suda on grounds that she had failed to menstruate thirty days after he had purchased her. The seller, 'Abd al-Karim "al-Baghl", took her back and was told three days later she had menstruated. According to Mahmud efendi, the slave did not menstruate until she had stayed with 'Abd al-Karim for two months and then he was convinced she had aborted the foetus.[37] Ahmad Shaqrun al-Maghribi sought to cancel a slave transaction on grounds that the woman he bought had irregular periods and provided the judge with specific evidence of their relationship. After he bought Za'faran al-Habashiyya, he stated, she menstruated within three days; then "he coupled with her after that and had sexual intercourse with her repeatedly, continuing with her in this way for two months; then she menstruated a second time." But when he decided to sell her after two months, the merchant who was to buy her declared she was four months pregnant.[38]

Za'faran al-Suda succumbed to plague before the dispute involving her pregnancy was resolved, and the judge refused to allow Ahmad Shaqrun to return Za'faran al-Habashiyya, but the unwillingness of merchants to take back "used" property and the difficulties involved in proving paternity did not deter Cairene buyers from often charging slave merchants with using their own slaves themselves. Merchant behavior in this regard was decried by the Swiss traveller Burckhardt – a view which Lane later incorporated into his *Manners and Customs of the Modern Egyptians* – and other western observers have mentioned the open prostitution of black and Ethiopian women by slave merchants in Egypt.[39] In assessing such charges, court judges could only rely on the testimony of merchants who would not in any case have wished to undercut the potential value of their goods. Indeed, the reluctance of buyers to purchase pregnant slaves because of the cost and "bother" of feeding a newborn child, providing clothes and finding additional space was a strong commercial reason for merchants to leave female slaves alone. Court judges could also rely on appointed doctors and midwives (*qawabil*) who at court order verified the

Black Slavery in Egypt

condition of suspect slaves. In almost every instance, they returned negative evidence and in one case pronounced the woman to be suffering from acute diarrhea.[40]

Nonetheless, Mahkama evidence suggests that merchants failed to heed sound commercial advice from time to time and that some slave merchants were notorious in this respect.[41] In a case brought in 1854, another Za'faran al-Habashiyya stated that while she had been in the possession of Sultan Ramadan, a slave merchant, "he had taken her as a concubine" and that when she was two months pregnant, she had been sold to another. She gave birth to a son, named Ibrahim, and was sold with him to a doctor. (It was he who presumably encouraged her to plead for freedom as the mother of the merchant's child.) Sultan refused, however, to acknowledge her as "the mother of his son" and her case was turned down.[42] In another example, Hasan Mustafa, a slave merchant from Ibrim (Nubia), complained that a slave he bought suffered from *bahaq* (leukoderma, a mild skin disease often mistaken for leprosy), adding that "he had not kept her company until the beginning of the present month and then found her pregnant for months." The seller, a merchant from Kurdufan, refuted the central charge – not that she was pregnant but that she suffered bahaq – by proving the buyer knew of her condition when he purchased her.[43] Charges of pregnancy among slaves were made and then disproved so often that one suspects their validity. In light of generally low birth rates among black slave women – which will be discussed below – or the converse, a strong tendency to abort foetuses, such charges may have been simple pretexts to get rid of slaves no longer wanted or desired.

Whatever personal degradation female slaves endured as a result of sexual services to masters, the birth of a child actually enhanced their position. This did not always lead to their enfranchisement, though it "often happened",[44] even when owned by notable men. *Mustawlidat*, or slave women who had borne children to their masters but were not manumitted, were not covered by inheritance law, being excluded from any part of the master's estate, but their children, if recognized, were considered his legal heirs and they themselves often received posthumous bequests (*wasiya*). In many cases, the inheritance enjoyed by a slave's children and vicariously by the mother, proved far greater than if the mother had been freed and married. It is ironic, moreover, that bequests to some mustawlidat actually exceeded the one-eighth share of a husband's estate given to the wife. Such economic reasons were no doubt strong individual arguments justifying institutional iniquities.[45]

As regards the private life of slaves, almost all became Muslim, even those owned by Christians and Jews,[46] and they seem to have brought to the practice of religion an unusual zeal. In the nineteenth century they became associated with performances of zar, a psychotherapeutic exercise that attempted to release female victims from the grip of evil spirits.[47] Female slaves were also evidently fashion-conscious. Al-Jabarti commented that when public criers announced in the spring of 1787 that women must stop wearing a costly hair-do called "Qazdughliyya", it had become so widespread "that even the black slaves wore it, [though] it cost up to a dinar to have it done."[48] On feast days and during mawlids and even on market days when they were free to leave the house, they could be found in *buza* shops, drinking a local fermented beer. These shops had, however, a bad reputation and brawls had sometimes to be settled in court.[49]

Though the slave population of Cairo fluctuated between 12,000 and 15,000 during most of the nineteenth century, slaves seem to have had a hard time escaping. Erstwhile owners, including slave merchants, had an uncanny ability to locate runaway slaves, even if "lost", as Mahkama documents euphemistically put it, somewhere in Upper Egypt many months before. In this regard, Government-paid ghafirs and local police kept a watchful eye on blacks who could not satisfactorily explain their presence in unusual places. About a dozen court cases refer to slaves who had been "lost" by owners in places as far away as Nubia, Kurdufan and Dar Fur, only to be found again in Cairo.[50] In one case, a merchant from Shandi, the famous market town in the Sudan, claimed that a slave he owned, named Bahr al-Nil, had fled from him a year and a half earlier while he was in Kobbei, the commercial capital of Dar Fur, and that when he reached Cairo he found her with another slave merchant. An owner could prove his ownership by producing two witnesses, but if he failed to do this, then the slave stayed with his current owner. Thus Bahr al-Nil was returned to her rightful owner, but another trader who claimed a slave had fled from him nine months earlier when he was in Kurdufan, could not produce the correct evidence of his ownership, and his case was dismissed.[51]

Freedom

The manumission (*'itq*) of slaves was considered a meritorious religious act in Islam, and the Mahkama archive contains copies of thousands of emancipation deeds registered by individual slave owners over a period of almost four hundred years.[52] Manumission could be gratuitous or conditional, freedom being stipulated only upon the death of the master (in which case the slave was called *mudabbar*) or in lieu of a future compensation (in which the term *mukatib* was used). In the mid-nineteenth century, British consular activity against slavery is evident in court registers as a flurry of '*itq* documents were recorded by British proteges in 1848,[53] but the veritable flood of emancipation acts that occurred in the later decades of the century – some 18,000 between 1877 and 1889[54] – were registered in manumission bureaus, not in the courts.

According to Mrs. Turgay, slaves in imperial service were customarily freed after nine years of servitude in the case of whites, seven in the case of blacks. Among less noble classes, there seems to have been no fixed rule about suitable years of servitude. Mahkama documents show nevertheless the concern that many masters felt about freeing slaves who had little job training other than domestic skills and who were often without normal family connections to assist them. Thus, documents registered in many cases not only the manumission of a slave but also the gift of a sum of money. In the middle part of the nineteenth century, this sum usually amounted to 500 piasters (£E5), about half the cost of a new slave.[55]

Mukatib slaves who earned their freedom would come to an agreement with the master over the sum to be paid and the period in which it would be delivered. This was usually done by installment, the master foregoing partial payment on the last installment. It is not known how often this type of agreement was made in the nineteenth century; the one example I found was concluded in 1605.[56] In the event, it would rarely have been reached between masters and female slaves since they ordinarily had no means of livelihood outside the household.

Slavery, as is well known, is not forbidden in the Qur'an, but the enslavement of free-born persons, namely those having a Muslim mother and/or father, was illegal. (Neither Muslim men nor women were permitted pagan spouses.) The problem of the enslavement of Muslims proved unexpectedly real in the nineteenth century as areas of black Africa that traditionally supplied slaves to Egypt were gradually Islamized. Courts were not infrequently asked to sit in judgment on cases brought by people who claimed they had been unjustly enslaved, many of whom came from Wadai and had been captured in wars with neighboring Dar Fur or kidnapped by passing merchants or raiding parties. Their testimony furnishes interesting details about the trade in slaves and will be given at some length. What is surprising, perhaps, is the support such individuals received from jallaba and slave merchants.[57]

Unjustly enslaved Africans were often rescued from servitude because, as these documents reveal, Africans from many parts of *bilad as-Sudan* came through Cairo on their way to the Holy Cities and stayed there for business reasons or in order to attend classes at al-Azhar. Sometimes they enlisted or were enlisted in the army. 'Abd Allah 'Uthman al-Takruri, for example, was a soldier in an Egyptian regiment, though he came originally from dar Sulayh, as Wadai was known at this time.[58] In 1803 he found his sister, Fatima, at the slave market in Cairo. With the support of the shaikh of Wakalat al-Jallaba, the venerable al-Hajj Sultan Isma'il, he sued her owner, testifying that around the year 1794, when their father had died, his sister "had gone out of her village, named Wara,[59] and had lost her way," that she was freeborn, having come "from a town (*balad*) inhabited by Muslims" and had been unjustly enslaved. The defendant, a long-distance merchant whose *nisba* suggests he came from Bani 'Adi, the entrepot in Upper Egypt for caravans travelling the *darb al-arba'in*, stated he had bought her from another merchant in R-qa,[60] "in the regions of the Sudan", and that Fatima had "been bought and sold numerous times over the last six years." Following his testimony, Fatima was asked about her forebears, to which she replied she was "Fatima bint 'Uthman, son of Adam, fruit of her father by his wife, Zahra Indara, and [was] a Muslim, free at birth, from Dar Sulayh of the regions of the Sudan." Her brother was required to produce witnesses, his testimony by itself being insufficient evidence, and after a month's delay brought two other soldiers, 'Umar Jum'a and 'Abd Allah Adam, who verified his statement, and his sister was freed. As was usual in such proceedings, the owner was instructed to recover his loss from the man who sold her to him. In this case, it amounted to 140 *mahbubs*, about 525 old piasters.[61]

Another case disclosed the plight and ultimate vindication of Maryam al-Samra. She claimed she was the daughter of Asad Adam "of a village of Muslims called Kara in the regions of Sulayh in Upper Egypt,[62] the fruit of her father by her deceased mother, Hawa bint Adam, and that some people from the area of Dar Fur, near her village, had made war on it and captured her, bringing her to Cairo."[63] She also stated that her master, a slave merchant named Muhammad Wirdi Yusuf, who attended the court proceedings, had fathered three children by her in the seven years he had owned her. In his testimony, Muhammad replied he had purchased her from another merchant at Wakalat al-Jallaba for 950 piasters and had "produced children by her in a blameless fashion." Maryam's claims were supported by two Wadaians in Cairo, al-Hajj Jabir al-Fiqi Adam, from Abu Qara, and

Black Slavery in Egypt

al-Hajj Tuqayl Muhammad from "Nimra al-'Adawiyya;[64] their testimony in turn was supported by two more Wadaians who attested to their honest character. Maryam was not only freed but married to her former master who granted her a brideprice of 300 piasters. Nasr al-Shuqayri, one of the long-time merchants at Wakalat al-Jallaba, was appointed her representative (*wakil*) in this matter.[65]

Finally, there is the example of Salih al-Habashi who claimed freeborn status, having been born in an Ethiopian village identified as Hirza. He was granted freedom with the help of Ethiopian students in the *riwaq* al-Jabart at al-Azhar mosque.[66]

Freed slaves had nonetheless to keep their manumission papers with them. Without such papers they could be picked up by the police, imprisoned and sent to the slave market. This happened to Sa'id al-Asmar in 1842 who was arrested while on the way to visit the Sharif of Mecca, residing temporarily at an estate in Giza. Once in the slave market he was able to contact friends and establish his freed status.[67] Other freed slaves were forced to go to the courts to prevent their former masters from reneging on a declared manumission or to stop slave merchants from selling them.[68]

Marriage

Social historians interested in the personal lives of slaves, their marriages, offspring, livelihoods and connections in urban society will find estate inventory data especially relevant. The inventories pertain to the personal belongings of freed slaves; unfreed slaves were considered part of the master's chattel – indeed, listed alongside his donkeys, cows, camels or water buffalo – and their marital partners, offspring and material possessions were not separately enumerated. Slaves were allowed to marry other slaves, only the master's consent being required, but they could not marry free persons without themselves becoming free.

The data below are based on 85 estate inventories of freed black slaves who died between 1701 and 1873. Considering the thousands of freed slaves who lived in Cairo during this long number of years, the assembled data can only be submitted as representative of what a fuller study would make clear. It should also have bearing on the condition of enslaved blacks, though obviously freed blacks were more fortunate. The bulk of the inventories, 58 out of 85, date from two nineteenth-century periods, and since their data can be somewhat better controlled, particular emphasis is given to nineteenth-century information.[69]

The material falls into the following chronological arrangement:

Dates	Number of inventories	M	F	Eunuch
1113-25/1701-13	8	2	6	–
1135-58/1722-46	19	6	11	2
1237-57/1821-42	32	6	26	–
1265-89/1848-73	26	3	23	–
Totals[70]	85	17	66	2

Eighty percent of freed black slaves were married. Of this number, almost two-thirds were married to whites, either free or freed, male or female. Fifteen percent contracted marriages were between black males and white females, about evenly divided between freed white female slaves, usually Circassian, and free white females of Egyptian origin, often daughters of former masters or of business colleagues. On somewhat scarce evidence there seems to have been more intermarriage between black males and white females in the eighteenth century, reflecting, perhaps, a higher status enjoyed by freed black slaves at that time. It was tradition, according to Mrs. Tugay, for black female slaves to be freed and married off to black male slaves, yet only 36 percent of freed black marriages in Egypt followed this particular pattern.[71]

Sixteen percent of freed blacks remained single, the marital status of the other four percent not known. The percentage was certainly higher than among freeborn Egyptians. Most of the unmarried blacks were women. Eunuchs, whom one would expect to be single, followed traditional household patterns and took wives, freed white slaves in two examples found.[72] They may have done this to conform to social dicta which prohibited unmarried men from living in private houses.[73]

Black women as a rule appear to have been married to men of above-average social standing, those who were numbered among the merchant community or were attached to various policing organizations, or were employed as retainers (*tabi'*) to important military personalities (in the old Mamluk fashion), or who held high- to medium-ranking positions in the Government. Among merchants, husbands are identified as slave merchants, perfumers, cloth sellers, stationers and brokers. Among higher ranking Government officers are found provincial governors, officers holding the title *kashif* or *bey*, and several *efendis* employed in the Treasury Department. Toward the latter part of the nineteenth century, husbands are often identified as African students at al-Azhar or as Sudan-trade retailers. This suggests that the increase in the number of slaves in Egypt brought about an overall lowering of status that blacks once enjoyed, and that the social system was no longer accommodating them with marriages to socially reputable men.

One of the puzzles in modern Egyptian social history is the minimal impact black Africans have had on the biological make-up of Egyptians. If it is true that as many as 800,000 Africans were forcibly settled in the country during the eighteenth and nineteenth centuries,[74] why is there so little "African" imprint on the general population? Leaving aside the important question of mortality rates among blacks – which clearly has fundamental bearing on the subject – an investigation into birth rates among blacks might also be pertinent. In truth, the full answer may never be known since there are no statistics for those centuries relating to the number of unrecognized offspring borne by blacks to Egyptian masters or by black slaves amongst themselves, or indeed on child mortality and birth rates for Egyptians as a whole. Nonetheless, Mahkama documentation gives some tantalizing clues to the central question of birth rates among blacks, or at least among one segment of that population, that may point to a partial explanation of why so few "African" traces show among the general population today.

Of 85 inventories surveyed, spouses are identified in 72. Eleven freed slaves were unmarried; the marital status of two others is not known. Two inventories pertain to eunuchs who, though technically married, could not produce children. The total number of potentially fertile people, adjusted accordingly, is 155, a figure which also includes *mustawlidat* who are specifically identified in the texts. The number of off-spring produced by these various relationships – and listed as heirs in estate proceedings – amounts to 21. Forty-six inventories list no offspring whatever, and if that number is added to unmarried and castrated slaves, then almost 70 percent of the freed black population of Cairo left no progeny. Moreover, the vast majority of black or inter-racial couples produced only one child. The birth rate among them, in short, seems to have been astonishingly low.

No satisfactory explanation can be given as yet for this phenomenon. There can be little doubt that inventories reflect the harsh realities of high infant mortality rates and high general mortality rates due to epidemics of cholera and plague. Only the survivors would have stood a chance to inherit. It is also possible that many black women were married when past their child-bearing years, having been freed only after long years of servitude and then to husbands who desired only a woman to manage the household. Certainly further research into the problem is needed.

For purposes of cross-checking our statistics, the 1868 census of

Egypt is useful. Accounted as "Nubians, Abyssinians and Sudanese," the black population, free and freed, numbered 16,442. This figure was broken down by age: 15,755 adults and 687 children.[75] It represents a probable negative growth rate even higher than that reflected in our findings. The 1868 census, however, may not have included half-Egyptian children under the category "Sudanien," while it would certainly have included a fairly large number of Nubian men who worked as domestics and concierges in Cairo, leaving wives and families in Nubia, as well as Nubian and Sudanese retailers with families elsewhere.

Yet it also seems clear that demographic research into birth and death rates among nineteenth-century Egyptians – a project which can be undertaken on the basis of Mahkama documentation – will show that high infant mortality and death from recurrent epidemics were not factors impeding the growth of individual ethnic communities. In my study of Sudan-trade and slave merchants in the nineteenth century, based on inventories dated 1812-66, I found that 36 merchants with 55 wives and concubines produced 66 children, evidence that negative birth rates prevailed also among indigenous communities.[76] But whereas 70 percent of freed blacks left no progeny, the corresponding figure among Sudan-trade merchants in Cairo was 27 percent.

There was an Arabic saying that went, "The Ethiopians are black, the Egyptians thieves, the North Africans cruel, the Damascans liars, and of these four peoples it is the Black who will soonest lose the imprint of the stamp which marks his nature."[77] While it may be true for biological reasons beyond ordinary competence that children of inter-marriages between black Africans and Egyptians tended to lose their color and other racial characteristics, it seems also true that much of the black population in Egypt – certainly in Cairo – failed to survive because of low birth and high mortality rates.

Inheritance and Estate

The wife of a deceased husband received one-eighth of his estate, the remaining seven-eighths going to his children. In the case of freed slaves with no offspring, the wife inherited one-fourth, with three-fourths reverting to her husband's former master or his nearest male relation, while a husband of a deceased freed female slave with no offspring split her estate fifty-fifty with her former master. If the former master was deceased and had no surviving heirs, then the half or three-fourths was claimed by the *bayt al-mal*, the public treasury. In short, the formidable bonds of patronage existing between slaves and masters continued to be exerted despite emancipation.

Islamic laws of inheritance were devised to safeguard shares in an estate for all members of the family, and most notably for female members. The one-eighth share allotted to the wife may seem somewhat paltry by western standards, but it was based on the assumption that wives were usually mothers and that ties between mothers and sons, who received the largest share, were indissoluble. In this respect, the fate of freed black women, and perhaps of many slaves, who did not or could not produce heirs, was cruel indeed.

The small estates left by them, which during the period 1821-42 averaged 1,547 piasters, about £E15½, and which during the period 1848-73 averaged 1,812 piasters, slightly more than £E18, placed that group among the poorer, though not the poorest, inhabitants of Cairo.[78] Of these women, freed Ethiopian slaves appear to have been better situated, with estates averaging 5,204 piasters in the first period, 4,049 piasters in the second. "Suda" slaves averaged 1,152 piasters in the years 1848-73 (figures for the earlier period are not extensive enough), and "Samra" slaves averaged 832 piasters in 1821-42 and 1,514 piasters in 1848-73.

Freed black males were generally better off than female slaves, having estates valued at 5,808 piasters for the 1821-42 period and 2,780½ piasters for 1848-73. This was true in the eighteenth century as well.[79]

Averages, of course, obscure the wide range of these estates. They ran from as little as 101 piasters and 10 para left by Mahbuba al-Samra, who died unmarried in 1841, to as much as 15,680 piasters and 23 para left by Za'faran al-Habashiyya, wife of al-Hajj Salim Agha Arna'ut, who died the same year leaving a husband and brother, Surur Agha, as heirs.[80] All inventories list in detail the possessions of the deceased, and the inventory of Nukh al-Suda, freed slave and wife of Husayn Agha Jarkis, may be typical if spartan. She died in 1857 with an estate valued at 220 piasters and 10 para which was split between her husband and a son.[81] Her property consisted of a few copper utensils – a *tisht* or large washbasin, a pot, a pan and a plate – worth 70 piasters; a good-quality mattress (*martaba*), valued at 50 piasters; another mattress with pillow and blanket, 31 piasters; a wood box worth 65 piasters; and a mirror, a few rags, a meat grinder and a pulley (*ma'allaq*) worth 3 piasters. For contrast, Za'faran al-Habashiyya owned a large assortment of silver bracelets, pins and anklets, a quantity of pearls and a pair of valuable armlets worth £E17.

There were, in fact, a number of well-to-do freed blacks whose wealth can be measured in terms of the charitable endowments they established for students and teachers at al-Azhar. Their waqfs continued to furnish yearly revenues to the al-Azhar budget as recently as 1962-3. Among donors were several eunuchs, three rich Ethiopian women and one freed slave of probable Sudanic origin.[82] Further examination of waqf titles will reveal the names of many more.

Blacks are identified in Mahkama documents as having been military personnel, retainers, merchants and cooks, yet the bulk of emancipated Africans probably functioned on the fringes of society, finding obscure livelihoods as diviners and occultists,[83] errand-boys, beer-hall operators and wood-gatherers. When in the late nineteenth century the number of freed blacks rapidly increased, many were forced to take to thievery for a living, and "gangs" of freed black slaves operated in several Delta provinces until brought under control by the police.[84] Chronic unemployment among them may have been one of the reasons prompting the Government to enlist blacks in expeditionary forces sent against the Mahdi in the early 1880s.[85]

Conclusion

This paper is not meant as a definitive study of blacks in Egypt. The modest aim has been to point out some important aspects of their lives as slaves and ex-slaves as seen in a survey of court documentation in Cairo. A more extensive search in these documents would produce other aspects, would establish birth and mortality rates on a stronger basis and would answer questions about occupations, marriage and wealth. If this paper serves any purpose, it will be to encourage more active research into the subject.

NOTES

1. Al-Jabarti's biography of Ibrahim Kathuda al-Sinnari, a black mamluk who rose through the ranks to become the right-hand man of Murad bey, ruler of Egypt in the late eighteenth century, shows that he began his career as a doorkeeper in Mansura and was never enslaved. 'Abd al-Rahman al-Jabarti, *'Aja'ib w'al-athar fi't-tarajim wa'l-akhbar*, 4 vols. (Bulaq, 1297/1879), III, 219-20; French tr., *Merveilles biographiques et historiques ou chroniques*, 9 vols. (Cairo, 1888-96), VII, 105-6.
2. For the story of 'Ali, *Lettres de Mold*, I (1881-2), 215; for Luigi Kuku, *La Nigrizia*, IV (1886), 41-50; for Maria Lishok Kegi, *ibid.*, 114-21; for Felice Giom'ah, *ibid.*, III (1885), 171-2; for Mabruk and Rahma, Lucy Duff Gordon, *Letters from Egypt* (London, 1902), 344-5, 339-40.
3. Gérard de Nerval, *Voyage en Orient*, 2 vols. (Paris, 1851), I, 203-5 (story of Zaynab); Charles Didier, *Nuits du Caire* (Paris, 1860), 62-4, 211-34 (stories of

Mahbub, Aminava and Ipsa); William C. Prime, *Boat Life in Egypt and Nubia* (New York, 1858), 455-9.
4. "The Trade between Egypt and *Bilad as-Sudan*, 1700-1820" (Boston University, 1975), to be published by the Institut Français d'Archéologie Orientale du Caire in their series, *Textes arabes et études orientales*, vol. VIII. Hereafter cited Walz, "Trade".
5. Court documents are footnoted by court series, volume, page, number and date. Court series are abbreviated as follows: (Mahkama) al-Bab al-'Ali (BA); (Mahkama) al-Salihiyya al-Najmiyya (SN); (Mahkama) Jam' Tulun (T); (Mahkama) Qism al-'Askariyya (Askar); al-I'lamat (M); al-Tarikat (TAR).
   The archive is presently located in the Maslahat al-Shahr al-'Aqari, Cairo. Research in the archive was undertaken with the support of generous grants from the Foreign Area Fellowship Program and the American Research Center in Egypt, 1970-3.
6. See my article, "Wakalat al-Jallaba: the Central Market for Sudan Goods", *Annales Islamologiques*, XIII, forthcoming.
7. Slave sales are sometimes obliquely mentioned by references to "monies due" and "monies received" by slave merchants. These merchants, previously identified as *al-yasirji fi'rraqiq al-aswad* or *al-asmar*, become identified as *al-mutasabbib fi bida'a al-sudaniyya* (retailers in Sudanese goods).
8. For an account of anti-slavery measures, Gabriel Baer, "Slavery and Its Abolition" in his *Studies in the Social History of Modern Egypt* (Chicago, 1969), 177 ff.; Muhammad Fu'ad Shukry, *The Khedive Ismail and Slavery in the Sudan (1863-1879)* (Cairo, 1938).
9. Edward W. Lane, *Description of Egypt. Notes and Views in Egypt and Nubia during the years 1825-26-27-28*, British Museum MS, ADD 34080-8, 9 vols., I, 165; Walz, "Trade," 363-66; Robert Hay, *Illustrations of Cairo* (London, 1840), plate XXV; Hector Horeau, *Panorama d'Egypte et de Nubie* (Paris, 1841), plate between 4 and 5; G. Ebers, *Egypt, Descriptive, Historical and Picturesque*, 2 vols. (London, 1898), II, plate facing 36.
10. John Bowring, *Report on Egypt and Candia*, Parliamentary Papers, Reports from Commissioners, XXI (1840), 93. For estimates of slave imports, Ralph Austen, "The Transsaharan Slave Trade: A Tentative Census," paper given at Northwestern University, 1976, subsequently revised, table 2.
11. Walz, "Trade," 412-28; (Mahkama archive), M 10, 177, no. 526 (2 Jum I 1258/1842).
12. David Roberts, *Egypt and Nubia*, 3 vols. (London, 1855-6), III, plate 239, "A group in the slave market in Cairo"; Robert Mantran, *Istanbul dans la seconde moitié du XVIIe siècle* (Paris, 1962), 340; John Lewis Burckhardt, *Travels in Nubia* (London, 1822), 199-200; (Mahkama archive), BA 401, 278, no. 1438 (18 Raj 1251/1835).
13. On expenses, BA 401, 278, no. 1438 (1251/1835): merchant spent 64 piasters on a slave during three months; 8 piasters per slave was allotted by Muhammad al-Hilali, great merchant of Asyut, for provisions during a ten-day trip by Nile to Cairo markets: Hilali Papers, in the possession of Dr 'Abbas al-Hilali, Asyut and Alexandria, Account Book, p.9 (1265/1848). A study of these and other private papers of Asyut merchants is in progress.
14. BA 320, 282, no. 643 (1212/1797); A. Cardin, tr., *Journal d'Abdurrahman*, 2 parts (Paris, 1838), I, 20. Al-Jabarti tells the story of another escaped slave who fled from Khan Dhu'l-Fiqar (where he was probably lodged with his master). He ran out into the street, shouting "To the Jihad, O Muslims, kill the French!" As this occurred during their occupation of Egypt, and shortly after the Cairo Uprising in 1798, he was captured and executed. *Merveilles biographiques*, VI, 118-19.

15. The color of many Egyptians, especially those from Upper Egypt, is usually described as *asmar* or *qamhi* (wheaty), a descriptive term also found in seventeenth-century court documents. The difference between *asmar* and *habashi* was explained to me several years ago by alluding to two national figures. Gamal Abdel Nasser would be called *asmar*, my informant said; Anwar al-Sadat, who has a Sudanese grandmother, would be termed *habashi*.
16. A slave woman Al-Malak was purchased "on condition she be Ethiopian"; later she was found to be Black: M 2, 99, no. 444 (21 Raj 1254/1838); a slave named Sa'id was purchased on condition "he be Ethiopian and free from legal defects"; the owner was later informed he was Black: M 12, 3, no. 10 (5 Shaw 1258/1842). Such stipulations also affected white slaves: a *jariya bayda* was discovered not to be Circassian as desired: M 7, 92, no. 325 (7 Hij 1256/1841).
17. Bayle St. John, *A Levantine Family* (London, 1897), 133; Mary L. Whately, *Letters from Egypt to Plain Folks at Home* (London, 1879), 116; John Lewis Burckhardt, *Arabic Proverbs, or Manners and Customs of the Modern Egyptians*, 3rd ed. (London, 1972), nos. 105, 347. On the hand-span (8 inches?), E. de Cadalvene and J. de Breuvery, *L'Egypte et la Turquie de 1829 à 1836*, 2 vols. (Paris, 1836), I, 277; Muhammad 'Umar al-Tunisi, tr. by Dr Perron, *Voyage au Darfour* (Paris, 1845), 207.
18. Walz, "Trade," 348-9 (10 slaves out of a total of 47). A biographical sketch of 'Abd al-Karim is found in my, "Notes on the Organization of the African Trade in Cairo, 1800-1850," *Annales Islamologiques*, XI (1972), 281-5; see also Walz, "Trade," 246-53.
19. I advanced this argument in a paper given at Northwestern University, February 1977, in comment on Austen's paper, "Transsaharan Salve Trade."
20. M 28, 55, no. 143 (10 Rabi' I 1269). Their market behavior differed from that of newly-imported slaves, being characterized, according to one European visitor, by "ill humour, and a certan audacious, impertinent manner, mixed with a degree of coquetry." H. Puckler-Muskau, *Egypt under Mehemet Ali*, 2 vols. (London, 1845), I, 185-6.
21. The inventory of al-Hajj Ahmad al-Kharubi al-Maghribi who died in Khartum (Askar 308, p. 532-4, 1253/1837) includes a long list of slaves just arrived in Cairo. Some are named al-Shuna or Shuna (granary – perhaps reflecting purchase from Government-stores in Khartum), Jurada (hoer), al-Daw', 'Amiya, Taranja. Other nineteenth-century documents contain more bizarre names: Umm Ballina (mother of whale?), Umm Hiyyat (mother of snakes), Barwana (grass-snake?), Bursiyya (tarantula?).
22. Edward W. Lane, *Manners and Customs of the Modern Egyptians*, Everyman Edition, 1963, 191; Emine Foat Tugay, *Three Centuries* (London, 1963), 310-11; Ellen Chenelles, *Recollections of an Egyptian Princess*, 2 vols. (London, 1893), I, 35. Some slave names reflect domestic work: Khadima (servant); Khadim Allah; Mantuf (hairdresser?); Nukh (carpet); Faraj (comfort, aid); Zulfa (toadyism). Their hard life, Mrs. Tugay commented, gave many of them a bad temper.
23. A slave named Sa'dana may have earned her name suckling children. BA 361, 39, no. 91 (1234/1819).
24. Thus names such as Murasaliyya, Mursil and Bashir, all implying carriers of messages or bringers of good news, were popular slave names.
25. Askar 297, p.430 (1247/1832), a slave woman with the title *Fusta* is valued four times the average price of black women; see also Lane, *Manners*, 191. An obituary of "Sitt Assa of Assiut", *Egyptian Gazette*, December 9, 1939, recalls the life of a Dar Fur black who worked in the Asyut Girls' School, and noted, "More than a cook, although she was an excellent one, she has taught and shown the culinary arts to daughters of the best families in Upper Egypt."

26. Inventory of 'Abd al-Karim "al-Baghl", TAR 5, p.229-30 (17 Raj 1259/1843), includes unwell and crippled slaves valued at 360 and 370 piasters respectively; the average price of healthy slaves was 1,250 piasters; Surur, an "unwell" eunuch, is listed at 200 piasters; the average was 1,275 piasters.
27. For a list of slaves suffering various ocular illnesses, Walz, "Trade," 357.
28. Lane, *Manners*, 190, relative to the health of Ethiopian slaves; Tugay, 304, considered the health of black slaves more precarious than that of whites.
29. Louis Frank, "Mémoire sur le commerce des Nègres au Kaire et sur les maladies auxquelles ils sont sujets en y arrivant," appendix in Vivant Denon, *Voyage dans la basse et la haute Égypte*, 2 vols (London, 1807), II, 245-8.
30. *Nubia*, 307; the slave population of Cairo in 1800 was estimated to be 12,000: E. Jomard, "Description abrégée de la ville et de la citadelle du Kaire," *Description de l'Égypte, État moderne*, II, part 2 (Paris, 1822), 694. The fear of plague shut down the slave market operations. See A.W. Kingslake, *Eothen* (London, 1935), 181; and BA 401, 278, No. 1438 (1251/1835).
31. J. Colucci bey, "Quelques notes sur le cholera qui sévit au Caire en 1850 et 1855," *Mémoires de L'Institut d'Égypte*, I (1862), 604, 606.
32. Burckhardt, *Nubia*, 304.
33. For specific examples and Arabic terminology, Walz, "Trade," 353-63.
34. *Manners*, 190. Further on inventories, see below
35. On family quarrels that erupted because of such a circumstance, St John, *Levantine Family*, 132
36. The phrase *'ala al-wajh al-mastur* is employed in M 14, 74, no. 304 (5 Jum I 1260/1844).
37. BA 401, 278, no. 1438 (1251/1835). For a complete translation of this case, Walz, "Trade," 388-96.
38. M 8, 81, no. 275 (18 Jum I 1257/1841). It is possible that vigorous sexual activity would produce bleeding in a pregnant woman which would have been misconstrued.
39. Burckhardt, *Nubia*, 300-01; Lane, *Manners*, 192; Cadalvene and Breuvery, I, 278-9, relating to a corporation of prostitutes in Asyut, ca. 1830.
40. M 28, 267, no. 730 (25 Hij 1269/1853).
41. In the dispute Mahmud efendi vs. 'Abd al-Karim, merchants and a client at Wakalat al-Jallaba all too readily suggested to Mahmud that his slave had been left alone with one Sulayman Agha al-Yasirji; this charge, too, was never proved.
42. M 30, 202, No. 641 (8 Rabi'I 1271).
43. M 22, 95, no. 237 (3 Qad 1265/1849).
44. Lane, *Manners*, 192.
45. Zahra al-Habashiyya, a *mustawlida* of Husayn al-Tawil, a wealthy merchant of Asyut, received nothing from his estate, but her two children were allotted 54 percent while the child by his lawful wife inherited a 46 percent share. Askar 269, p.144 (1235/1820).
 As regards *wasiya*, Jabir Ahmad "al-Jallab" bequeathed 50 riyals to each of his *mustawlida*, Nasra and Fatima, while his wife inherited only 13½ riyals plus the last installment of her brideprice (10 riyals). Askar 196, 475, no. 466 (1188/1774).
46. An exception was Maryam 'Abd Allah al-Habashiyya al-Nasraniyya, freed by a Christian master, Mu'allim 'Antun Ghabriyal: BA 85, 398, no. 2221 (19 Jum II 1014/1605). The Shanudas, a merchant family of Asyut, owned and freed a white slave called "Matta al-Mamluk" who is buried in the family graveyard: interview with Yusuf Habib Shanuda, 19 August 1971.
47. Tugay, 311; Niya Salima, *Harems et musulmans d'Egypte* (Paris, n.d.), 255-89.
48. *Merveilles biographiques*, VI, 272; see also Sonnini de Manoncour, *Voyage dans la haute et la basse Egypte*, 3 vols. (Paris, year VII), III, 95, who speaks of *perruques à l'anglaise* worn by black slaves.

49. Clients of *buza* shops were called "riff-raff" by 'Ali Mubarak, *al-Khitat al-tawfiqiyya*, 20 vols. (Bulaq, 1306/1888), XII, 104. For a brawl, T 186, 379, no. 1244 (23 Shab 1006/1599).
50. SN 757, 156, no. 347 (1162/1749); SN 522, 391, no 864 (1172/1759); BA 279, 67, no. 120 (1186/1772); SN 528, 185, no. 368 (1187/1773); M 6, 49, no. 233 (1256/1840); M 6, 60, no. 286 (1256/1840); M 8, 30, no. 99 (1257/1841); M 14, 235, no. 896 (1260/1844); M19, 172, no. 599 (1264/1848); M 23, 236, no. 634 (1266/1850); M 28, 173, no. 464 (1269/1852).
51. M 6, 49, no. 233 (1256/1840); M 19, 172, no. 599 (1264/1848).
52. Salwa 'Ali Milad, "Registres de la Salihiyya Nagmiyya," *Annales Islamologiques*, XII (1974), 199: 6 manumission deeds registered during the first year of the oldest Mahkama court in Cairo (1524).
53. 25 deeds are found in M 20 (for the year 1264 A.H.)
54. Baer, "Slavery and Its Abolition," 179-81.
55. Tugay, 311; Mahkama notations: Sa'ida al-Gharbawiyya (al-Suda), freed on deathbed of her master and given 500 piasters (M 17, 29, no. 129, 1263/1847); Bahr al-Zayn, freed and given 500 piasters (M 12, 236, no. 738, 1255/1839); Sa'id al-Habashi and Amina al-Samra, freed and given 500 piasters each after death of their master (M 31, 17, no. 91, 1272/1856); Sunbul-tan al-Habashiyya, freed and given 1,500 piasters (M 50, 116, no. 179, 1290/1873).
    The Egyptian pound was pegged slightly higher than the pound sterling during the mid-nineteenth century.
56. BA 85, 179, no. 927 (? Safar 1014). The agreement was between Amir Isma'il Muhammad Mirdawan and his Ethiopian slave, Ja'far, the sum amounting to 100 dinars. Upon delivery, the slave was declared *hurran min ahrar al-muslimin*, "free as Muslim free men."
57. Examples:
    Asil 'Abd al-Halim, a broker in black slaves, went to court on behalf of Sa'da, daughter of al-Hajj Muhammad al-Salihi of Dar Sulayh (Wadai), supported by Hasan 'Ali Fa'id al-Burnawi and Yusuf 'Ali al-Burnawi; she was freed. SN 757, 253, no. 523 (20 Jum II 1162/1749).
    Ahmad 'Abd al-Rasul Husayn, a slave merchant at Wakalat al-Jallaba, and two *jallaba* support the case of Muhammad al-Asmar ibn Musa Husayn al-Sinnari, of the Bani 'Abbas in the Sudan, who had been unjustly enslaved and placed in the Egyptian army; he was freed. M 8, 207, no. 756 (2 Shab 1257/1841).
    Tayyib Muhammad al-Jallab of Dongola and three others from Ibrim and Shallal, Nubia, support the claims of Bakhit and 'Abd al-Rajal (?), sons of 'Abd Allah, whose manumission certificates were registered in Mahkama Kubran, "outside Khartum," and had been taken away from them by a boat captain and subsequently enslaved. They also testified on behalf of Bahkhit and Murjan, two other unjustly enslaved freed slaves held by another boat captain. M14, 278, nos. 1045 and 1047 (12 Muh 1261/1845).
58. He may have been among Takruri pilgrims that the Ottoman viceroy pressed into military service in 1801-2. Nicholas Turc, *Chronique d'Egypte, 1798-1804*, tr. Gaston Wiet (Cairo, 1950), Arabic text, 123, 176; French text, 151-2, 227.
59. The old capital of Wadai.
60. Possibly Runqa, with *nun* missing, Dar Runqa lay on the southern Dar Fur-Wadai border and was raided for slaves by both sides. See R. S. O'Fahey, "Slavery and the Slave Trade of Dar Fur," *Journal of African History*, XIV, 1 (1973), 34-6.
61. BA 327, 205, no. 466 (16 Muh 1218/1803).
62. It was customary for Cairenes to speak of many parts of the Sudan as situated in Upper Egypt (*al-Wajh al-Qibli*). "Kara" or "Kura" is not identifiable. Nachtigal noted a "Karé" in his map of Wadai, located in Salamat country. Gustav

Nachtigal, *Sahara and Sudan, IV: Wadai and Dar Fur*, tr. by Allan G. B. Fisher and Humphrey J. Fisher (London, 1971), map at end.
63. On the war in the 1830s between Dar Fur and Wadai, R. S. O'Fahey and J. L. Spaulding, *Kingdoms of the Sudan* (London, 1974), 174.
64. Probably Nimro, the commercial center of Wadai. Many *jallaba* were settled there. See Nachtigal, 50, 57, etc.
65. M 14, 74, no. 304 (5 Jum I 1260/1844). On Nasr al-Shuqayri, Walz, "Trade," 317, 392. The other Wadaians were named Sulayman Bashir and Muhammad Sahil.
66. M 26, 283, no. 758 (10 Shaw 1268/1852). The village, which is not yet identifiable, is spelled H-w-za or H-r-za (Hirza?) or H-w-ra (Hura?).
67. M 10, 177, no. 526 (2 Jum I 1258/1842).
68. 'Abd al-Ra'uf, freed by Nasr Yusuf al-Birkawi al-Jallab, sued his former owner for trying to re-enslave him: SN 520, 511, no. 1060 (? Shaw 1169/1756); Mahbub al-Asmar al-Dar Furi, freed by al-Hajja Amuna "al-Shamiyya" Muhammad, sued Muhammad Husayn al-Bibawi for attempting to sell him: M 9, 161, no. 466 (10 Qad 1257/1842).
69. I have been unable fully to account for the inflation rate which between 1822 and 1834, when a monetary reform was enacted, amounted to 66 percent in the value of the "hard" Austrian and Spanish dollar. See Helen Anne B. Rivlin, *The Agricultural Policy of Muhammad Ali in Egypt* (Cambridge, Ma., 1961), 121. However, most of the nineteenth-century inventories fall between 1251 and 1289 (1853-73) when the piaster was stabler.
70. Female slaves outnumbered male slaves three-to-one, coinciding neatly with these figures. There are no statistics on the ratio between castrated and uncastrated males. The operation, once performed in Upper Egypt, was prohibited in 1841 (O. Abbate, *Aegyptica*, Cairo, 1909, 650) and thereafter eunuchs were imported from black Africa.
71. *Three Centuries*, 311.
72. Bashir Agha al-Tawashi, married to Safiya al-Bayda, both freed slaves of Muhammad Kathusa Bayraqdar; Ahmad Agha al-Tawashi, married to Khalifa al-Bayda: Askar 131, 67, no. 139 (1142/1730) and Askar 131, 435, no. 823 (1143/1730).
73. Lane, *Manners*, 20. Gérard de Nerval, a bachelor, resolved his difficulties by purchasing a female slave: *Voyage en Orient*, I, 105 ff.
74. Austen, Table 2.
75. Egypt, Ministère de l'Intérieur, *Statistique de l'Égypte, 1873*, 22-5.
76. It is significant that children of merchants who lived outside Cairo, in Upper Egypt and the Sudan, seem to have had greater survival chances.
77. Quoted in J. J. Marcel, tr., *Contes du Cheykh el-Mohdy*, 3 vols. (Paris, 1835), I, 147.
78. No study has yet appeared on income averages among Cairo's various ethnic groups and social classes during the nineteenth century. (For the eighteenth century, see the pioneer work of André Raymond, *Artisans et commerçants au Caire au XVIIIe siècle*, 2 vols. (Damascus, 1973-4). Among merchants at Wakalat al-Jallaba, I have found the following "income" averages (based on inheritances registered at the Mahkama during the years 1831-66): long-distance merchants (*jallaba*): 3,734 piasters; retailers and "lesser" merchants: 5,463 piasters; "great" merchants (i.e. market shaikhs, "elders" and property owners): 58,215 piasters. This may be compared to selected estates left by more prominent nineteenth-century personalities: 'Umar Makram, religious notable (d. 1823), 25,700 piasters; 'Abd al-Rahman al-Tuwayr, great merchant and head of the North African community in Cairo (d. 1844): 966,200 piasters: Muhammad Amin, great

merchant and *Shahbandar tujjar* (head of the merchant community) (d. 1848): 756,035 piasters (excluding many debts); Ahmad pasha Yagen, former war minister under Muhammad 'Ali and related to the khedivial family (d. 1857): 16,029,801 piasters; Ibrahim pasha, son of 'Abbas pasha, Muhammad 'Ali's son (d. 1860): 3,057,163 piasters.

79. For the period 1722-46: black males; 9,027 *nisf fidda*; black females: 3,401 *nisf fidda*.
80. TAR 4, 73, no. 108 (13 Muh 1257); TAR 4, 172, no. 291 (21 Shab 1257). It is not rare to find brothers and sisters listed as heirs of freed slaves, or as being sold together.
81. TAR 15, 17, no. 29 (15 Saf 1274).
82. Wizarat al-Awqaf wa'l-shu'un al-Azhar, *Al-Azhar, tarikhhu wa tatawwuruhu* (Cairo, 1964), 175-91, especially 178-85. The endowments usually went to support students and teachers from Sudan, Chad and Nigeria. A study of West Africans in Cairo and at al-Azhar in the nineteenth and early twentieth centuries is forthcoming.
83. See, for instance, Hamont, "Souvenirs d'Egypte. Magiciens et psylles," *Revue de l'Orient*, II (1843), 155-6; A. Chelu, "Magie et sorcellerie, Etude de moeurs égyptiennes," *Bull. Union Géographique du Nord de la France*, XII (1891), 1-22.
84. *Egyptian Gazette*, issues of 26 February and 10 March 1883; 31 March 1884; 20 January 1886; 4 January 1887.
85. *Ibid.*, 5 and 13 December 1883; 2 January 1884.

IX

The Slave Mode of Production Along the East African Coast, 1810-1873

A. M. H. Sheriff

1. *The Slave Mode of Production: The Argument*[1]

Theoretically, a slave mode of production can exist autonomously, reproducing its productive labour through slave breeding. However, this increases the cost of that labour since it requires the maintenance of women and children during their unproductive periods, and limits the amount of surplus product that can be appropriated by the slave-owning class.

To overcome this contradiction two alternatives are open to the slave owners. The first is to use the slaves extensively, maintaining a large number of slaves who produce their own subsistence from allocated plots of land during certain assigned days of the week. Under such a system, approaching a squatter system, the slave helps in the production of foodstuffs for subsistence.[2] The extensive use of slaves, however, increases the cost of supervision and endangers the safety of the comparatively small slave-owning class.

The second alternative is to use the slaves intensively by developing their skills and improving their tools to increase their productivity. If subsistence is kept to the minimum necessary for survival, the slave owners can increase the proportion of their appropriation of surplus product from the slaves. However, with the increase in the rate of exploitation and the more developed consciousness of the skilled slaves, there may be an increase in class antagonism and resistance in the form of destruction of the more delicate tools, or escape. Although skilled slaves have existed historically in many parts of the world, it is the unskilled slave who is the common feature of the slave mode of production. Thus the slave relations of production hinder the development of skills and productivity of the slaves, the development of the productive forces in a slave mode of production.

Since neither of these alternatives resolve the contradictions in the slave mode, historically it has flourished generally when there were external sources of slave labour, when it can articulate[3] with subordinate and weaker modes of production from which the slaves can be appropriated through slave raids and wars without having to bear the cost of production of that labour power.

However, the slave mode of production that developed along the East African coast during the nineteenth century developed at a time when the capitalist mode was becoming a world-wide system, subordinating other modes throughout the world to its accumulation needs. The development and reproduction of the slave mode in East Africa, therefore, began to be determined by the laws that govern the capitalist mode. The latter thus imparts a number of specifically capitalist features, though not the capitalist relations of production, to the subordinate slave mode. The slave mode of production in East Africa therefore consisted of a double articulation, on the one hand with the communal and transitional modes in the African interior which it subordinated for its labour needs, and on the other hand with the capitalist mode to which it was itself being subordinated.

II. The Genesis of the Slave Mode of Production in Zanzibar and Pemba

With the overthrow of the Portuguese control over the Omani coastline in 1650, the Omani society began to undergo a transformation. With the accumulation of wealth from raids against Portuguese shipping and trade in the Indian Ocean there emerged a powerful class of Omani merchants who began to play an increasingly dominant role in the politics of Oman. This ultimately culminated in the accession to power of the mercantile Al-Busaidi dynasty and in the transfer of the capital from the interior to Muscat. The wealth of this class, however, was not based merely on trade but also on production of dates by slaves especially in the coastal belt. One of the rulers of Oman is credited in the local chronicles with renovation or construction of irrigation canals, ownership of 1700 slaves and of a third of the date-palms of Oman. If a rough correlation exists between the number of slaves and date palms owned, and assuming the mortality rate among the slaves to be 15% to 20%, the annual demand for agricultural slaves was probably between 1000 and 1500 slaves a year during the eighteenth century.[4]

The decreasing profitability in the West African slave trade and the development of sugar plantations in the French islands of Mauritius and Reunion during the last third of the century led to the extension of the French slave trade to the eastern coast of Africa. The larger source was Mozambique which expanded its supply from an average of about 3000 per annum in the 1770s to about 9000 in the 1780s. To meet this expanding demand, however, the coast of East Africa began to be drawn into the French-dominated slave trade. The supply of slaves from East Africa doubled to an average of over 2000 during the same period, partly at the expense of the northern Omani slave trade because of the better prices offered by the French.[5]

Napoleonic wars from the early 1790s disrupted this lucrative slave trade, and the conquest of Mauritius by the British in 1810 pulled the rug from under the feet of the Omani and Swahili merchant class in East Africa. The Moresby Treaty of 1822 prohibited the export of slaves from East Africa to the south altogether. Though slaves continued to be smuggled to the south during the 1810s and subsequently, the southern slave trade had definitely suffered a mortal blow by the early 1820s. The southern slave trade had been "a lucrative trade for the Island [Zanzibar], and the people in office made a great deal by it"; its collapse was therefore "a grievous blow to the fortunes of the merchant class in East Africa. Prior, who visited Kilwa in 1812, commented that at present the demand is confined to the Arabs, who do not take many".[6] There may have been a decline in the use of slaves in the date plantation economy of Oman during the last quarter of the eighteenth century, probably because of the greater competition from the French slave traders and the consequently higher prices for slaves. By the 1830s Oman was importing less than 1200 slaves, half of whom were re-exported to the Persian Gulf to be used in pearl diving, as crew on dhows, or for the unproductive sector as domestics or concubines. British efforts to prohibit the export of slaves to the north after the treaty of 1845 may have contributed to the decline, but it was not until the late 1860s that they embarked on a comprehensive campaign. In 1870 they laid a wide-spun web to search every dhow going north, and they searched in all more than 400 dhows, but only 11 dhows were found carrying slaves. What is remarkable is the fairly constant number of slaves captured between 1868 and 1870, numbering about 1000 slaves a year, though, with increasing risk of capture, the trade was becoming a more specialized activity with a decreasing number of dhows carrying an increasing number of slaves on average.[7]

Contrary, therefore, to the exaggerated estimates of the northern slave trade by British anti-slavery crusaders of the 19th century and the colonial historians of the 20th century, that portion of the trade was fairly modest and the demand fairly inelastic. Therefore the amputation of the southern arm of the slave trade from the end of the 18th century constituted a crisis for the merchant class in East Africa. Not only was a market for a substantial number of slaves lost; there was also a decline in the price of slaves to nearly a half by 1822. It was this same class which took the initiative in seeking an alternative use of the slaves to maintain their own prosperity.[7a]

Saleh b. Haramil al-Abray appears to have been the doyen of this class at Zanzibar. Born at Muscat in c.1770, he left his native country when young and visited the Seychelles, Ile de France (Mauritius) and Bourbon (Reunion). By the first decade of the 19th century he was described as "a perfect Frenchman". He was a friend and interpreter of the Omani governor of Zanzibar, probably the same but unnamed interpreter who was described by Dallons in 1804 as "a subtle and pliant man on whom all success depends" in the conduct of the French slave trade. It is also probably the same Arab whose share, according to Burton, in a single adventure in the southern slave trade was worth $218,000. According to Albrand, Saleh more than once came close to paying dearly for his intimacy with the French, and he built up a party at Zanzibar to protect himself from the Harthi, another Omani clan, long established at Zanzibar, who may have been more identified with the northern slave trade. Saleh apparently continued to trade in slaves to the south despite the 1822 Treaty which prohibited it. Seyyid Said, therefore, probably in 1828, confiscated his properties, profiting thereby "with all the appearance of justice", and Saleh died a pauper.[8]

Burton credits this same Arab with the introduction of cloves to Zanzibar, which Albrand dates fairly precisely, to 1812, and adds that by 1819 when he visited Zanzibar, they were already fifteen feet high. The selection of cloves was influenced by the astronomically high prices as a result of Dutch monopoly over the spice. As late as 1834, when the monopoly had already begun to crumble, it was yielding a profit of over 1000% on original cost of production. Zanzibari traditions, dating back at least to the end of the 19th century, attribute this initiative definitely to Saleh who obtained the seedlings from the French Islands in the Indian Ocean and who planted them on his plantations at Mtoni and Kizimbani. These were among the plantations which Seyyid Said confiscated. In addition Seyyid Said bought the plantation at Mkanyageni belonging to the sons of Saleh which was already planted with cloves. A French visitor to Zanzibar in 1822 found cloves growing on two plantations belonging to the governor of Zanzibar, but this governor was probably Saleh's relative who succeeded Abdullah b. Juma al-Harthi, according to Farsi. The only other clove plantation which had cloves before Seyyid Said visited Zanzibar in 1828 appears to be the one at Bumbwini which belonged to his slave "Al-kida Tengueni", at least as far as our records go.[9]

However, in view of the fact that there is a long gestation period in the production of cloves – five to seven years before the first small crop, and several more before the average for a mature tree is reached – the transformation of the merchant class into a class of slave-owning producers, and the expansion of clove production, may have been slow, so long, especially, as the slave trade could be carried on legally or otherwise. Bombay trade figures show that between 1823/4 and 1832/3 small quantities of cloves were already being imported from East Africa, the first crops of trees planted undoubtedly before Seyyid Said's first visit to Zanzibar.[10]

Seyyid Said himself, as the sovereign of Zanzibar and as a merchant prince, felt the pinch of cessation of the slave trade to the south even more acutely than his mercantile subjects. He claimed that the Moresby treaty of 1822 cost him $40,000 to $50,000 in lost revenue, though this may be an exaggeration, and additional amounts in commercial profit. In 1828 Seyyid Said informed the Bombay government:

> In consequence of the abolition of the slave trade the collections [revenue] of Zanzibar have been diminished; it has therefore been deemed necessary to make eleven plantations of sugar cane in the island.[11]

An American visitor reported in 1828 that the government of Zanzibar "for some time past have turned their attention to the cultivation of spices, the sugar cane, coffee, etc., all of which . . . will shortly be articles of export". In 1819 there were two sugar mills which had recently been established, one belonging to the Harthi governor, which were capable of producing enough sugar and syrup only for local consumption. Seyyid Said sought to expand this industry with the help of "technical aid" and personnel from the Mascarennes and England. In 1834 the industry was still in its "infancy". In the early 1840s Said went into partnership with an Englishman under which the latter provided machinery and supervision while the former supplied labour, slave labour, a formula which was an obvious subterfuge for the employment of slave labour. This was one of a series of joint ventures between the Sultans of Zanzibar and European capitalists culminating in Majid's agreement with Fraser, under which the latter was to supply machinery and supervisory staff while the former was to provide land and 500 slaves. When the agreement broke down,

Fraser contracted with four Arab slave-owners for the supply of 400 "labourers" who were to be "at the sole disposal" of Fraser & Co. for five years and were thereafter to be freed. The Arabs received their "wages" for one year which amounted to $24 per "labourer", probably a fair price for experienced slaves. When British Law officers pronounced the contracts to be subterfuge for the employment of slave labour, the British Consul induced Majid to emancipate the 711 slaves on Fraser's plantation at his own expense and offered in return the portrait of Queen Victoria. Though the climate of Zanzibar was unkind to many of the European settlers, the industry did obtain a footing, with sugar mills being established at Kizimbani and Mkokotoni, among other places. In 1847 about 10,000 *fraselas* of sugar were produced which Seyyid Said wished to send to the U.S. or England for refining. The Americans, fearing his penetration of the U.S. market, tried to discourage him, and a British embargo on the importation of sugar from the "slave states" may have hindered the expansion of this industry.[12]

More spectacular and of greater long-term significance, however, was the expansion of clove production on plantations confiscated or otherwise acquired by Seyyid Said. In 1834 Ruscenberger saw about 4000 clove trees at Kizimbani, ranging in height between five and twenty feet, suggesting that the smaller ones were planted since he confiscated it from Saleh b. Haramil. A similar expansion occurred on his other plantations which, by the time of his death, numbered forty-five. The smaller ones employed fifty to sixty slaves and the larger ones about 500, while the one visited by Guillain had six to seven hundred slaves. In all he is said to have owned 10,000 slaves. In 1840 the production of cloves from his plantations amounted to between five and six thousand *fraselas*, and by the late 1840s to between twenty and thirty thousand. Each of his numerous children, concubines and eunuchs also had their plots, and one of his elder sons, Khalid, owned "the grand and superb plantation 'Marseilles'," so named because of his "predilection for France and everything French". Seyyid Said's kinsman and governor of Zanzibar, Suleiman b. Hamed al-Busaidi, was one of the richest landowners whose plantations were furnishing five to six thousand *fraselas* of cloves worth over $10,000 by the late 1840s.[13]

The Busaidi ruling dynasty were at the head of what was developing as the landed aristocracy. Seyyid Said is said to have compelled his Omani subjects to plant a certain proportion of clove to coconut trees, threatening confiscation of the land for failure to do so. By the mid-1830s Ruschenberger reported that "the easy profits which clove

The Slave Mode of Production

plantations yielded made all the inhabitants of Zanzibar turn their eyes towards the crop", but he goes too far when he says that "almost everybody on the island is now clearing away the coconuts to make way for them." Loarer aptly described this feverish expansion, still raging in the 1840s, as a clove "mania". Members of other Omani clans also participated in this "mania", including the powerful Harthi clan whose leader in the late 1850s owned 1500 slaves, though most owned two to three hundred slaves.[14]

Though the Omani was a favoured ethnic group providing the ruling dynasty, ownership of clove plantations was not confined to that group. Evidence of participation in the clove economy by the indigenous Shirazi population is somewhat limited. Burton reported in 1857 that one of the Swahili had "lately purchased an estate of $14,000", and that the indigenous ruler of the Hadimu of Zanzibar, the *Mwinyi Mkuu*, lived on the proceeds of clove plantations. When the latter died in 1865 his two daughters inherited two of his plantations at Dunga and Bweni. But this remnant of the pre-existing ruling class was already merging with the new Omani dominated class, and both of these daughters themselves married prominent Omani landlords. By the 1840s some of the Indian merchants had also begun to pay "their tribute to this mania", according to Loarer, each having his small Shamba. Ibji Shivji, the brother of the farmer of customs of Zanzibar, acquired a new Shamba in 1844, and another merchant had three plantations and 175 slaves when he went bankrupt in 1846.[15]

Though production on non-Busaidi plantations had lagged behind, it rapidly caught up with, and by 1845 surpassed royal production by two to one. Cloves also spread to Pemba during this lucrative phase when the forest began to be cleared by *busaidi* and other rich landowners of Zanzibar. Though slave labour was used as in Zanzibar, it has been suggested that a very common method of establishing a plantation was for an Arab to supply clove seedlings and the indigenous Shirazi to clear the forest. The land was then divided between them under the "*nus bin nus*" system, though this system may have been more common after the abolition of the slave trade. This system may have allowed a greater participation by the indigenous population in the clove economy in Pemba. Production in Pemba rose steeply from about 2000 *fraselas* in 1845 to 10,000 in 1849.[16]

By the late 1840s, therefore, a landed aristocracy had emerged which, though predominantly Omani, was not exclusively so. And it was as a class that it enjoyed economic privileges, the most important of which was freedom from taxation. Only when over-production threatened its prosperity did Seyyid Said impose a tax of $¼ per *frasela* of cloves from Pemba in an effort to slow down expansion there. Coupled with the falling prices of cloves by the late 1840s, this postponed the rise of Pemba as the major producer until the hurricane of 1872. Although the landed aristocracy was emerging as the privileged ruling class of Zanzibar, the source of capital for the clove economy was commerce which provided most of the Sultan's revenues as well as commercial profit to the merchants, some of whom invested it in landed property in Zanzibar. Many caravan traders into the interior of Africa, after three or four journeys, settled down to a more leisured life in Zanzibar, the most outstanding case being Tippu Tip who reportedly owned seven *shambas* and 10,000 slaves, worth £50,000 at the end of the 19th century. Other Arab merchants involved primarily in coastal trade, such as Muhammad b. 'Abd al-Kadir, diverted their capital from commerce into clove production especially during the highly lucrative early phase. Finally, members of the Indian mercantile community also invested in clove production as detailed above.[17]

The development of the clove economy contributed to the marginalisation of the greater part of the Shirazi peasantry, especially in Zanzibar, in terms of both land and labour. Previous studies have tended merely to assert that the Shirazi were expropriated of the clove lands but producing little evidence beyond recourse to common sense.[18] It appears that during the initial feverish phase of expansion of cloves, the foothills of the four longitudinal ridges situated in the western half of Zanzibar, which were under coconuts and foodcrops, were cleared and planted with cloves. In these areas many cases of forcible expropriation appear to have occurred. Unfortunately, the soil here is not as fertile and the rainfall is only moderate, and these areas were to emerge as the poor clove lands of Zanzibar. The best clove plantations, however, were established along the ridges in Zanzibar and the more numerous hillsides in Pemba which enjoyed a heavier rainfall and had deep and well-drained soils. These areas appear to have been heavily forested early in the 19th century, used merely as refuge in times of trouble, or to hunt and collect firewood. Middleton was informed that "although the Shirazi sometimes planted plots in the forest area, these were covered with weeds so fast that cultivation became impossible". He argues, moreover, that the large villages in the plantation belt were not indigenous, lacking the social characteristics of the indigenous ones like Donge, Chaani and Dunga. In these areas expropriation of land from the Shirazi may not have been as widespread. However, the loss of access to forest products may have upset the economy of the Shirazi in the surrounding foothills, and this

The Slave Mode of Production

may have contributed to their displacement from the clove areas into the less fertile eastern parts of the islands.[19]

As the cultivation of cloves spread there was an increase in the demand for labour. Contrary to the assertion of Hamerton in 1841, the indigenous Muslim population of the islands were not enslaved, although it is possible that when the cleared and cultivated lands were expropriated, the resident peasants may have been allowed to squat in return for a contribution of labour at harvest time. Seyyid Said appears to have attempted to obtain a share in the traditional tribute in labour, amounting to a fortnight a year, which was due to the *Mwinyi Mkuu* for state purposes such as cutting and transporting timber for building purposes. Increased demands for labour sharpened the contradictions between the Omani ruler, the *Mwinyi Mkuu* and the Hadimu peasants which forced the conversion of the tribute into a poll tax in cash which was shared between the two suzerains until the *Mwinyi Mkuu's* dynasty died off in 1873. The Hadimu peasants thus withdrew even further from the clove economy, preferring to produce other commodities for exchange to pay the tax.[20]

With the already limited source of non-slave labour drying up, the plantation economy came to depend almost entirely on slave labour. The growth of the slave trade was due, therefore, not to any expansion of the export of slaves to the north as the British anti-slavery crusaders believed, but to the development of a slave mode of production within East Africa. In fact, British measures to prohibit the export of slaves to the south in 1822 and to the north in 1845, ironically, contributed to this development. But the slave mode, once launched, had its own momentum, more than making up for the loss of the external markets. Whereas at the beginning of the 19th century, a larger proportion of the estimated six to ten thousand slaves were for export, by the 1860s only about 15% of more than 20,000 slaves were exported outside Eastern Africa. Of the remainder at least 10,000 were retained within the islands of Zanzibar and Pemba, and the balance absorbed along the coast of Kenya and Somalia (see next section). The proportion of slaves retained in the plantation economy of Zanzibar is quite reasonable considering the mortality rate among the slaves and the size of the slave population in Zanzibar. Albrand estimated the slave population of Zanzibar in 1819 at about 15,000, and Burgess in 1839 at about 17,000. As the clove economy developed the figure rose to about 60,000 by 1847. Considering that the population of Zanzibar island in 1910 was just over 100,000, it is highly unlikely that the slave population exceeded 60,000 before the abolition of the slave trade. Since the mortality rate among slaves during this period was 15—20%, between nine and twelve thousand slaves would have been required per year to replenish the requirements for slave labour in Zanzibar.[21]

III. *Articulation with other Modes of Production in the African Interior*

Since the indigenous Muslim population of the islands and the coastal belt could not be enslaved for religious reasons, and it would not have been able to provide so many slaves annually anyway, the slave mode of production could develop only through articulation with other weaker social formations in the African interior for the supply of slave labour. These social formations had begun to be tapped from the 18th century to supply Oman and the French islands, and during the 19th century the numbers were to be expanded to supply the needs of Zanzibar. In 1811 Smee commented that "the various tribes of negroes brought to this port for sale are too numerous to describe," but he listed the Makua, the Yao, the Ngindo among the southern, and the Zigula, the Sambaa, the Doe and the Nyamwezi among the northern social formations as the principal ones providing slaves. A list of slaves liberated from a vessel captured in 1810 listed, in addition, the Makonde among the southern, and the Nyika, the Mrima and the Chaga among the northern groups as well as the Galla and others whose names are undecipherable. There is little doubt that throughout the 19th century the southern region yielded the majority of slaves, though the precise proportions varied according to conditions in the African interior at different times. In 1860 Rigby reported that out of 19,000 slaves brought to Zanzibar that year, 15,000 came from "the neighbourhood of the great lake of Nyassa", and 4,000 from the Mrima coast opposite Zanzibar. Seyyid Said's fiscal policy, charging a tax of $1 on slaves coming from the south, $2 from the northern coastal area, and $3 from Unyamwezi and other interior regions, may have contributed to this specialisation in the slave trade in the south.[22]

What is significant for our purposes is that, with few exceptions, the social formations listed above were characterised by a communal mode of production in transition to more differentiated ones during the 19th century. The Makua and the Yao appear to have been practicing extensive agriculture with limited division of labour in different economic activities except that based on sex and age. Many of the activities were carried on communally. The basic unit of social organisation was the kinship group. However, participation in long-distance trade had begun to give rise to social differentiation and to "a number of petty despotisms" based on the territorial principle and on

The Slave Mode of Production

increasing appropriation of the surplus by the chiefs. Social differentiation and the development of slavery as an institution within the chiefdom and the contradictions between the chiefdoms thus provided a fertile ground for the slave trade. Alpers argues that among the matrilineal Yao, the assimilation of female slaves provided an important mechanism for expansion in the scale of political organisation in the era of long-distance trade, thus giving impetus to the slave trade. The Nyassa, who had a more developed economy and social organisation before the 18th century, were going through a period of disintegration during the 19th century, and the dense population around the lake, therefore, provided a rich source of slaves for the coastal plantations.[23]

In the north the major source of slaves was the matrilineal tribes in the hinterland immediately behind the coast opposite Zanzibar and Pemba. The Zigula lived in the low plains sandwiched between the Shambaa and the Doe, practicing a mixed economy in an area prone to periodic famine as well as to raids from more powerful neighbours. Coupled with internal contradictions among these decentralised social formations, these factors contributed to the supply of slaves from these areas. The devastating famine of 1836 is remembered as a time when many Zigula sold themselves into slavery to escape starvation. However, the rising demand for slaves and the introduction of firearms among them led not only to attempts to resolve internal conflicts through wars and raids, and the sale of the vanquished to buy more firearms and other imported commodities, but also to expansionism. Kisabengo was typical of the new leaders who built up political power on the slave trade, expanding at the expense of the other stateless tribes, the Doe, Kami and Kwere, but also turning the tables on the Shambaa kingdom which was still committed to a pre-colonial rather than to the new proto-colonial mercantile economy and politics. As a well-developed feudality the Shambaa kingdom depended on subjects as payers of tribute rather than as a source of slaves for export. Therefore, apart from the occasional criminal, the only major source of slaves were the conquered enemies who could not be subjugated. It was only when the kingdom began to disintegrate after the death of Kimweri in 1862 that it became a major source of slaves.[24]

Smee had mentioned the Nyamwezi among the principal sources of slaves at the beginning of the 19th century. However, as the demand for ivory developed with a steeply rising price, it was apparently more profitable to engage in the ivory trade. By the 1840s sources are emphatic that the Nyamwezi did not supply slaves to the coast. In fact the Nyamwezi, the Gogo and the Kamba consumed slaves themsleves to produce foodstuffs for sale to the caravans passing through their territories. The fact that slave trade thrived in some parts of the deep interior, such as between E. Zaire and W. Tanzania, and yet few of these slaves reached the coast, may suggest a limit beyond which slave trade to the coast was uneconomic.[25]

The slave mode of production that developed in Zanzibar and Pemba, therefore, flourished only as a result of its ability to exploit the labour resources of a vast hinterland without having to contribute to the production of that labour. By the 1860s the boundary of that hinterland ran fairly close behind the coast of northern Tanzania but in the south it extended as far as Lake Nyassa. Although the boundary obviously shifted at different times during the 19th century, and in the north it may even have retreated closer to the coast, it does not seem as if it was annually being pushed deeper into the interior as the tribes closer to the coast were exhausted, as Rigby implies. As early as the 1770s Morice suggests that the hinterland of Kilwa had already extended as far as Lake Nyassa. Moreover, as has been suggested above, it may have been uneconomic to extend the distance over which the slaves had to be fed and marched. It is more likely that the existing sources were more thoroughly exploited. In this process the more fertile and thickly populated regions may have been able to withstand the increased demands without the collapse of the whole economic system. On the other hand in the area between Kilwa and Lake Nyassa, which was fairly sparsely populated when Bocarro passed through in 1616, and which was just being penetrated by the Yao and the Makonde from the south, the consequence of slave trading and slave raiding appeared to have been utter devastation and depopulation that Rigby, perhaps with some exaggeration, describes in 1860:

> Natives of India who have resided many years at Kilwa ... state that districts near Kilwa, extending to ten or twelve days' journey, which a few years ago were thickly populated, are now entirely uninhabited; and an Arab who has lately returned from Lake Nyassa informed me that he travelled for seventeen days through a country covered with ruined towns and villages which a few years ago were inhabited by the Mijana and Mijan [Yao] tribes and where no living soul is to be seen.[26]

IV. *Articulation with the Capitalist Mode of Production*

While, on the one hand, the slave mode of production in Zanzibar subordinated the communal and transitional modes in the African interior to supply its own labour needs, it articulated, on the other

The Slave Mode of Production

hand, with the capitalist mode of production which was becoming a worldwide system. The main instrument in that articulation was merchant capital in its different forms. It has already been suggested above that a considerable proportion of the capital invested in the slave mode was accumulated through trade in slaves and ivory. Secondly, what was being created at Zanzibar was an export economy since only a minute proportion of the cloves was consumed within East Africa. In 1859 more than 50% were exported to Europe and the U.S. and 40% to British Inida. Finally, as the clove economy entered a period of crisis of overproduction it became increasingly dependent on money-lending capital, itself largely accumulated in trade. Thus, the slave mode was gradually subordinated to the capitalist mode of production and its fate, and that of the landowning class, began to be determined by the laws of development of the capitalist mode which imposed on the slave mode a number of capitalist features.[27]

As the cultivation of cloves spread in Zanzibar and Pemba, so production increased, after the five to seven year gestation period, from the small quantities during the early years to a mature crop when the tree is about twenty years old. Bombay trade figures show the importation of cloves from the African coast, as well as from the Persian Gulf and Kutch, both areas in close commercial contact with East Africa, from 1823/4. However, for the first decade or so the quantities were limited, averaging just over 3,000 Rupees worth of cloves, the first crops of the plantations established before Seyyid Said's first visit to Zanzibar. As the trees on these plantations began to mature, and new trees planted since 1828 began to yield their first crops, production rose to an average of over Rs. 54,000 (about $25,000) worth of cloves during the late 1830s and early 1840s. Also during this period increasing quantities of cloves began to be exported directly to the U.S., reaching an estimated $24,000 worth of cloves in 1839. However, the full significance of the clove "mania" that raged during the 1830s began to be felt only by the late 1840s. Production of cloves from Zanzibar and Pemba rose from about 10,000 *fraselas* in 1840 to the staggering figure of 135,000 *fraselas* 1849. Though production fluctuated widely from year to year, it seems that by that date production had begun to level off and was to remain at that level until the hurricane of 1872.[28]

Such a rapid expansion of this export industry brought in its train a host of problems typical of a monoculture which have continued to haunt the economy of Zanzibar ever since. The most immediate effect of bursting the dam of Dutch monopoly over the spice was a precipitous decline in the price of cloves on the international market.

Already by 1834, as a result of expanded clove production in the Mascarenes, Guyana and Zanzibar, the profit margin was nearly halved, and by the end of the decade the monopoly was more or less dead and buried. At Bombay and Zanzibar the price of cloves declined to nearly a tenth by the 1850s compared with prices reigning in the 1820s and 1830s. Seyyid Said himself "saw with pain the depreciation of his beautiful plantations". When Loarer proposed to him to control further planting by imposing a tax on new clove trees and to prohibit the destruction of coconut trees, he replied that the measures proposed "will need surveillance which will cost money, whereas he wished to save money". Nevertheless, a duty of $1/4 per frasela was imposed on cloves from Pemba to restrict expansion there, and Seyyid Said threatened to confiscate plantations which did not replant a certain proportion of coconut trees to clove trees. However, the low prices of cloves were probably more effective in hindering further expansion of cloves. Grant commented in 1860 that plantation owners did not replace the dying clove trees.[29]

With the decline in the price of cloves there was a substantial decrease in the profitability of clove production. It has been estimated that a slave could harvest cloves from 10 to 20 trees during the short harvest season, and at an average of 6 lbs. of dry cloves per tree, this would give the slaves productivity of 60 to 120 lbs. of dry cloves per season. Translated into monetary terms, the slave harvested $17 to $34 worth of cloves in 1830 when the price was $10 per frasela, and $1.75 to $3.50 worth of cloves in 1865 when the price was $1 per frasela. Assuming an average working life-span of five to six years, in view of the high mortality among slaves, the gross returns from an investment in a slave made clove production rather uneconomic by the 1850s and 1860s.[30]

The decrease in the profitability of clove production was bound to have an effect on the price of the producers. Data for slave prices at Zanzibar during the 19th century are defective but a compilation of the available data shows that in fact there was an overall decline in the price of slaves. Whereas in 1784, at the height of the French slave trade, the price was about $40, it had declined to about $20 in 1822, to an average of $15 in the early 1840s, and to between $8 and $10 by the early 1860s. Thus the price of slaves halved between the 1820s and 1860s, but this did not adequately compensate for the decline in the price of cloves.[31]

Under these conditions the landowners attempted to diversify their economy, and with lower prices for slaves, these attempts stood a better chance of success. Guillain and Hines record greater interest in

The Slave Mode of Production

the production of indigo and coconuts. The quality of the former, however, prevented it from entering the Indian market. On the other hand, French demand for vegetable oils led to an increase in the production of coconut products for export from about $50,000 in the late 1840s to three or four times the amount by the mid-1860s. The sugar industry also received a fresh stimulus, attracting British and Indian merchant capital in addition to that of the Sultan. In the mid-1860s Sultan Majid entered a partnership with Fraser & Co. for the production of sugar at Mkokotoni (see *supra*). By then even Indian merchants began to show an interest in the industry, two of them offering to put up $45,000 for the project. However, since by then they had been declared British citizens, they were not allowed to employ slave labour, and free labour was unobtainable.[32]

A more spectacular result of the lower price of slaves, however, was the development of a slave mode of production on the coast of Kenya for the production of foodstuffs and oleaginous grains which became more competitive. The hinterland of Mombasa had been cultivated since the 18th century, and Emery recorded in 1826 that many of the inhabitants of Mombasa had their *shambas* there. However, with the loss of her independence in 1837 and the decline in Mombasa's direct foreign trade, Mombasa may have turned more agricultural. From the 1840s there was a marked expansion of production of food grains for export to the Arabian coast. Krapf commented about encroachment on Mijikenda land and increase in the employment of slaves on plantations. In 1866, 725 slaves were officially exported from Zanzibar to Mombasa apart from those shipped directly from Kilwa.[33]

The development at Malindi was even more striking. The town was revived in the late 1850s or early 1860s apparently on the initiative of the Sultan of Zanzibar to produce foodstuffs for export to Zanzibar and Arabia. By 1873 Kirk estimated an annual importation of 600 slaves just to maintain the stock of 6,000 slaves. He estimated an annual export of grain worth $166,000, though Grefulhe, a French commercial agent directly involved in the trade, estimated it at between $80,000 and $120,000. While other ethnic groups took part in this development, it is significant that at the beginning of the 10th century Omani Arabs owned nearly 54% of the plantation acreage, led by the family of the Busaidi governor who owned 30% of it.[34]

A similar development occurred in the hinterland of Lamu and southern Somalia. In the 1840s Loarer and Guillain reported that the area produced a large quantity of food grains largely for export to Arabia. In 1853 it was reported that cultivation was on the increase and that many dhows were being sent as far as Mozambique to procure slaves. Here again the Omani Arabs, and especially members of the Busaidi ruling clan, took a leading role. An important stimulus was given to agricultural growth by French and German demand for sesame for the production of vegetable oil, and orchella weed, used in the production of dyes, for export to Europe. During the early 1860s Zanzibar exported an average of nearly $170,000 worth of sesame and other oil seeds, 70% of which went to France and Germany.[35]

The more or less successful attempts at diversifying the economy perhaps partly explains why the decline in the price of slaves did not correspond to the same degree with the decline in the price of cloves. The consequence of this for the plantation owners in Zanzibar was that those who had invested their capital in establishing clove plantations during the booming period of the 1830s when the price of slaves was also higher, could only look on helplessly as the value of their investment progressively declined and their annual income diminished substantially. This inevitably led to indebtedness and even loss of land to the money-lenders. As early as 1843 Hamerton reported that many Arab plantations were mortgaged to Indian money-lenders "who cultivate them and in this way repay themselves", and Burton reported in 1857 that "the Indians have obtained possession from the Arabs, by purchase or mortgage, of many of the landed estates". In 1860/1 Rigby emancipated over 8,000 slaves owned by Indians who, as British subjects, were not allowed to possess slaves. According to Rigby about a third were domestic slaves and some were employed in the city and on the mainland as porters and in other commercial activities such as cleaning copal. The rest were employed on plantations. From a partial register that has survived, recording more than a third of the slaves emancipated, it appears that 30% of the slaves were owned by 77% of the Indian slave owners, probably as domestics, at an average of three slaves per owner, while 70% of the slaves were owned by only 23% of the Indian slave owners at an average of 24 slaves per owner, undoubtedly mostly as plantation workers. The largest owner was the prominent firm of merchant, financier and farmer of customs, Jairam Sewji, who owned 460 slaves.[36]

However, this represents only the land which had already passed into the hands of the merchant capitalists as a result of foreclosure. But money-lenders are normally not too anxious to be involved in actual production themselves, and they were undoubtedly even less anxious in Zanzibar at this time due to the very low profitability of the enterprise. Therefore, the extent of actual ownership of land by the merchants was only the tip of the iceberg of impoverishment of the landed class by the 1860s. Moreover, the emancipation of the slaves

The Slave Mode of Production

held by the Indians denied the latter the option of foreclosure, and they therefore had to resort to very high interest rates as a guarantee against losses and to establish a claim directly on the crop, retaining the landowner as little more than a manager. The indebtedness of the landowning class, therefore, continued to mount. By 1873 a single, though most prominent, Indian firm had loaned out to Arab landowners on the islands and the mainland nearly $285,000, and Frere was assured that few of the larger Arab estates in Zanzibar "are unencumbered by mortgages in Indian capitalists, and that a large proportion are so deeply mortgaged as virtually to belong to the Indian mortgage".[37]

V. Conclusion

Merchant capital was thus the universal mechanism by which the slave mode of production developed at Zanzibar. It was merchant capital which financed slave trade deep into the African interior to expropriate cheap labour from the weaker social formations there without having to pay for its production. Though the rise of capitalism dictated the abolition of slavery on a world scale, in East Africa it did so only gradually, initially only by restricting the export of slaves. This had the effect ironically of internalising the slave economy and establishing a slave-based production system within East Africa. Capital accumulation from the preceding trade in slaves, and later in ivory, financed a substantial portion of the clove plantations.

However, what was being created was an export-oriented dependent economy. Only a minute proportion of the cloves were consumed within East Africa, the rest being destined for the international capitalist-dominated market. Concentration on the production of this luxury diverted a considerable amount of land, labour and capital from other economic activities, including food production, so that Zanzibar was transformed from a more or less self-sufficient island into an importer of food and other commodities. The economy of Zanzibar was thus asymmetrical, exporting much of what was produced, and importing manufactured goods increasingly from the industrialised capitalist countries of the West, in exchange not only for cloves but also for slaves from the interior. This provided a wide scope to merchant capital as a conduit by which a large part of the surplus appropriated from the social formations in the African interior without compensation, and that produced by the slaves in the clove plantations of Zanzibar, was conveyed directly or indirectly to the capitalist mode of production through the mechanism of unequal exchange.

In its money-lending form merchant capital was able to take advantage of the crisis of overproduction faced by the landowners to fleece them of much of the surplus produced by the slaves. By impoverishing the landowners through money-lending, merchant capital undermined the position of the landowning class. However, merchant capital which is not involved in production, is dependent on the class that organises production. It therefore attempts to buttress that class against total collapse. Moreover, for it to exist and flourish it has to accumulate and invest capital primarily in the sphere of circulation, which means the withdrawal of the life-giving surplus from the sphere of production. In both these aspects merchant capital plays a reactionary role, hindering the transformation of the society.

Merchant capital is therefore incapable of promoting the transition from one mode of production to another. However, by providing the mechanism for articulation of the slave mode with the dominant capitalist mode, it was instrumental in imposing on the former the logic of the latter, which was the ultimate annihilation of the slave mode of production.

NOTES

1. This section is partly based on B. Hindess and P. G. Hirst, *Pre-Capitalist Modes of Production*, London, 1975, Chapter 3.
2. This occurred in Zanzibar throughout the slave period. The slaves were allowed two free days a week to grow their own food, and to sell the surplus, if any, on their own account. W. S. W. Ruschenberger, *Narrative of a Voyage round the World*, London, 1838, Vol. I, pp. 40-41. R. F. Burton, *Zanzibar*, London, 1872, Vol. I, p.466. Kirk to Foreign Office (F.O.), 22/9/1871, Public Record Office: FO 84/1344. J. Christie, "Slavery in Zanzibar as it is", in E. Steeve, ed., *The East African Slave Trade*, London, 1871, p.34. Only Putnam in 1849 mentions three free days, and he was only a short-term visitor. N. R. Bennett & G. E. Brooks, *New England Merchants in Africa (NEMA)*, Boston, 1965, p.427. It is curious that Nicholls should have adopted his evidence against the other more reliable ones, some of which she lists in a footnote. C. S. Nicholls, *The Swahili Coast*, London, 1971, p.289.
3. For a discussion of the concept of circulation, see C. Bettleheim's "Theoretical Comments", in A. Emmanuel, *Unequal Exchange*, New York, 1972, pp. 296-8.
4. Salil b. Razik, *History of the Imams and Seyyids of Oman*, London, 1871, pp. 69, 89, 92-3, 201-2, 216. R. D. Bathurst, "The Ya'arubi dynasty of Oman", Oxford, D.Phil., thesis, 1967, pp. 137, 205-6. Hamerton to FO 2/1/1844, FO 54/6, estimated mortality rate at 22-33%. In 1883 it was estimated at 8-12%. F. Cooper, "Plantation Slavery on the East Coast of Africa in the Nineteenth Century", Yale Ph.D., 1974, p.300 n. C. Lloyd, *The Navy and the Slave Trade*, London, 1968, p.240.
5. E. A. Alpers, "The French Slave Trade in East Africa (1721-1810)", *Cahiers D'Etudes Africaines*, X, 1 (1970), pp. 100-12, 113-14.

The Slave Mode of Production 179

6. G. S. P. Freeman-Grenville, *The East African Coast*, Oxford, 1962, p.210.
7. Wilson to Norris, 28/1/1831, Maharashtra Archives: Political Department (MAPD): 1/1830-2, pp. 18-21. Robertson to Willoughby, 4/3/1842, MAPD: 78/1841-2, pp. 346-62. Kemball to Robertson 8/7/1842, MAPD: 80/1842-3, pp. 289-99. J. E. Harris, *The African Presence in Asia*, Evanston, 1971, pp. 48-9. G. L. Sullivan, *Dhow Chasing in Zanzibar Waters*, London, 1873, p. 307. C. Lloyd, op. cit., p.278.
7a. Freeman-Grenville, op. cit. pp. 196-7, Cooper, op. cit., pp. 87-8.
8. F. Albrand, "Extrait d'un Mémoire sur Zanzibar et sur Quiloa", *Bulletin de la Société de Géographie*, Aôut, 1838, p.78. Fisher's Report, 1809, PRO: Admiralty 1/62, Freeman-Grenville, p.199. R. F. Burton, *Zanzibar*, op. cit., Vol. 1 pp. 294-5, 361. M. Guillain, *Document sur l'histoire, la géographie et le commerce de l'Afrique Orientale*, Paris, 1856, Vol. II, p.49.
9. Albrand, p.69, Ruschenberger, pp. 73-5. R. H. Crofton, *A Pageant of the Spice Islands*, London, 1936, p.80. W. A. Fitzgerald, *Travels in the Coastlands of British East Africa and the Islands of Zanzibar and Pemba*, London, 1894, pp. 553-4. A. S. Farsy, *Seyyid Said b. Sultan*, Zanzibar (1942), p.29. Guillain, II, p.49. Cooper, p.99.
10. G. E. Tidbury, *The Clove Tree*, London, 1949, p.108. Bombay Commerce, 1801/2-1847/8, India Office: P/419/Vols. 39-106.
11. Said to Shoostree, n.d., consultation 9/7/1828, MAPD: 8/1828. Bruce to Warden, 25/2/1822, MAPD: 82/1822.
12. Roberts to Woodbury, 19/12/1828, Library of Congress: Roberts' Papers, Vol. 6. Albrand, p.76. Captain Hart, "Extracts from Brief Notes of a Visit to Zanzibar", Bombay Records XXIV, 1855, p.280. Hamerton to FO 24/9/1846, FO 54/10; s. to s. 13/4/1844, FO 84/540. Extract of Freemantle's Journal, 20/5/1842, FO 54/5. Memorial of W. Henderson & Co. to the Treasury, 18/12/1844, FO 54/8. Said to Palmerston, 30/6/1847, FO 54/11. *NEMA*, 253, 257, 384, 390, 398. Playfair to FO 3/5/1865, Seward to Goune, 14/7/1866, 25/10/1866, FO 84/1261; s. to FO, 20/2/1867, FO 84/1279. Frere's Memo, 10/2/1873, Parliamentary Papers, 1873/61, pp. 805-6. Loarer, "sucre", Archives Nationales: Section Outre-Mer (A.O.M.) Ocean Indien (O.I.) 5/23/5.
13. Ruschenberger, I, pp. 70-1. Loarer, "girofle", *ibid.* R. Said-Ruete, *Said b. Sultan*, London, 1929, p.87. Guillain, 11, p.48. Ward to Ward, 22/11/1847, Essex Institute (E.I.) Ward's Letter Book, 1848-9. *NEMA*, 256. Burton, *Zanzibar*, I, p.98.
14. R. Coupland, *East Africa and Its Invaders*, Oxford, 1938, p.322. Rushchenberger, I, 51. Loarer, *loc. cit.*, Rigby to Bombay Government, 4/4/1859, National Archives of India: Foreign Department (NAI:FD) 17/6/1859-P.C.-5.
15. Burton, *Zanzibar*, I, pp. 278, 432. J. Gray, *History of Zanzibar*, London, 1962, p.168. *Zanzibar Gazette*,592/2. Loarer, *loc. cit. NEMA*, 376. Waters' Notes, 8/9 & 22/11/1843, Peabody Museum.
16. Loarer, *loc. cit.* Loarer, "Pemba", AOM:O.I. 2/10(2)D.
17. C. E. B. Russel, *General Rigby, Zanzibar and the Slave Trade*, London, 1935, p.328. Loarer, "girofle". D. Mackenzie, "Special Mission to Zanzibar and Pemba", *The Anti-Slavery Reporter*, June-August 1895, pp. 92-3. H. Brode, *Tippu Tib*, London, 1907, p.48. Cooper, 143. Waters' contracts with various landowners, Waters Papers, Peabody Museum.
18. Cooper, 112-13. Gray, 167-8.
19. Ruschenberger, I, 51. Broquant to Ministère des Affaires Étrangères (MAE), Correspondence Consulaire et Commerciale: Zanzibar (CCZ), Vol. I, 220-31. Burton, *Zanzibar*, I, 363. L. & W. Christopher, "Extract from a Journal..." Transactions of the Bombay Geographical Society, Vol. VI, p.377. Tidbury, 108-9. Gray, 167-8. Albrand, pp. 66, 70. J. Middleton, *Land Tenure in Zanzibar*, London, 1961, pp. 11, 42. A. H. J. Prins, *The Swahili-speaking Peoples of Zanzibar*

and the *East African Coast*, London, 1961, p.62. E. Burgess, "Probable openings for missionaries at Zanzibar", *Missionary Herald*, 31 (1840), pp. 118 *seq.*
20. Ruschenberger, I, 64. Hamerton to Bombay Government, 2/1/1842, FO 54/4. Gray, 161-2. J. M. Gray, *Report on the Inquiry into claims to certain land at or near Ngezi* — Zanzibar, 1956, p.10. M. H. Jabir, personal communication, 1976.
21. Burton, Vol. II, 493. Albrand, 73. Burgess, 118-21 *NEMA*, 400. Zanzibar Protectorate, Report on the Native census, 1924, Zanzibar, 1924, p.5. See fn.4 above.

Slave Trade on the East African Coast, 1862/3-1872/3

	Exported from Kilwa to Zanzibar	Elsewhere	Retained in Z'bar & Pemba	Re-exported to the Kenya coast	Total
1862/3	13,000	5,500			18,500
1863/4	14,000	3,500			17,500
1864/5	13,821	3,000			16,821
1865/6	18,344	4,000			22,344
1866/7	17,538	4,500	14,142	6,434	25,076*
1867/8				7,819	
1868/9		3,000	4,089	7,855	14,944
1869/70				5,099	
1870/1			2,120	3,412	
1871/2			8,930	9,392	
1872/3			8,845	6,284	18,129*
Average	15,341	3,917	7,625	6,614	19,045

*Apart from Kilwa the other major, though intermittent source of slaves was the Mrima coast. This explains the discrepancy in 1866/7 between the total export from Kilwa, 22,038, and the total trade, 25,076 (adding coluns 2, 3 and 4). In 1871/2 also, about 3,000 slaves were imported into Zanzibar from the Mrima.

Sources: Burton, I, 464-5, 372. Seward to Bombay Government, n.d., MAPD: 73/1866, pp. 7-25. *Parliamentary Papers* (P.P.) 1867/67, c. 3761, pp. 284, 288. Seward to FO, n.d. (3/1867), FO 84/1279. Churchill to Bombay Government, 4/4/1868, FO/84/1292. Kirk to FO, 1/2/1870, FO 84/1325; s to s., 27/6/1871, FO 84/1344; s. to s., 25/1/1872, FO 84/1357; s. to s., 13/1/1873. *P.P.*, 1874/62, S.T. 8(1874), p.7. Only about 1000 slaves being exported to the north were intercepted in the late 1860s. See p.163 above.

22. Smee, in Burton, II, 346, 510-11. Albrand, 80. "List of different tribes comprising the cargo of slaves taken by the Sir Edward Hughes Indiaman", 1810, India Office: Marine Records Misc. 586, Russell, p.333. R. F. Burton, *The Lake Regions of Central Africa*, London, 1860, Vol. II, 376. Loarer, "Tougni", "Lindy", "Quiloa Quevindja", AOM:O.I. 2/10/2. "Esclavage", *ib.*, 5/23/5. Guillain, III, 327-8.
23. E. A. Alpers, *Ivory & Slaves in East Central Africa*, London, 1975, pp. 8-29.
24. H. M. Stanley, *How I found Livingstone*, London, 1872, p.243. J. L. Krapf, *Travels, Researches and Missionary Labours in Eastern Africa*, London, 1860, p.121. C. Pickering, *The Races of Man*, London, 1850, p.197. S. Feireman, *The Shambaa Kingdom*, Madison, 1974, pp. 137-44, 165, 175-7.
25. Smee, in Burton, *Zanzibar*, II, 510-1. Farquhar's Memo, 12/1821, British Museum: Add. Mss. 41265. Krapf, 357-8. Guillain, III, 267-8. Pickering, 194, 196-7. Rigby to Bombay Government, 13/9/1858, MAPD: 167/1858, pp. 28-31. E. A. Alpers, *The East African Slave Trade*, Nairobi, 1967, p.21.

26. Alpers, *Ivory & Slaves*, p.239. G. S. P. Freeman-Grenville, *The French at Kilwa Island*, Oxford, 1965, pp. 76, 119, 137. Freeman-Grenville, *The East African Coast*, pp. 165-8.
27. Rigby to Secretary of State for India, 1/5/1860, FO 54/17.
28. Tidbury, 108. "Bombay Commerce, 1801/2-1847/8". Loarer, "girofle". Burton, *Zanzibar*, I, 364-5. Essex Institute; Salem Custom House Records, Inward Invoice (1839).
29. Loarer, "girofle". Burton, *Zanzibar*, I, 219. J. A. Grant, *A Walk Across Africa*, London, 1864, p.15. Seward's Report on the Trade and Commerce of Zanzibar, 1864/5. *P.P.*, 1867/67, C.3761, p.285. Prices of cloves at Bombay worked out from "Bombay Commerce, 1801/2-1847/8"; at Zanzibar from Peabody Museum: Waters' Shephard's and West Papers.
30. O. Sullivan-Boere's "Report on the Island of Pemba, 1900", *P.P.*, 1901/81, No. 2653, p.11. Tidbury, see p.2.
31. Freeman-Grenville, *The East African Coast*, pp. 196-7. Cooper, 87-8. MAPD: 78/1841-2, pp. 7-9. W. E. Devereux, *A Cruise in the Gorgon*, London, 1869, pp. 70, 104, 114, 368-9. MAPD: 54/1864, pp. 16-33. R. N. Colomb, *Slave Catching in the Indian Ocean*, London, 1873, p.57. *P.P.*, 1865/53, C.3488, pp. 176.
32. Guillain, *NEMA*, 528, 553. Pelly to Forbes, 10/1/1862, NAI: FD-4/1862-Pol.A-185, pp. 261-2. Pelly to Stewart, 10/7/1862, NAI-FD-10/1862-Pol.A-24; s. to s., 10/6/62, Stewart to Secretary to the Government of India, 16/10/1862, NAI:FD-11/1862-Pol.A-32. Seward's Report, *P.P.*, 1867/67, C.3761, p.284.
33. Loarer, AOM:O.I.:2/10/2, 5/23/5. Emery's journal, PRO: Adm. 52/3940. F. J. Berg, "Mombasa under the Busaidi Sultanate", University of Wisconsin, Ph.D. 1971, pp. 196, 202, 216-23, 245, 263-6, 277.
34. Cooper, 173-85. Kirk to Granville, 6/11/1873, *P.P.*, 1874/62, pp. 101-2. E. B. Martin, *The History of Malindi*, Nairobi, 1973, Ch. IV.
35. Loarer, "Lamo", AOM:O.I.-2/10/2. Sunley to Clarendon, 23/8/1853, FO 84/919. H. Grefulhe, "Voyage de Lamoo à Zanzibar", *Bull. de la Société de Géog. de Marseilles*, II (1878), pp. 328-31. Rigby to Anderson, 11/2/1860, MAPD: 159/1860, pp. 219-53. M. Ylvisaker, "Shamba na Konde", University of Nairobi, History Seminar, Oct. 1971.
36. Hamerton to Bombay Government, 9/10/1843, INA:FD. Rigby to Anderson, 14/5/1861, FO 84/1146. Burton, *Zanzibar*, I, pp. 316-7. Zanzibar Archives: Secretariat G.I. I am indebted to Martha Honey for a copy of the register.
37. Frere's "Memo regarding Banians," *P.P.*, 1873/61, C.820, p.102.

GLOSSARY

'Abd (pl., *'abid*): slave, esp. "black" slave; (*'abidiyya* = "royal" slaves; slave settlements).
Ama (pl., *ima'*); female slave.
Dhimmi: a protected person; a Christian or Jew protected by Muslim law, and allowed to practise his religion in return for his recognition of the supremacy of Muslim law and Muslim rule.
Ghazwa (also, *salatiyya* with the same meaning): a raid or armed expedition formed for the acquisition of slaves.
Ghulam: a beardless youth, young slave; house servant.
Habash (*Habasha, Hubush*): Ethiopians (Abyssinians); slaves from Ethiopia or the Ethiopian region.
Ham: one of the sons of Nuh (Noah), popularly thought to be cursed (owing to a sin against his father) in that his descendants were turned black in color and made slaves.
Haratin (sing., *hartani*); a horse of mixed breed, hence, "half breed"; a sedentary population of North African oases of apparent slave origin.
Harim: female preserve or part of household: metaphorically, a point of separation between the sexes. In custom (especially Turkish), penetrated only by men who are without sexual threat to the women therein (e.g. *khasi* = eunuch).
Hurr: "freeborn"; *hurriyya*: "freedom"; *hurthani*: free man.
Jabarti: Muslim Galla merchant in Ethiopia.
Jallaba: itinerant Muslim traders; slave traders.
Jihad: "struggle in the path of Allah", the only sanctioned war in Islam; an expedition for the expansion of Islam wherein slaves were often taken.
Jizya: a compensation paid to Muslims by Christians or Jews in return for the privilege of practising their religion.
Kafir: heathen; pagan; one susceptible to enslavement (pl. *kuffar*); *kufr*: heathenism; paganism.
Khadim (pl. *khaddam*): domestic slave or servant.
Khazi: eunuch.
Mamluk: "white" (originally, Circassian) slave.
Mawla (*mawali*; *muwallad*); freedman; client through conversion to Islam or by "kinship" affiliation.
Mudabbar: manumitted on the death of the master.
Mukatib: manumitted for future compensation (often by instalment) or in lieu of future compensation.
Raqaba: "neck"; slave.
Riqq: slavery; slave trade (*raqiq*: slave newly caught).
Rumada: slave settlements of the Fulani.
Sa'iba: untamed, wild beast; free and put out to pasture; she-camel once domesticated and then turned loose to pasture; slaves and societies beyond reach of Muslim control and authority.
Sirriyya: female slaves.
Sudan: black (sing. *aswad*); *bilad al-Sudan*: land of the Blacks.
Tilad: slaves or pasturing beasts that breed in one's own abode or house and become old, long possessed.
Wakil: agent (*muwakkil*: prinicpal).
Wala': either of manumission or alliance; (*wilaya*: forced affiliation); the means by which the freedman effects a "kinship" bond with his master's line.

Glossary

Wasif: black servant or slave (sing. *wasfan*).
Zanj: a enslavable "barbarian" from the East African Coast; a "black".
Zariba: permanent thorn enclosures for ivory traders and slave traders of East African region; place where such traders and their servants (and slaves) establish themselves.

INDEX OF ARABIC WORDS AND TERMS

Note: An asterisk before a word indicates that a definition is given in the Glossary on page 181.

ab shaykh dali, 89
'abaq', 139
*'abd (pl. 'abid), 2, 14n, 54, 84
'Abid al-Bukhari, 2, 14n
'abidiyya, 92
ahmar al-jilda, 4, 5
'ala al-wajh al-mastur, 157n
'ala sabil al-amana, 141
'alim, 91, 130
'amil, 66, 71, 81n
amir, 62, 98n
aro, 47n
ashab al-Jabal, 85
askar, 110, 113, 114
asmar, 140, 156n
aswad, 140, 155n
awlad al-salatin, 89

Bab Sharqi, 63
Bab Zuwayla, 59
bahaq, 145
baiwa (pl. bayi), 46n
balad, 148
bara, 38
bayt al-mal, 152
bazinear, 113
beni bio, 43
bey, 150
bey al-nuba, 67
bi'l-mazad al-'alani, 87
bilad as-Sudan, 148
bitana, 23
buza, 146, 158n

daadiŋa, 92
dabari, 11
daftar bi-asma' al-'abid alladhina kanu fi 'askar al-Dhahabi al-Sa'di, 2
dagaci (pl. dagatai), 46n
darb al-arba 'in, 87, 148
dawawin, 3
daym, 106
dendal, 64
*dhimmi, 19, 54
dhurra, 63
dimajo (pl. dimajai, rimaibe), 40, 41, 43, 47, 48n
dinar, 61

diya, 93
djose, 43
djund, 31n

efendi, 150

falaqna, 88, 98n
fanfa, 25
faqih, 89, 92, 93, 94, 95, 97n, 99n, 100n
farukh, 113
fashir, 88, 89
fatwa, 7, 8, 13, 26, 28
fayruz akhdar, 55
fiere, 68
firman, 74
frasela, 166, 167, 173
fuqqarat, 58
furusiyya, 84

gabar, 126
Galadima, 70
galla, 40
gandu, 38, 45, 50n
ganga, 64
*ghazwa, 86, 87, 93, 95
*ghulam, ix, xin
gurma, 18, 25

*Habasha, 125, 128
habashi, 140, 156n
al-haddadiyyat al-zamirat, 22
hajaray, 85
hakimi (pl. hakimai), 39, 47n
hakura (pl. hawakir), 93
Harat Zuwayla, 59
*Haratin (sing. Hartani), x, 1-13 (passim), 14n;
*harim, ix, 54, 63, 78, 88, 89
hausa, 18
Hayy al-Nazila, 63
Hayy al-Ra'is, 63
Hayy al-Zawiya, 63
hubs, 26
Hugu-korei-koi (or Hu-kokorei-koi), 23
hurma, 25
hurran min ahrar al-muslimin, 158n

imam, 9, 100n, 114

Index of Arabic words and terms

irade, 74
istirqaq, 7, 10
'itaqnameh, 82n
'itq, 146, 147

jabalawiyya, 98n
jabalawiyyin, 85
*Jabarti, 125
jabir al-dar, 90
*jallaba, 93, 102, 103, 105, 106, 108-9, 111, 113, 114-15, 118, 138, 147, 158
jariya baydi, 156n
jaysh, 24, 50n
*jihad, ix, 18
jins, 86
jund, 24, 50n
jund Songhay, 24

Kabara-farma, 23
kashif, 150
katib, 114
Kaygama, 70
khabir, 100n
*khadim, 84
Khammas, 4
kharaj, 66, 68
Kislar Agha, 30n
kizlar agas, 54
korayat, 88, 98n
koy, kurra (pl. *abdiana*), 84
kubaniyya, 86
kuuriŋa, 92
kɔrkwa, 88, 89, 98n

libn, 62

ma'allaq, 153
mahbub, 76, 148
Mahkama al Shar'iyya, 137
mai, 60
majidi, 87
malam, 36
malik, 97n
malik al-'abidiyya, 92
*mamluk, 25, 54, 60, 70
mander, 129
martaba, 153
masarif ma'kal wa mashrab ar-raqiq, 139
*mawali, 28
Misiriyya, 85
mithqal, 61, 66, 67, 70, 72

*mudabbar, 147
Mudir, 74
*mukatib, 147
muluk al korayat, 89
murabits, 66
mustawlida, 157n
mustawlidat, 145, 151
mut'a, xin
al-muta sabbib fi bida 'a al-Sudaniyya, 155n
Mutasarrif, 75
mutawa 'ik, 142
Mwingi Mkuu, 167, 169

narakik, 113
nisba, 148
nisf fidda, 160n
nus bin nus, 167

qadi, 3, 96n, 114
qa'id, 61
Qa'im Maqam, 74, 76, 79
qamhi, 156n
qanat, 58
qawabil, 144
qayn (female *qayna*), 22, 30n
Qur'an, ix, 112, 115, 147

rahat, 139
al-ra'iyya, 24
raqiq, 54, 84
razzia, 113
*riqq, 84
riwak, 125
riwaq, 149
*rumada (pl. *rinji*), 40, 47n, 92
rumbde, 48n
rumda, 40
runde, 42

saariŋa, 92
salamathu, 87
*salatiyya, 86
saqat, 142
sariyya, 19
Shahbandar tujjar, 160n
Shamba, 167, 168, 175
Shanqalla, 128
Shari'a, 7, 17, 19, 84, 96n, 112
sharif, 27, 62, 69
somiŋ dogala, 88, 89, 91
sudasi, 87
sulh, 95

Sultan al-Ghazwa, 105
Sunna, viii, ix, 12
sunnu, 25
Suq al-Bashar, 52

tabi', 150
tarbush, 91
ta 'rikh, 29
temhi (temhy), 56
tibr, 66
*tilad, xin
tisht, 153
Topkapi Sarayi, 77
trona, 72

'ulama', 71, 100n, 112; Fas, 1-13 (passim)
uroso, 43
'usta, 142

Veli, 51, 52, 67, 77
vilayet, 52

al-Wajh al-Qibli, 158n
*wakil, xn, 110-11, 125, 130, 131, 149
waqf, 26, 154
wasf (pl. awsaf), 86
wasiya, 145, 157n
wazir, 89, 90, 91, 104

al-yasirji fi'rraqiq al-aswad, 155n

zaga, 43
*zanj, 78
*zariba, 107-20 (passim)
zurqa, 95
Zuwayliyin, 59
ɔrre baya, 88
ɔrre de, 88

INDEX

Abadie, M., 31n
Abbadie, Antoine d', 135n, 136n
Abbadie, F.N.A., 135n, 136n
'Abd al-Bari, 91
'Abd al-Basit bin Halil, 61
'Abd al-Hamid II, Sultan, 52, 76, 77
'Abd al-Jalil (chief of the Sayf al-Nasr), 53, 71-2, 73
'Abd al-Karim, 144, 156n, 157n
'Abd al-Rahman, Sultan, 89, 91, 92
'Abd al-Rahman al-Jabarti, 146, 154n, 155n
'Abd al-Rahman Ibn Ziyad, 11
Abdal-Salam ibn Jasus, 7, 8, 9; fatwa, 9-13
'Abdalla al-Rusi (Governor of Fas), 5, 6
'Abdallah al-Tijani, 80n
'Abdallah Ibn 'Umar, 11
el-Abdin, Zein, 100n
'Abdul Majid al-Abadin, 136n
Abéché, 94, 100n
'Abid al-Bukhari (slave army), 2, 14n
Abir, Mordechai, 123-34, 135n, 136n
Abraham, R.C., 40
Abron, 50n
Abu-'Abdallah Sidi Muhammad al-'Arabi Ibn Ahmad Bardulah (Qadi of Fas); fatwa against enslavement, 13-14
Abu Adam 'Abdallahi, 98n
Abu 'Ali al-Rusi (Governor of Fas), 6, 7
Abu Muhammad Sidi al-Hajj 'Abdal – Salam ibn Ahmad see 'Abdal-Salam ibn Jasus
Abu Qila, 68
Abu Sumat, 112, 116
Abu 'Ubayd al-Bakri, 80n
Abubakar Tafawa Balewa (former Prime Minister of Nigeria), xin
Abu 'l-Fida', 60
Abu 'l-Qasim, 98n
Abyssinia see Ethiopia
Adam Bosh (slave wazir), 90-1, 98n
Aden, 55; British conquest, 132
Adham, al-Hajj 'Abd al-Salam, 82n
Afar, 132, 134
Agades, 67, 76
Aghlabids, 59
agriculture; East Africa, 170; Fazzan, 63; slave labour, 25, 27, 54, 95; slave production, 161-2; Songhay, 31n; see also farm-slavery
Ahir, 74
Ahmad al-Huwaydi al-Khurmani, 66
Ahmad Baba, 17, 19, 21, 31n
Ahmad Bey al-Na'ib al-Ansari, 77, 80n, 81n, 82n
Ahmad ibn Nasir, 68, 69
Ahmad 'Izzet Pasha, 74
Ahmad Pasha, 68, 69
Ahmad Rasim Pasha, early career, 51; measures against Libyan slave trade, 77-9
Ahmad Sidqi al-Dajjani, 80n
Ahmad Tanga tanga, al-hajj, 94
A'imma, 8, 9, 10
Air region, 18, 20
Akansus, Abi 'Abdalla Muhammad b. Ahmad, 2, 14n
'Alawite regime, 2
Albrand, F., 164, 179n, 180n
Alfa Ka'ti, 25, 27
Algeria, 73
'Ali, Bara ruler, 76
Ali, Abbas Ibrahim Muhammad, 96n
'Ali Abu' Amuri, 115
'Ali al-Mukni (al-Mukkani), 67
'Ali al-Rusi, 9
'Ali Amuri, 108
'Ali b. Jami, 89
'Ali Bey (*Qa'im Maqam*), 74
'Ali Dinar (Sultan of Dar Fur), 85, 89, 91, 93, 99n
'Ali Pasha Qaramanli, 69
'Alilish see Muhammad 'Alilish
alkali's courts, 35, 46n
Allen, C., 30n
Alpers, E.A., 171, 178n, 180n, 181n
'Alu (eunuch), 23
Alvarez, Francisco, 135n
Ambomu, (Azande people), 117
American Civil War, effect on slave holding, 107
Anstey, Roger, xn
anti-slavery convention, Egypt-Great Britain, 138
Anunga (Azunde people), 115, 117
al- 'Aqib al-Insamni (Anusamani) of

Takedda, 27
al-Aqqad, Salah, 14n
Arbi people (servile group), 17, 25-6
Arkell, A.J., 55, 80n, 97n, 121n
army *see* slave soldiers
Arnold, T.W., 136n
Ashanti, 39; slavery, 49n
Askia Dawud, 19, 21, 22, 23, 24, 25, 27
Askia Ishaq II, 22, 23, 27
Askia Isma'il, 18, 20
Askia al-Hajj Muhammad I, 17, 18, 19, 22, 23, 24, 25, 26, 27, 29n-30n, 31n
Askia Muhammad Bani, 23
Askia Muhammad Bunkan, 22, 24
Askia Musa, 18, 22
Askia dynasty (Songhay empire), 16
'Atiq 'Ali Pasha (slave dealer), 73
Austen, Ralph A., xn, 155n, 156n, 159n
Avungara (Azunde clan), 102
Awjila, 59, 69
Awlad Muhammad (Fazzan dynasty), 53, 61-2, 64, 65, 70, 81n
Awlad Sulayman (nomads), 71-2, 75
Ayandele, E.A., xn
Ayyub, Muhammad Sulayman, 55, 56, 58, 61, 62, 80n, 81n
Azande kingdoms, and Khartoumers, 109, 112, 115-17, 121n; slaves, 102-3
Azawad, 18

Baba Guru b. al-hajj Muhammad al-Amin Ganu, 32n
Badis ibn Mansur (Zirid prince), 59
Baer, Gabriel, 122n, 155n, 158n
Baggara (nomads), 103, 105, 106
Baghirmi, 31n, 78
Bahr al-Ghazal, 85, 92, 95, 98n, 101; indigenous slavery, 102-3; slave trade, 103-6; spheres of influence, 109-10; and Zariba system, 114; and al-Zubayr, 115
Baker, Sir Samuel, 83, 101, 109, 113
Bakhit b. Adam Bosh (slave), 90 98n
al-Bakri, 59
Balama al-Sadiq, 22, 23
Bambara (tribe), 20
Banda, (Fartit people), 85
Banu Bashir (nomads), 71
Banu Khattab bin Izliten (dynasty) 53, 57-8; overthrow, 59-60

Banu Khurman (dynasty), 53, 66; rule in Fazzan, 61
Banu Nasur, 61
Baqirmi, 105
Baqqara (nomads), 95
Bargery, G.P., 47n
Barth, H., 96n
Basset, R., 135n
Batagarawa, 47n
Batavia, 125
Bathurst, R.D., 178n
Batran, Aziz Abdalla, 1-13
Baxter, P.T.W., 121n
Beccari, C., 135n
Beigo people, 91, 99n
Beke, C.T., 136n
Benghazi, 75, 76
Benin, 44, 49n
Bennett, N.R., 178n
Berbera, 124, 132
Berbers, and the camel, 57
Berg, F.J., 181n
Berti people, 99n
Bettleheim, C., 178n
Bilma, 57, 69
Binga, 85
Biri (river), 108
Birmingham, D., 136n
birth rates, black slaves in Egypt, 151-2
Bizemont, H. de, 96n
Bjørkelo, Anders, 99n
blacks, in Egypt, 137-54
blacksmiths, Bongo, 112; Songhay, 22
Boahen, Adu, 74, 82n
Bobo, 21
Bombay, 173, 174
Bongo people, 108, 112
Borgu, 18, 21
Bornu, 21, 31n, 66, 70, 71, 73, 77, 78; and Fazzan, 61; revolt, 72
Bosworth, C.E., xin
Boutillier, J.L., 43, 49n
Bovill, E.W., xin
Bowring, John, 139, 155n
Breck, M., 80n
Brehm, A.E., 100n
Brenner, L., 98n
Breuvery, J. de, 96n, 156n, 157n
Britain and Showan slave trade, 133; and slavery in Hausaland, 39, 42, 47n, 48n-49n; slave trade suppressions, 163-4

Index

Brode, H., 179n
Brooks, G.E., 178n
Brown, W.A., 32n
Browne, W.G., 87, 96n, 97n, 98n
Bruce, J., 136n
Brun-Rollet, M., 96n
Buba Maryam, 27
al-Bukhari, 11
Burckhardt, J.L., 31n, 135n, 136n, 143, 144, 155n, 156n, 157n
Burdula (Qadi of Fas), 3, 4
Burgess, E., 180n
Burton, R.F., 164, 176, 178n, 179n, 180n, 181n
Busa, 21
Busaidi (dynasty), 162, 166-7, 175, 176
Butt, Audrey, 121n
Byzantines, and Garamantes, 53, 56
Cadalvène, E. de, 96n, 156n, 157n
Caillié, René, 30n
Cairo, 59; slave market, 137-42; slave population, 146, 157n
Camels, and trade, 57
Capitalism, and slave production, 177-8
caravan trade, Ethiopia, 127-36 (passim)
carbuncles (garnets), 55-6
Cardin, A., 155n
castration, xin, 23, 31n, 42, 98n; *see also* eunuchs
Catalans, 55
cattle raiding, Khartoumers, 107, 108
Caucasus, slaves, 127-8
Chad, Lake, 55
Chapelle, 61, 81n
Chelebi, Evliya, 59, 80n
Chelu, A., 160n
Chenelles, Ellen, 156n
children; of slave concubines, 19-20; of slaves, 44, 50n, 103; *see also* pederasty, women
cholera, slave mortality, 143
Christianity, 54; Ethiopia, 123-4, 127; Garamantes, 56
Christie, J., 178n
Christopher, L., 179n
Christopher, W., 179n
Circassians, 156n
Clauzel, J., xn
clientage, 45; Hausa states, 38
clove production, Pemba, 167-8, 172-7; slave economics, 174; Zanzibar, 164-7, 172-7
coconut production, 174, 175
Colin, G.S., xn, 14n
Colomb, R.N.., 181n
Colucci bey, J., 143, 157n
Combes, E., 135n
cooks, slave, 142, 156n
complexion, Egyptians, 156n; in freed slave marriages, 150
concubines, viii-ix, 37, 88, 103, 143-4; Circassian, 107; Songhay empire, 21-2; status of children, 19-20; zariba system, 14
confessions, forced, 7-8, 10
conscription, Haratin, 1-13
Cooper, F., xn, 178n, 179n
copper smelting, 20
Cosmas (Indicopleustes), 56
cotton cultivation, 107
Coupland, R., 179n
crime and punishment, Khartoumers, 112
Crimean War, 74
Crofton, R.H., 179n
Crone, A.J., 30n
Cunnison, I., 96n, 100n
Cuny, C., 98n
Curtin, Philip D., xn
Cushitic peoples, 128
Cush, 123, 124

Dagomba, 21
al-Dajjani, Ahmad Siddiqi, 82n
Dallons, 164
Damagaram, 77
Dampierre, E. de, 97n
Dankali merchants, 130, 132
Dar Fartit, 103, 106n, 108, 116; slave trade in, 84-7, 105
Dar Fongoro, 86, 93
Dar Fur, vii, 78, 103, 109, 147, 159n; defeated by Al-Zubayr, 119-20; domestic and pastoral slavery, 94-6; estate slavery, 91-4; horse and slave prices, 87; royal slaves and confidants, 88; slave owning, 103-4; slave raiding, 95; slave trade, 85-7; trade, 84-5
Dar Runga, 89
date production, vii, 162
Daym Gudyoo, 106
Daym Zubayr (zariba), 116, 117
Debo, Lake, 25

Defrémery, C., 30n
Delafosse, M., xin, 29n
Della Diserittione dell' Africa (Leo Africanus), 17-18
demography, black slaves in Egypt, 151-2
Dendi, 25, 28
Derman, W., 41, 48n
Devereux, W.E., 181n
Dialan, 18
Didier, Charles, 154n
Dinka, 102, 107, 108, 114
Dioula, 43
Doe people, 170, 171
Dogon tribe, 20
Dongalawi merchants, 105
Dongola, 78
Durar al-hisan (phantom chronicle), 29
Duveyrier, H., 61, 64, 81n
Dyawambe (Zaghrani) tribe, 20
Dyoor (river), 108

East Africa, slave mode of production, 161-78; slave trade statistics, 180n
Ebers, G., 155n
Egypt, 84, 128, 132; abolition of slave trade, 116, 138; in Bahr al-Ghazal, 118; black slavery in, 137-54; slave markets, 137-42; slave population, 152
Emmanuel, A., 178n
Enarea, 128, 129
Epaulard, A., 29n
estate inventories, freed slaves, 143, 149-52
estates, royal, in Sudan, 99n
Ethiopia, 54; Christian kingdom, 134; foreign trade, 124-5; Muslim harassment, 124; Solomonic dynasty, 123-4; slave trade, 123-34
Ethiopians, 136n; in Ottoman Empire, 125; slaves, 68
eunuchs, xin, 30n-31n, 42, 54-5, 77, 103, 159n; Dar Fur, 89, 104; as gifts, 78-9; marriages, 150; soldiers, 23; Songhay empire, 22-4
Europeans, in Red Sea trade, 125, 127
Evans-Pritchard, E.E., 121n

Fage, J.D., 46n
false testimony, 11

Farina 'Ali Kushiya (Songhay official), 20
farm-slavery, farm-slaves: origins, 37, 44, 48n; economics, 36-7, 38, 44-5; Fulani and Hausa, 40-1; manumission, 38; owners' characteristics, 42-3; owners' responsibilities, 37-8; ransom, 38, 44; reproduction rates, 42-3; selling limitations, 38, 43, 44; sex ratio, 37; and status, 39; second generation, 43, 49n; Zaria Emirate, 40-1
Farsy, A.S., 164, 179n
Fartit people, 84-6, 95
Fas, Fez, 1; Haratin in, 4-5; professional army, 2; 'Ulama' of, 3
Fashil, 92
al-Fashir, 87, 88, 91, 94; population, 100n
al-Fasi, Muhammad, 14n, 15n
Fatimids, 59
Fawzi, Taha, 82n
Fazari (Beigo tribesman), 91
Fazzan, agriculture, 63; growth of slave trade, 53-8; history, 53; al-Mukni coup, 71; Ottoman penetration, 64-7; slave trade and Ottomans, 73; trade, 67-8, 69-70, 72
Feireman, S., 180n
Felkin, R.W., 87
female slaves, *see* slaves
Féraud, L.C., 76, 81n, 82n
Feroge, 85
Fez *see* Fas
Finley, M.I., 33, 34, 37, 46n, 47n, 49n
firearms, 171; Ethiopia, 133, 134
Fisher, A.G.B., 159n
Fisher, H.J., 31n, 159n
Fitzgerald, W.A., 179n
Florus (poet), 56
Ford, Daryl, 121n
Fortes, M., 49n
Fouta-Djallon, 41
Frank, Louis, 142-3, 157n
Fraser, 165-6, 175
Freeman-Grenville, G.S.P., 179n, 181n
Frere, 177
Fulani, 40
Fulbe tribe, 20, 21, 22, 27
Funj Sultanate, 84
Fur peoples, 103

Index

Furwa, 120; nobility, 104, 105
Futuh Misr (Ibn 'Abd al-Hakam), 57

Gagliuffi (British vice-consul), 74
Galla, 125, 127, 128, 134; Islamization, 131; merchants, 129-30
Gao, 17, 18, 19, 25; slave quarter, 22
Garama (Jarma), 55, 56; Muslim raids on, 57
Garamantes, 53; history, 55-7
Gardane, Ange de, 69
Gellner, E., 14n
German (town), 53
Gessi, 120
Ghadamis, 53, 55, 63, 75, 76
Gharyan, 61, 79
Ghat, 53, 55, 63, 75, 76
Ghattas the Copt, 111, 115
Ghuma al-Mahmudi, 73
Giolotti, Giovanni, 79
Gobir, 23
Gogo people, 172
gold, 133; mining, 54; trade, 31n, 61n, 72, 123
Golo people, 108
Gondar, capital of Ethiopia, 130, 131
Gordon, Charles, 83, 120
grain trade, Kano, 36
Gray, J., 179n,
Gray, J.M., 180n
Gray, R., 121n, 122n, 135n, 136n
Grefulhe, H., 175, 181n
Guillain, M., 166, 174, 175, 179n
Gurague, 128, 129
Gurma, 18, 21, 24
Gurmantche, 18
Gyaman, 50n

Hadimu people, 167
Hair, P.E.H., 97n
al-Hakam, Ibn 'Abd, 80n
Hake, A.E., 121n
Halim Bey, 76
Hamdan Abu 'Anja, 95
Hamdun al-Rusi (Governor of Fas), 6, 7
Hamerton, 169, 176, 178n
Hamilton, A., 135n
Hamont, 160n
Harar, 132, 134
Harari merchants, 125, 132
Harari plateau; Muslim strongholds, 123
Haratin, slave soldiers, x, 1-13, 14n

Hardy, P., xin
harem, Murzuq, 68-9; Songhay, 22-3
Harris, J.E., 179n
Harris, Sir William Cornwallis, 136n
Hart, Captain, 179n
Harthi clan, 164, 167
Hasan, Hasan Iman, 96n
Hasan, Yusuf Fadl, 96n
Hasan Bey al-Bel'azi Pasha, 73
al Hasha'ishi, Muhammad b. 'Uthman, 75, 82n
Hashim bin 'Umar al-Kanemi of Bornu, Shaykh, 78
Hausa states, 18, 19, 21, 55, 67, 106; eunuchs, 30n-31n; farm slavery, 33-45
Hawwara Berbers, 57
Hay, Robert, 155n
Hebbert, G.K.C., 100n
Hemsö, Graberg de, 72, 82n
Herodotus, 55, 56, 80n
Hijaz, 128, 132
al-Hilali (Bulali, Belali), 118, 119
Hill, L.G., 100n
Hill, Polly, vii, 33-45, 46n, 47n, 50n
Hill, R., 100n
Hindess, B., 178n
Hirst, P.G., 178n
Holt, P.M., 121n
Holy, L., 99n
homosexuality, and slavery, xin
Hope, A.C., 97n
Hopkins, A.G., 46n, 48n
Horeau, Hector, 155n
Horneman, F., xn, 68, 69, 70, 81n
Houdas, O., xin, 29n
Hufrat al-Nahas, 85
Hunwick, J.O., viii, 16-29, 30n, 31n
Hurgronje, C. Snouck, xin
Husayn al-Na' 'al, 81n

Ibadi dynasty (Berber), 57
Ibn 'Abd al-Hakam, 57
Ibn 'Abdal-Bar, 10
Ibn Abi Dinar, 80n, 159
Ibn al-Hajj, 5, 7, 15n
Ibn al-Hajjib, 10
Ibn al-Mukhtar (Mahmoud Kati ben el Hadj el-Motaouakkel), xin, 16, 29n, 30n, 31n
Ibn 'Arafah, 10
Ibn Battuta, 20, 30n
Ibn Duqmaq (Ibrahim b

Muhammad b. Aydamur al-'Ala'i, 59, 80n
Ibn Fadl Allah al-Umari, 135n
Ibn Ghalbun, 64, 65, 66, 67, 81n
Ibn Khaldun, 21
Ibn Khattab, 59
Ibn Majah, 11
Ibn Yunis, 10
Ibrahim Qarad, Sultan, 90
Ifara, 79
Ifriqiya, 58
Igbafe, P.A., 49n
Ighi Zuma, 55
Ihsan, Akmal al-Din Muhammad, 80n
'Imad al-Din Abu 'l-Fida, 81n
India, 124, 125
Indians, in Zanzibar, 176
inflation, Egypt, 159n
inheritance and estates, 152-4; slaves, 158n
Inikori, J.E., xn
International Encyclopaedia of Social Sciences, 33
irrigation, 58-9
Islam, in Ethiopia, 123-4
Islam in Ethiopia (Trimingham), 113
Islamic law: & farm-slavery, 35-6, 41; property inheritance, 46n; *see also* slaves (categories of enslavement)
Ismail (ruler of Egypt), 118, 120
Istanbul, 51, 73
ivory trade, 107, 108, 109, 116, 121n, 123, 133, 138, 171
Izmir (Smyrna), 73

Ja 'alyn merchants, 105
Jabal Marra, 86, 91, 93, 103
Jabart, 135n
al-Jabarti *see* 'Abd al-Rahman al-Jabarti
Jabartis, 129, 130, 134; Ethiopian trade monopoly, 127
Jabir, M.H., 180n
Jackson, H.C., 121n, 122n
al-Jahiz (Abu 'Uthman 'Amr b. Bahr al-Fuqaymi al-Basri), xin
Jahn, Karl, 82n
Jalaba, 130, 134
Jamaica, 47n
James, W., 96n
Janakhara, 85
Jarma (Jirma), 53, 55
Jenne, 18, 21

Jews, 54
John of Biclar, Abbot, 56, 80n
Johnson, R.W., 30n
Johnston, C., 136n
Jomard, E., 157n
Jones, John Winter, 135n
Judar, Pasha, 27
Julien, Captain, 99n
Jur people, 108
Justin(ian), Emperor, 56

Kabara, 17
Kaffa, 130
Kamba people, 172
Kambe, Kambebe (Dogon of the plain), 21
Kami people, 171
Kammerer, A., 135n
Kanem state, 53, 57, 59; expansion into Fazzan, 60
Kano, 21, 30n, 35, 46n; Close Settled Zone, 35, 36, 48n; farm-slavery, 33-45
Kara, 85, 92
'Karamallah Kurkusawi, 98n
al-Kashf wa'l-bayan li-asnaf majlub al-Sudan see *Mi'raj al-su'ud*
Katsina, 21, 39, 41, 65, 72
al-Kattani, 15n
Katte, A. von, 136n
Kawar, 58
Kebabo, 78
Kebbi (Kanta), 18, 25, 29n
Keira dynasty, 84
Kel Owi Tuareg, 69
Kenya, 54; food production, 175; slave statistics, 180n
Khalil (wakil), 111
Khan al-Khalili (market), 137-8
Kharputli, Kamal al-Din, 82n
Khartoum, 101, 109
Khartoumers: characteristics, 113; failure to proselytize, 112; and zariba system, 106-15
Khayr Qarib (slave), 90, 98n
Khoja Ahmad, 81n
Khuda bint Sharuma bin Muhammad al-Fasi, 64, 65
Khurasan, 58
Kilwa, 172; slave statistics, 180n
Kimweri (Shambaa king), 171
Kinglake, A.W., 157n
Kirdi, Kirdawi, 85
Kirk, 175, 178n

Index

Kisabengo (chief), 171
Kitab al-Istibsar, 59, 80n
Kobbei, 87, 94, 146
Kopytoff, Igor, xn, 43
Kordofan, 78, 84, 89, 92, 94, 100n, 105, 109
Kotokoli, 21
Koulango, 43
Krapft, 136n
Krause, G.A., 81n
Kresh, 85
Kuchuk Ali (zariba owner), 118
Kukawa, 71
Kunayr (battle), 65
Kwere people, 171

Lampen, G.D., 96n
Lamu, food production, 175-6
Lane, Edward W., xin, 138, 143, 144, 156n, 157n, 159n
Last, Murray, 47n
Lawata group, 57
Leo Africanus, 17-18, 19, 21, 22, 23, 31n, 62, 81n
Levtzion, Nehemiah, 17, 29n
Lewis, Bernard, xn
Leyder, J., 97n
Libya, 54, 55, 57, 73; slave trade, 76; suppression of slave trade, 79
Lloyd, C., 178n, 179n
Loarer, 167, 174, 175, 179n
Lodulphus, J., 135n
Lombard, Maurice, 80n
Lugard, F.D. (High Commissioner of Northern Nigeria), 36, 42, 48n, 49n
Luxorius (poet), 56, 80n
Lyon, G.F., 71, 81n

Mackenzie, D., 179n
McLoughlin, Peter F.M., 96n, 100n
MacMichael, H.A., 97n, 99n
Madden, R.R., 135n
Maghariha, 71, 72
al-Maghili (scholar), 16, 17, 19, 20, 23, 26, 29n, 30n, 31n
Mahdi, the, 120, 154
al-Mahdi (Fatimid caliph), 59
Mahdiyya, 59, 95
Mahkama Archives, 137
Mahmud, Hasan, 82n
Mahmud b 'Umar (qadi of Timbuktu), 19, 26, 27
Majid, Sultan, 175

Makhluf al-Balbali (jurist), 26
Makonde, 172
Makuma people, 170
Malfante, Antoine, 21
Mali empire, 17, 18, 21
Malindi, slave labour, 175
Mami (Mahmud), 'Bey of the Fazzan', 65
Mami (Moroccan *qa'id*), 20
Mamman Hajji, 76
Mandala, 95
Mande, 43
Manners and Customs of the Modern Egyptians (Lane), 144
Manoncour, Sonnini de, 157n
al-Mansur, Sultan, 16, 27
Mansur ibn Nasir, 65
Mantran, Robert, 155n
manumission, 12, 82n; by Ahmad Rasim, 77; court cases, 147-9, 158n; Egypt, 146-9; by foreign consuls, 79; Ottoman decree of 1863, 74-5; Songhay, 19, 27-8
Marcel, J.J.,159n
Marione, Giovanni, 30n
Marra Mountains, 84
marriage: eunuchs, 150; slaves, 149-52
Martin, B.G., vii, 51-79
Martin, E.B., 181n
Marwa people, 57
Marxism, and farm-slavery, 50n
Maryam Dabo (captive and mother of Askia Isma 'il), 18
Marzuk, 79
Mason, M., 50n
Massawa, 124, 131
Massawa, A.E.C., 136n
Massawa, C., 136n
Ma'tuq Bu Humayra, Hajj (slave dealer), 73
Mauritius, 163
Mazata group, 57
Mbomu River, 85
Mehmet Amin Pasha, 73
Meillassoux, G., 43, 50n, 96n
Meinhof, C., 97n
Mema, 18
men, predominance in Trans-Atlantic slave trade, xn
Mengin, F., 96n
Meshra' al-Req, 108, 110
Meyers, A.R., 14n
Micaud, C., 14n

Middleton, J., 168, 179n
Midilli (Mytilene), 73
Miers, Suzanne, xn, 43
Milad, Salwa 'Ali, 158n
Miner, Horace, 22, 30n
Mira people, 57
Mi 'raj al-su'ud (Ahmad Baba), 17, 21
Mire, Lawrence, 101-20
Misurata, 61
Mitamura, Taisuke, xin
Miteri people, 85
Mofio (Azande king), 103, 106
Mollien, G., 41, 48n
Mombasa, 175
Moresby Treaty, 163, 164, 165
Mori Hawgaro, 25, 27
Morice, 172
Morocco, 14n; and M. Ismail, 3, 4
Mossi, 18, 20, 21, 24
Mozambique, 175; slave production, 163
Mrima, 180n
Mubarak, 'Ali, 158n
Muhammad, Prophet, ll; and slavery, viii-ix
Muhammad (son of 'Umar al-Tunisi), 91
Muhammad 'Abd al-Rahim, 87
Muhammad Ahmad al-Mansur al-Dhahabi, 4
Muhammad al-Amin al-Kanemi, 71, 72
Muhammad al-Fadi, Sultan, 90, 91, 99n
Muhammad al-Fasi, 62, 63, 64
Muhammad al-Ghuzayl, 67
Muhammad al-Husayn, Sultan, 90, 93
Muhammad al-Lamtuni, 20
Muhammad al-Mukni, 70-1
Muhammad al-Rashid, 1
Muhammad al-Sharif, 70-1
Muhammad al-Tijani (traveller), 60
Muhammad al-Tunisi, 86, 98n
Muhammad Ali (ruler of Egypt), 128, 139; slave raiding, 106
Muhammad b 'Ali Ku 'bar, 78
Muhammad 'Alilish, Faqih, 2, 6, 7
Muhammad b. 'Ali Dokkumi, 90
Muhammad bin Juhaym, 66
Muhammad Bu Humayra, Hajj (slave dealer), 73
Muhammad Ibn Abdal-Hakam, 11

Muhammad Isma 'il ibn al-Sharif ('Ulama' of Fas), 1-13; reasons for conscription, 9-10
Muhammad Kebkebe, 99n
Muhammad Kurra, 89-90, 98n
Muhammad Tayrab (Sultan of Dar Fur), 89, 92
Muhammad 'Umar al-Tunisi, 87, 89, 91, 98n, 99n, 156n
al-Mu'izz li-Din Allah, Caliph, 59
al-Mukni family, 67, 70-1
Muntasir bin Nasir ibn Muhammad al-Fasi, 64, 65
Murzuq, 53, 55, 61, 62-3, 69, 72; castle, 63; description, 63-4; and ban on slave trade, 75; trade, 63
Musa al-Hajj (Mudir of Ghadamis), 74
music, Songhay, 22
musicians, 54
Muslims, enslavement, 19, 20, 21, 146, 147
Mynors, T.H.B., 97n

Nachtigal, G., 61, 87, 95, 97n, 98n, 99n, 100n, 121n, 122n, 159n
Nadel, S.F., 50n
Naji, Mahmud, 80n
names, characteristic slaves', 141-2, 156n
Nasir, Sultan, 62, 63, 65
al-Nasiri, Ahmad b. Khalid, 4, 14n, 15n
Nasser, Gamal Abdel, 156n
Nasuf (slave trader), 75
Na 'um Shuqayr, 98n
Ndoromo (Azande ruler), 117
Nerval, Gérard de, 154n, 159n
Ngindo people, 170
Nicholls, C.S., 178n
Nimro, 159n
Nuba, 85
Nupe, 31n, 50n
Nur al-Din (ruler of Damascus), 60
Nuri, Mehmet, 80n
Nyamwezi people, 170, 171-2
Nyassa people, 170, 171

O'Fahey, R.S., vii, 80n, 83-96, 98n, 99n, 121n, 122n, 158n, 159n
Oman, 170; slave trade, 162-4
Omani Arabs, 175, 176
Ottoman Empire, 64; and Ethiopia, 124; penetration into Fazzan,

Index

64-7; reestablish power in Fazzan, 72
Pallme, I., 100n
palm groves, xn
patronage, 153; Haratin, 5-6
pederasty, ix
Pemba: clove production, 167-8; sources of slaves, 170-2
Penzer, N.M., 30n, 78, 80n, 82n
Perron, N., 98n
Persia, 124
Persian Gulf, 128, slave trade, 163
Petherick, John, 107-8, 122n
Pickering, C., 180n
pilgrim caravans, Fazzan, 68
plague, and slave population, 143
plantation system, East Africa, 169-70, 175
polygamy, viii
Poncet, C.J., 135n
population density, and slavery, 36, 48n
population movement, and slave raiding, 86, 97n
Portuguese, 124, 162
pregnancies, and slave sales, 144-5, 157n
Prime, William C., 155n
Prins, A.H.J., 179n
property, Islamic law on inheritance, 46n
Puckler-Maskau, H., 156n
Purchas His Pilgrims, 135n
Putnam, 178n

Qadadifa group, 72
Qal'at Awlad Muhammad (castle), 62
Qaradaghli Muhammad Pasha al-Imam, 67
Qaramanli dynasty, 53, 68, 72, 73
Qaraqush (mamluk), 60
Qatrun, 68

Ramusio, Giovanni-Battista, 29n
Rattray, R.S., 49n
Raymond, André, 159n
Red Sea trade, 125, 127, 132
rice production, Songhay, 25
Rigby, 170, 172, 176
Rizqayat Arabs, 117-18, 119
Roberts, David, 155n
Rohl (river), 108, 114

Roque, J. de la, 135n
Rossi, Ettore, 57, 59, 61, 67, 68, 76, 80n, 81n, 82n
Rotter, Gernot, xn, 80n
Rouch, Jean, 31n
runaway slaves, 146
Runga, 85
Russel, C.E.B., 179n
Russia, 107, 128

Sabha, 55, 64, 65
Sabi'u Nuhu, 47n
al-Sadat, Anwar, 156n
al-Sa'di, 16, 24, 29n, 30n, 31n
Sahih al-Burkhari (traditions of the Prophet), 14n
Sahnun, 11
Said-Ruete, R., 179n
St. John, Bayle, 156n, 157n
Salah al-Din (Saladin), 60
Saleh b. Haramil al-Abray, 164-5
Salifou, André, 79, 82n
Salil b. Razik, 178n
Salim, M.I., Abu, 99n
Salima, Niya, 157n
salt production, vii, xn, 18, 20, 54
Sambaa people, 170
Sandison, P.J., 98n
Sanguinetti, B., 30n
Santandrea, S., 96n
Sanusi sufi order, 73
Sawkna, 69
Sayf al-Nasr, 71-2
Schweinfurth, G., 112, 121n, 122
Sennar, 124
serfdom; Ethiopia, 126; and slavery, 41-2, 46n, 48n
Serjeant, R.B., 135n
servile tribes, Songhay, 17, 24, 25-6; *see also Haratin*
Seyyid Said, 164, 166, 169, 170, 173, 174
al-Shahi, Ahmed S., 96n
al-Shaikh Abu-Talib al-Makki, 11
Shakka (entrepôt), 118, 119
Shambaa kingdom, 171
Shandi, 146
Shankalla, 85
Sharifi, 116
Sharifi 'Alawi dynasty, 14n
Shatt community, 85, 92
Shaw, F.L., 122n
Sherriff, A.M.H., 161-78
Shirazi people, Zanzibar, 167, 168

Shol (Dinka queen), 108, 112
Showa kingdom, 131-3
Shukry, Muhammad Fu'ad, 155n
Shuqayr, 99n, 100n
Sibiridugu, 29n
Sidama tribes, 123, 128
Sidi al- 'Arbi Burdula, 7
Sidi al-Hajj Abdal-Salam ibn Jasus, 7
Sidi Muhammad al- 'Alim, 6
Sidi Muhammad al-Mashshat, 8, 9
Sidi Muhammad ibn 'Abdal-Qadir al-Fasi (sage and scholar), 1, 2, 3, 5-6
Sijilmasa, 58
singers, 54; slave women as, 22
Sinnar Sultanate, 84, 91
Skolle, J., 31n
Slatin-Pasha, R., 99n, 121n
slave caravans, Ottoman suppression, 79
slave holders, Dar Fur, 94, 100n
slave markets, 19, 20; Daym Zubayr, 117; Egypt, 137-42; Sudan, 87
slave raiding, consequences, 172; Dar Fartit; 105; Dar Fur, 86-7, 95; Fazzan, 58, 71, 74; Songhay, 18-19; Sudan, 85-6
slave routes, Africa, 54-5
slave soldiers, 1-13, 54, 59, 124; Dar Fur, 103, 104, 106; Ethiopian, 128; Songhay, 24; and zariba system, 113-114
slave trade, Atlantic, vii, xn; Bahr al-Ghazal, 103-6; and Dar Fur, 85-7; East African sources, 170-2; East African statistics, 180n; economic aspects, 75; Egyptian suppression, 138; Ethiopia, 123-34; Fazzan, 52-79; French, 162, 163; Garama, 56-7; Islamic, scale estimate, xn; Oman, 162, 163; Showa, and the British, 133; trans-Saharan, vii-viii, 21; Turkish suppression in Fazzan, 73-9; Waday-Tripoli route, 75-6; Zanzibar, 163
slave-villages, 34, 39; Dar Fur, 92 Nupe, 50n; status of inhabitants, 41-2
slaves, slavery, vii-x, 102-3; authority exercised by, 25, 104; agricultural employment, 25, 27; assimilation, 43, 47n; birth rates, 49n, 151; career opportunities, 88; categories of enslavement, 17, 19, 54-5, 85; Dar Fur Sultanate, 83-96, 104; definitions, 33-4, 84; duties, 142; East Africa, 161-78; economic aspects, vii, 20-1, 22, 36-7, 47n, 58, 75, 102, 161-78; estates and inheritance, 37, 38, 91-4, 152-4; free days, 178n; Ethiopian, 124, 126-7; expenses, 155n; as gifts, 27, 91, 98n; health, 142-3, 157n; marriage between free men and, 44; medieval categories, 54; mortality, 178n; Muslim attitude to, viii-ix, 10-11, 135; Muslims as, 19, 20, 21, 146, 147; names, 141-2, 156n; ownership transfer, 26-7; prices, 50, 87, 174; private lives, 146; ransoming, 47n, 49n; runaways, 97n, 146; sale of farm-slaves, 38; sale laws, 140-1; sex ratio, 138, 159n; slave races, 25-6; Songhay empire, 16-29; sources of slaves, 54-5, 102-3, 138-9, 170-2; taxes, 73, 104, 139, 170; temporary, 45n; treatment, 46n, 74, 139-40; West Indian and Islamic, 47n; women, vii-viii, 22, 103, 143-5; Zanzibar emancipation, 176; *see also* concubines, farm-slavery, manumission
Smith, M.G., 40, 41, 47n, 92
Smith, Mary, 50n
Socotra Island, 55
Sokoto, 72
Somali merchants, 130, 134
Somalia, 54; food production, 175-6
Songhay empire, 29n, 92; court eunuchs, 22-4; economic role of slavery, 20-1; Moroccan invasions, 23, 25, 28; servile tribes, 17; slave soldiers, 24; slavery, 16-29; succession, 22
Sorko people (servile group), 17, 24, 25, 26
Sourdel, D., 31n
Spaulding, J.S., 96n, 98n, 159n
spice plantations, vii; *see also* cloves
Stanley, H.M., 180n
Stenning, D.J., 47n
Sudan; conquest, 106, 139; dependence on slaving, 75; Muslim

Index

society in North, 84; North-South conflict, 83-4; *see also* Dar Fur, zariba system
Sudd barrier, 106, 107
sugar production, 54; Zanzibar, 165, 175
Sulayman, (son of al-Zubayr), 120
Sulayman *or* Safar Day (Governor of Tripoli), 65
Suleiman b. Hamed al-Busaidi, 166
Sulivan, G.L., 135n, 179n
Sullivan Boere, O., 181n
Sunni (Songhay dynasty), 16
Sunni Abu Bakr, 18
Sunni Ali, 17, 18, 19, 23, 24, 26, 27, 29n, 30n, 31n; harem, 21-2
Sunni Sulayman Doma, 18
Surur (Azande ruler), 116
al-Suyuti, 20

Tabakali (eunuch), 23
Taghaza, 18; salt pans, 20
Tahert, 58
Tahir Ahmad al-Zawi, 80n
Tahir ibn-Nasir, 66
Takedda, 20
Tamisier, 135n
Tanghe, B.O., 97n
Tanzania, 54
Ta(o)udeni, 30n, salt pans, 20
Taqwim (Abu 'l-Fida'), 60
Ta'rikh al-Fattash (Ibn al-Mukhtar), 16, 17, 23, 27
Ta'rikh al-Sudan ('Abd al-Rahman al-Sa'di), 16
taxes, cloves, 174; slaves, 73, 104, 139, 170
Tayrab *see* Muhammad Tayrab
Teizeira da Morra, A., 80n
Terray, E., 50n
Thevenot, Monsieur de, 135n
Thuriaux-Hennebert, A., 121n, 122n
Tibbu people, 69
Tibesti, 74, 75
Tidbury, G.E., 179n
Tikima (Azande king), 115-16, 119
Timbuktu, 17, 18, 19, 20, 21, 22, 27, 30n, 72
Tinimu dan Sulayman (Amir of Zinder), 78
Tippu Tip (caravan trader), 168
Tiryaqi Ibrahim, 68
Tombo (hill Dogon), 21

Tondibi (battle), 23
Tondy (river), 108
el Tounsy, Mohammad ibn Omar, 96n, 97n, 121n, 122n
trade: classical period, 55; Dar Fur, 84-5; Egypt, 138; Ethiopia, 123; Fazzan, 67-8, 72; Murzuq, 63; *see also* caravan trade, slave trade
Traghen (Tarajin), 60-1
Tremearne, H.J., 31n
Trimingham, J.S., 41, 48n, 113
Tripoli, 52, 59, 61, 64, 73, 76, 77; slave market, 74
'Troglodytes', 55, 56
T(o)uareg, 18, 74
Tubu (Temhu) people, 56, 75
Tugay, Emine Foat, 147n, 150n, 156n, 157n, 158n
Tunis, 59, 61; refugees, 52
al-Tunisi (Muhammad 'Umar al-Tunisi), 87, 89, 91, 98n, 99n, 156n
Turc, Nicholas, 158n
Turuj, 85, 92
Tuwat, 21
Tymowski, Michal, 31n, 99n

'Umar al-Maqdisi (Mai of Bornu), 66
'Umar 'Ali bin Isma'il, 73, 74, 81n, 82n
'Umar Lel, 98n
Umm al 'Abid, 65-6
'Uqba ibn Nafi', 57
'Uthman *or* Atman (Hausa slave), 76

Valentia, Viscount G., 135n
Vallière, 69
Viet, G., 135n

Wadai, Wada'i, 72, 86, 91, 105, 120, 147, 159n
Waday-Tripoli route, 75-6
Wadi al-Ajal, 53
wage labour, 37, 47n
Wakalat al-Jallaba, 137-42
Walata, 18, 20, 30n
Walz, Terence, 97n, 137-54, 155n, 156n, 157n, 159n
Warburg, G., 100n
Ward, Philip, 81n
Warfalla group, 72
Watson, J.L., 46n
Weld Blondel, J., 136n
Wele (river), 119

Wello, 131
West Africa; farm-slavery, 33-45; French, 49n
Whately, Mary L., 156n
White Nile, 109, 116
Wilks, I., 49n
Willis, J.R., vii-x
Wollega, 130
Women, family obligations, xin; manumission cases, 147-8; *see also* concubines, slaves
women and children, predominance in Islamic slave trade, xn
Works, J.A., Jr, 100n
Wright, John, 71

Yao people, 170, 171, 172
Ya'qubi (Persian geographer), 57
Yemen, 124, 128
Ylvisaker, M., 181n
Yoruba, 21
Yulu, 85
Yusuf (Qaramanli Pasha), 70-1, 72
Yusuf Bey al-Mukni, 67

Zabid, 55
Zaghawa people, 57
Zaghrani tribe, 20
al-Zaki, Tamal, 95

Zanzibar, agricultural diversification, 175-7; capitalist production, 172-7; clove production, 166-7; Omani ruling class, 167; slave conditions, 178n; slave emancipation, 176; slave statistics, 169-70, 180n; slave trade, 163; sources of slaves, 170-2
Zaria Emirate, 47n, 49n, 76; farm-slavery, 40-1, 50n
Zariba system, 108-14, and al-Zubayr, 115-20
al-Zayani, 14n
Zayla, 124, 132
Zigula people, 170, 171
Zinder, 31n, 78, 82n
Zirids, 59
Zoroastrians, 54
al-Zubayr Pasha Rama Mansur, 84, 90, 101, 104, 112, 115, 117; defeats Dar Fur, 119-20; impresses Gordon, 120; governor of Bahr al-Ghazal, 118-19; role in zariba system, 115-20
Zulaykha bint Hamad al-Malik Jawish (slave), 141
Zuwayla, 53, 55, 56-60; early slave trade, 57-8; fall, 60
Zyhlarz, E., 96n